1 MONTH OF
FREE
READING

at

www.ForgottenBooks.com

D1363887

By purchasing this book you are eligible for one month membership to ForgottenBooks.com, giving you unlimited access to our entire collection of over 1,000,000 titles via our web site and mobile apps.

To claim your free month visit:

www.forgottenbooks.com/free141344

ISBN 978-0-484-07876-4
PIBN 10141344

NARRATIVE

OF THE

FRENCH REVOLUTION OF 1848.

By WALTER K. KELLY.

WITH PORTRAITS AND OTHER ILLUSTRATIONS.

LONDON:
CHAPMAN AND HALL, 186 STRAND.

MDCCCXLVIII.

LONDON:
PRINTED BY GEORGE BARCLAY, CASTLE STREET,
LEICESTER SQUARE.

CÒNTENTS.

ILLUSTRATIONS.

NARRATIVE

OF THE

FRENCH REVOLUTION OF 1848.

CHAPTER I.

INTRODUCTION.

THE Revolution accomplished in Paris on the 24th of February, 1848, is without a parallel in history. The immediate spectators of the wondrous event declare, that when all was over they felt like men waking out of a dream,—so quick and sweeping had been the changes effected; so disproportioned the apparent means to the end; so sudden the bursting of the storm, so rapid and entire its subsidence; so utterly transcending all human experience the whole manner, course, and issue of the movement. It was with the same feeling of stupefaction we received the news in England. Narrowly as we had watched of late the conduct and disposition of the French government and people, and thoroughly convinced as we were that Louis Philippe had sealed the perdition of his own dynasty, yet was there not one amongst us who looked for the fulfilment of that inevitable doom in such wise or so soon. Even now, though we have recovered from the first stupor of surprise, the event seems to us almost præternatural; and so must it continue to seem, until it ceases to be what it now is—the solitary example of a new order of facts.

This Revolution, at once the most bloodless and the most

B

complete of modern times, was the spontaneous, unpremeditated act of the unarmed people of Paris. No long-matured and widely-ramified conspiracy preceded the outbreak, as in 1830; no delegated agents of the middle classes in secret goaded, restrained, and, when the moment was come, let loose the fiery passions of the multitude; no leaders in fine cloth organised the rude strength of the men in blouses, put weapons in their hands, and shewed them where to strike, and how. Alone the people did it all.

And never was so much work done, and well done, in so brief a space of time. The Three Days of July, glorious as they were to the great-hearted victors, resulted in nothing more than a transposition of the established order of things; they shifted the parts in the political drama from one set of actors to another, but the play remained the same. The Three Days of February were days both of destruction and creation, and produced a fundamental change in the whole political and social system of the country. Between the ancient France of Louis Philippe and the new-born Republic there lies the interval of a deluge.

Those who are fond of noting minute coincidences in outward things have not failed to remark, that the two popular victories of July and February were both achieved on the same days of the week; that the one was preceded by the conquest of Algiers, the other by the capture of Abd-el-Kader; and both by the freezing of the Seine in the previous winter, &c. We leave these facts to the astrological almanac writers, who will henceforth adopt it as a canon that Tuesday, Wednesday, and Thursday, are favourable days for making revolutions. To us it seems far more interesting to remark the differences between the two events than their fortuitous coincidences, because the former all testify the progress which public opinion has made in France since 1830. We believe with M. Quetelet, that the surest measure of the amount of civilisation in any people is the mode in which its revolutions are accomplished. Admitting this axiom, the following extract from the "Charivari" will enable us to apply it to the case of France :—

"In 1793, the first King that was dethroned inspired uneasiness, and he was guillotined. In 1830, the second King whom the people deposed was escorted to the sea-side, and a strict watch kept over him until he had set sail from the shores of *la belle France*. In 1848, the people treat the ex-King with sublime disdain—they give themselves no trouble whatever concerning him. The King goes whithersoever he will; no one looks after him, no pains are even taken to ascertain if he does go or not. A few days afterwards some report that he is dead, and the reply is 'Ha!' Others affirm that the poor devil is very well, and the reply is still 'Ha!' No one cares to be assured whether he be dead or alive. As little uneasiness is felt as if he had never been in existence. Is it possible to suppress a king and a whole dynasty more completely, or with greater generosity? Let us trace the steps of the declining scale :—The movement of 1789 lasted three years. That which resulted in the Restoration lasted three months. The Revolution of 1830 lasted three days. The Revolution of 1848 lasted three hours."

The Three Days, or the Two Days of February, is a phrase warranted both by fact and usage, but in one respect it is a misnomer. The great work was really achieved, as the "Charivari" asserts, in the space of about three hours on the 24th. At half-past ten that morning the King was still confident in his own strength, and his arrogant determination not to make any concession remained unbroken Before two o'clock the monarchy had ceased to exist, and he and his family were scattered abroad as hopeless fugitives. But give this Revolution the longest duration we can assign to it, from the first challenge on Monday evening, the 21st of February, when the banquet was prohibited, to the consummation of the people's victory and the final restoration of order, and we shall find the whole vast action comprised within the compass of a week. Louis Philippe fled on Thursday the

24th of February; on the following Thursday so little was he thought of, that his name was not once mentioned in any Paris paper sent to press on that day.   By the 3d of March the capital had fallen into a complete lull; there were no longer any sounds to be heard either of tumult or rejoicing, but the thinking and acting faculties of the people were wholly absorbed in the pursuit of their ordinary occupations, which the late crisis had suspended, or in the discharge of the duties imposed on them by the new state of things.   The correspondent of the "Atlas" newspaper, from whose remarkable letters the English public have derived so much gratification, depicts the state of affairs in one striking phrase,—"There is absolutely no news whatever. *The revolution is already old.*"

Already old!   What a world of self-control, resignation, goodness, and practical wisdom, do those words reveal!   The hungry, ragged, squalid people were absolute masters; the silken minions, whose opulence had flouted their misery, were at their feet; the wealth of luxurious Paris was theirs for the taking.   They were flushed with victory; the memory of life-long hardships, oppressions, and indignities burned in their hearts; the breath in their nostrils was tainted with the reek of blood—the blood of their slaughtered friends and kindred. Anarchy invited them to indemnify themselves by one sweet, delirious draught of license and tyranny, for their social degradation and political serfdom; nor were evil counsellors wanting to second the promptings of their own evil passions, and yell them on to vengeance, havoc, and spoliation.   Yet not one slightest act of violence to person or property sullied the pure triumph of those heroic men.   They were turbulent and threatening, indeed, at the Chamber of Deputies and the Hôtel de Ville; but their fierce souls, even in their wildest mood, were still obedient to the voice of reason and humanity as it flowed from the eloquent lips of genius.   Talk no more of Cincinnatus quitting the dictatorship to return to the plough; Paris has seen that sublime lesson bettered by scores of thousands of her poorest sons.

This is the light by which we should read the future destinies of France.　If the maxim of Montesquieu be true, that virtue is the one thing needful for republics, why should we look despondingly on the prospects of the young republic? It may have rough trials to encounter; internal strife and foreign war may prey upon its strength; but the virtue and intelligence of its people will carry it safe through all its struggles.　It is not usual, we know, to couple the words France and Virtue together, and many an ear will revolt at so strange an assortment of sounds.　But let us not be deceived by that figure of speech which puts a part for the whole.　The ruffian turpitude of France has its peculiar *habitat* in the classes most favoured by the late monarchy, and there it flourishes with a luxuriance unsurpassed among the *forçats* of Toulon or the convicts of Van Dieman's Land.　The moral dry-rot is confined to the upper orders, and those who minister to their pride and pleasure; the great bulk of the community, the men whom Guizot thought unworthy to be either electors or eligible, are sound to the core.　Let us at last be just to those who have given such shining proofs of their heroic integrity; let us believe in the worth of that people who command the love and admiration of Béranger.　It is not of a reprobate race that the greatest genius in France, and the most incorruptible of men, would say,—*Le peuple, c'est ma Muse*—"My Muse is the people!"

Whatever, then, be the troubles through which France may yet be doomed to pass, before her new constitution is finally consolidated, sure we are that the right of property will remain inviolate.　The poor will not combine to despoil the rich: how long have the rich conspired to rob the poor!

"Not for a single instant have we felt alarm," says the writer in the "Atlas," whom we have already quoted.　"There has been no one example of the slightest violation or despoilment of private property.　The National Guard has proved to the bands of desperate malefactors whom the great political convulsion has let loose upon society, that the vigilance of a hired police can never equal, in energy or power, the efforts of men who are bent on defending their own hearths and houses. At this moment the city of Paris presents one of the most extraordinary spectacles which, perhaps, has ever been afforded by history for the contemplation and instruction of the human race. The timorous and weak-minded may call this revolution a subversion of order; but those who seek for proofs of that providential government of the world, in which the best and wisest of mankind hesitate not to believe, will find in it another example of the justice of the Almighty, and of the power of His divine will. This truth is felt with such intensity by the whole mass of the population, that the churches are filled from morning till night, and the Curé of St. Louis d'Antin told me yesterday, that he was almost worn out with the numbers of penitents begging the sacrament, not in fear and trembling, but in order to bear witness to the glory of God. The clergy are busy about the streets carrying hope and consolation everywhere, and meet on their way with aid and respect from the people. The Abbé Lacordaire resumed his conferences yesterday at Notre Dame, and was listened to with eager interest by the most crowded audience yet gathered there. At one period of his discourse, the awe and enthusiasm surpassed in intensity any thing I ever witnessed. ' Some of you have said there is no God!' exclaimed he; 'because there is no justice on the earth, there can be no God in heaven. Throw wide the doors this moment and behold—now tell me, if ye dare, that there is no God.' The doors burst open as if by magic; the rays of the sun poured into the building and disclosed to view the whole of the National Guard of the arrondissement assembled before the guard-house, opposite the cathedral, to replace the old flag chosen by Louis Philippe with the new one of the Republic. The Archbishop of Paris was just at that moment entering the portal of the Hôtel Dieu, attended by his clergy, to bear help and succour to the wounded; the smoke from the Pont Louis Philippe was still ascending to the clear blue sky. No words can describe the impression of that scene, and when the doors were closed again one loud gushing sob was heard within the edifice, and in silence and in awe the whole congregation sank upon their knees—rich and poor mingling together in one prayer of glory and thanksgiving."

Till "Time is old and hath forgot itself," the emotions of that solemn moment will find their response in every conscience. The world will recognise in the ignominious fall of Louis Philippe the just punishment of his enormous treachery. He was a double traitor: first, to the weak, confiding sovereign, whom he fawned on and cajoled whilst he was plotting his ruin; secondly, to the nation, which he swindled of the rights it had purchased with its blood. His reign of seventeen years and a half was one continuous act of deliberate perjury. He owed his crown to the free choice of the people, and the title by which he wore it was expressive of that tenure. Throwing away the old feudal ideas of a territorial inheritance and ancient prerogative, his constituents called their new chief " The King of the French"—a king who reigned by right of the good will of the people. He pledged himself that he would surround the throne with republican institutions, and his *mot pour le peuple* was,—" Henceforth the Charter shall be a reality." He was liberal indeed of promises, and every promise was a lie. As an illustration of his mendacity, we may be permitted to relate an anecdote derived from unquestionable authority.

When the Quadruple Treaty between Great Britain, France, Spain, and Portugal, was concluded, Pozzo di Borgo, the Russian minister, waited on the King of the French, and remonstrated against the measure. Louis Philippe jumped up from his chair, caught the offended diplomatist by both hands, and earnestly exclaimed,—" I give you my word of honour, that if I did sign that treaty, it was solely with the intention of not fulfilling it."

That was exactly the spirit in which he bound himself by treaty to his new subjects.

His purpose, from the very first, was to farm the state only for his own private advantage. All the foreign ambassadors in Paris, in July 1830, not excepting Lord Stuart, the English minister, protested in the names of their respective Governments against Louis Philippe's usurpation, and threatened him with a new invasion. Terrified by these menaces, and not anticipating such a display of enthusiasm as was made in England in favour of the Revolution, he "hastened to declare, that he had taken no part in the Revolution, and solemnly promised that, although he had been compelled to accept the crown, he would resign it to its rightful owner as soon as, by his skilful exercise of the royal authority, he had reduced the people to their former condition of helplessness and passive obedience. The Duc de Montemart, who was the first person summoned to the Palais Royal by the Duke of Orleans on his arrival from Neuilly, and who by the last ordinances of Charles X. had been appointed President of the Council, has publicly stated the fact. These promises were subsequently renewed in his autograph letters written by the King of the French to William the Fourth, to the Emperors of Austria and Russia, and to the King of Prussia. To England he further engaged to fulfil the promise of Charles X. to abandon Algiers. Thus, at the beginning of his reign, the new King had bound himself to govern in opposition to the principles of the Revolution; and it was with the view of proving his sincerity that he called into his ministry Casimir Perrier, who had also been appointed Minister by the last ordinance of the former King, and also Guizot, who had fled to Ghent during the Hundred Days; who, on his return, was a violent Legitimatist, and, afterwards, went out of place an equally violent Oppositionist; and who, in the protest of the Deputies against the violation of the Charter, on the 28th of July, 1830, had inserted the ordinary formulas of fidelity and devotion, which were unanimously rejected by all the members of the Assembly. For the same purpose he sent, as ambassador to England (the only country which would then receive his envoys) Talleyrand, who had signed the treaties of 1814 and 1815, so disastrous to France."*

The King and his counsellors soon perceived how incompatible with their designs was the existence of a free press to expose their wicked practices; they therefore subjected it to the most iniquitous system of restraint ever endured in a country affecting to call itself constitutional. A free press is the first vital necessity of a free state, and there needs no stronger proof of the thorough depravity of Louis Philippe's government, than his intense hatred of that best guardian of the public liberties. From the beginning of his reign no means were neglected to corrupt the Parisian press. The leading daily papers were literally bought and paid for in money or in well-remunerated offices; the rest were gagged by penal laws; and as a further security against opposition, the caution-money deposited by the proprietors of French newspapers was increased, so that the press became again a monopoly, as it had been under the Restoration. A newspaper under this system could only be the organ, not even of a party, but of a faction of the governing party; and the Paris press was divided between those factions. The provisions of the infamous laws of September were as follows :—

" All mention of the King with regard to any political measure, except in praise, was prohibited; all blame directed against the Government; all attacks upon any class; all censure against either of the Chambers; all criticisms of the institutions of the country; all vituperation of any law, however unjust in principle and injurious in its consequences, were declared *délits* or crimes; and the penalties extended from 600 francs to 50,000, and from six months' to ten years' imprisonment; nay, the judges were empowered to double the *maximum* of the penalties, and to sentence to imprisonment for life and to transportation. To secure the payment of the highest fine, the caution-money was raised to 100,000 francs, and the re-

* France, her Governmental, Administrative, and Social Organisation. London : Madden, 1844.

sponsible editor was compelled to be proprietor of one-third of that sum.   The caution-money had to be made up to its original amount after every penalty, or the newspaper could not be published.   Nay, more; after two condemnations of a newspaper, the judges could interdict its publication."

Corrupt courts of law and packed juries made acquittals things of rare occurrence; but, as a further safeguard, the law empowered the servile Court of Peers—all appointed by the King—to judge writers in the papers, or others; and to encourage and protect the jurymen and the judges, the newspapers were prohibited from giving their names or reporting their deliberations; and, finally, they were prohibited from opening subscriptions for the payment of the fines, and publishing lists of donations on their own behalf for the same purpose.

This was not all.   The printers and booksellers, who were all under the control of the ministry, could be deprived of their licenses even without a trial; so that very few of them durst publish an Opposition paper, or any work in which the Government was in any way censured.

By means of these atrocious laws, fifty-seven journals were, during the first sixteen years of the Orleans rule, compelled to discontinue publication.   Their writers were sentenced, in the aggregate, to an imprisonment of 3141 years and eight months, and their proprietors were fined 7,110,000 francs.   Such, says the "Presse," has been the result of 1129 prosecutions commanded by the King, who inaugurated his accession to the throne by a formal promise that no prosecution should in future be directed against the press.

Let us examine some more of the broken pledges of this felon king.   Civil and religious liberty was the first promise made by him when he visited the Hôtel de Ville, after the Three Days of July; and when pressed by Lafayette to be more explicit in his declaration of principles, he immediately promised that the freedom of the press, the freedom of public meetings, the freedom of public instruction, and the trial by jury, should be the basis of the new constitution. Now the civil liberty existing in France, before February 1848, was of this sort :—A Frenchman was liable to arrest and imprisonment on the order of the mayor or his deputy, or on the denunciation of any paid spy or of an enemy; and he might be kept without any communication with his family and his friends, without being taken before the examining justice, for many days, for many weeks, nay, for many months. His examination was always secret; he was not allowed to call witnesses, or even counsel; he was not confronted with his accusers, nor allowed to hear the evidence against him. When his innocence was evident, many days, and in political cases many months, elapsed before he was set at liberty; and he could obtain no redress for the injury done to his character or property by his unjust imprisonment. If he was sent to trial for a political offence, his acquittal was almost impossible.

Public instruction was a monopoly secured to the University, that is, to the Government, by one of the earliest enactments of ministerial despotism; and the spirit in which the law was devised and administered was soon tested in the case of the Count de Montalembert, M. de Coux, and the Abbé Lacordaire, who were indicted and fined 100 francs for opening a free school in 1831. Are those who sound M. Guizot's praises, and boast of what he has done for the cause of education—are they aware that in 1844 one-half the inhabitants of France were unable to read or write; that 7,000,000 could read imperfectly, and could not write; that 7,000,000 could do both, but imperfectly; and that only 3,000,000 were fully educated? This was no very grand result to be obtained by an annual expenditure of about 380,000l. But another purpose was served by the system; if it kept the poor in ignorance, it enabled the Government to mingle a large portion of error with the education given in the superior schools, and to keep in pay an army of placemen. Russia, the most backward in education of all *quasi*-civilised nations, has a very showy, extensive, and costly system of public instruction.

After the events of February, it is unnecessary to say how far the French were indulged, under the Orleans dynasty, in the constitutional privilege of meeting to discuss the measures of the Government, or other topics of national or local interest. Even private meetings of more than twenty persons were prohibited, if in any way connected with politics. Napoleon's law, made more stringent in 1834, has been strained to prevent the meeting even of an Anti-Slavery Society.

Thus vexation and oppression were the common lot of the French people, from which none were exempt but the servile partisans of the Government, who formed the standing army of corruption. " The individual liberty of a French citizen," says the able and well-informed author of " France," writing in 1844, " consists in a perpetual vassalage to all the delegates and hirelings of the Minister of the Interior and of his police, and in a perpetual fear of the officials of the Minister of Justice."

Was there, at least, any good thing to set off against all this wrong and degradation ? Was the physical condition of the people improved, or were their pecuniary burthens alleviated ? On the contrary, the expenditure of France has increased continually since 1830, and taxation has gone on increasing in the same proportion. The Government of the Citizen King wrung from the nation more than the ambition and the conquests of Napoleon, and more than the aristocracy and the clergy of the Restoration, had ever cost. The war estimates during the Empire amounted on an average to 330,000,000 francs. In 1813, when after the disasters of the campaign in Russia the whole army was reorganised, the total expenditure was 420,000,000 francs. The average of the expenses of the Ministry of War, under Louis Philippe, has been 480,000,000 francs. The same Government that refused to provide any constitutional safety-valves through which the high-pressure steam of public opinion might find issue, thought it necessary to let the hot blood of France run to waste on the sands of Africa. The war in Algeria was purposely protracted to this end, as well as to afford a pretext for swelling the budget of the War Ministry, which certainly rendered distinguished services to the king, if not to the country. Almost all the principal towns of France have been attacked, captured, and partially pillaged by a French army, for resisting the administrative despotism. Lyons, in the short space of three years, was twice besieged and bombarded. Paris itself has not escaped. In June 1832, and April 1834, it presented a spectacle of a stormed city; and on many occasions was all but in a state of siege.

Under the Empire, the budget of the Ministry of the Interior, in which were included the public works, agriculture, and commerce, was 15,000,000 francs. In 1847 the same administration cost 70,000,000 francs.

The total amount of the expenditure for all the services of the Government, except the army and navy, were, under Napoleon, 300,000,000 francs a-year. During the last seventeen years the expenditure for the same services exceeded 900,000,000 francs a-year.

The Revolution of February found France already on the verge of bankruptcy. The public debt (deducting the sinking fund), which in January 1841 was 4,267,315,402 francs, had risen on the 1st of January, 1848, to 5,179,644,730 francs. The budget, which in 1830 was 1,014,914,000 francs, was settled for 1847 at 1,712,979,639 francs. And, notwithstanding a successive increase of receipts, the budget shewed a considerable annual deficit. From 1840 to 1847 the expense outstripped the receipts by 604,525,000 francs; in other words, an addition of 24,000,000 sterling was made to the national debt in the space of seven years. During the last 268 days of its existence, the fallen Government expended beyond its ordinary resources 44,000l. per diem.

Such a financial system absorbed all the resources of the people, and abstracted from them all the means of bettering their condition, improving in industrial, agricultural, and commercial pursuits, and advancing in instruction and morality. "Let it not be said that the greater proportion of the taxes bore upon the rich; it was quite the contrary. Most of them were almost exclusively paid by the poorer classes and the tradespeople. The 750,000,000 produced by the excise, the tax on salt, the customs, and the stamp duty, fell entirely upon these classes; which, besides, participated in a due proportion in the payment of the other taxes. The fact cannot be controverted, and official returns, carefully collated, prove that the total amount of taxes paid by the ruling or governmental class, the 240,000 electors and jurymen, never exceeded 54,000,000 francs; that is [less than] the twentieth part of the whole amount of the contributions levied upon the people. In England, the rich man pays in some degree for the gratification of his pride, of his tastes, for the enjoyment of his pleasure, and for his luxuries : he pays for his servants, for his carriage, for his horses, for his hounds, for sporting a coronet, a helmet, a buck's head, or any other family devices. In France, such taxes were not known; but then the beverage of the artisans, the spade of the labourer, the axe of the woodman, paid 100 per cent of their value."

The financial profligacy of the late Government would have been sufficient, even without the co-operation of other causes, to produce disruption of the social and political system. "There are few matters," says a writer in "Tait's Magazine," "to which statesmen less readily ascribe revolution than to finance." If this be so, statesmen and historians are strangely at variance, for the latter almost invariably find in the bankrupt condition of nations the most prominent causes of great political convulsions. All statesmen profess to be historians, and to build their theories of government on the broadest basis of experience; but somehow we find them too often, like M. Guizot, belying their theories by their practice, reserving the former for occasions "when there is no need of such vanities," and acting on diametrically opposite principles in the affairs of real life. "They imagine that, because the expenditure of a government is less frequently the object of complaints in the press than other departments of general politics, the people are not earnest friends of economy. They blunder in this business, and the British Government will discover, without the enlightenment of a revolution, that the middle and lower classes of this country are heartily hostile to a large expenditure, and dispirited by the hopeless burden of taxation pressing upon them."

Living beyond one's means is, for governments as well as individuals, the sure road to ruin. The Government of a wealthy people might have more slowly reached that inevitable goal, but the French are not a wealthy people. Property amongst them is more generally distributed than with us; but there are in France large numbers of persons in extreme destitution. The state of the peasant proprietors, as depicted by Michelet, is one of abject and increasing penury. Capital and skill, and the needful encouragements to apply them, have been alike wanting to the agriculture of a nation which yet depends mainly on the produce of its soil. The elasticity of its trading and manufacturing industry has been compressed by an iron band of privileges and monopolies, and by a system of customs that would seem to have been expressly organised for the utter ruin of the country. The calamity that swept over Europe in 1845, 1846, and partially in 1847, fell heavily on France, and sharpened the pangs of her chronic malady. The pressure on the money-market, and the necessity of raising loans and converting the unfunded into funded debt, compelled the Public Companies and the Government to reduce, or altogether stop, the expenditure on railway and other works. The little savings of the labourers were gradually exhausted, and there were no colonies to offer them the employment they could not find at home. The destitute, whose numbers every passing week augmented, flocked into Paris and other large towns, filling them with a seething mass of wretchedness and discontent. The mine being thus charged, it needed but a spark to shiver into dust the monstrous fabric of imposture and tyranny so elaborately reared by the Citizen King.

The enormous sums extorted from France by the house of Orleans went partly to fill the family coffers, partly to defray the expenses of family jobs, such as the Spanish marriages; the rest was employed in corrupting and enslaving the nation. Besides his belt of fortresses round Paris and his military force of 400,000 men, Louis Philippe had another, and far more efficient, standing army of placemen and expectants. In 1847, the number of persons employed in the civil service, by the Government of England, was estimated at 25,000, with salaries something under three millions in the aggregate; the registered electors of the kingdom being about 1,000,000. In France, in the same year, whilst the registered electors numbered only 240,000 or thereabouts, the civil offices held at Ministerial pleasure were 628,000, or almost thrice the number of the electors, at a cost of ten millions sterling annually. The main end of this system, though by no means the sole one, was to enable the Government to secure a majority in the Chamber of Deputies, and this it effected with the utmost facility.

The Chamber of Deputies consisted of 459 members; 300 would, therefore, constitute an excellent working majority for the Government. The means of supply exceeded the demand, for there were 350 poor electoral arrondissements, the total number of electors in which was at most 100,000. Sixty thousand places granted to as many electors of those arrondissements, would give the Minister of the day a majority of 20,000 votes in the colleges. These being secured, the large towns, the industrial and enlightened departments, might vote as they pleased; it was a matter of perfect indifference. Such was the electoral science professed and openly practised by the Doctrinaires. The Minister of the Interior, the grand elector of France, had nothing to do, in order to insure a subservient Chamber, but to issue his orders to the Prefects and Sub-

Prefects. If the Ministerial candidates were defeated, out went those two functionaries and all their subordinates in every branch of the public administration.

In order to make assurance doubly sure, the Minister of course took çare to pack the Chamber with placemen. M. Guizot had at the beginning of this year a majority of 78, and nearly two-thirds of his supporters were persons holding office. Is it wonderful that the country should have insisted on a reform of such monstrous abuses? A very moderate concession would have satisfied the Opposition; they only asked for a reduction of the two hundred officials forming the Ministerial majority, and the paltry addition of 20,000 electors to the 240,000 already on the lists. The ex-King and his Ministers, in the royal speech, attributed these very modest demands to " blind and hostile passions." The Peers almost unanimously, and the Deputies by a large majority, re-echoed the royal insult; and eight days had hardly elapsed when King, Peers, and Deputies, had disappeared without leaving a trace, except the blood which was running in the streets of Paris.

And what a time was chosen by these forcible-feebles for refusing so insignificant a concession to equity and public opinion!—the very moment when all France was filled with indignation and disgust at the proved infamy of the Court, the Government, and the classes that basked in the sunshine of royal favour. The Teste and Cubières affair had afforded judicial proof of that venality and corruption in high places, which the public voice had never ceased to denounce throughout the whole reign of Louis Philippe. The murder of his wife by a member of the aristocracy, and a friend of the Orleans family, his subsequent suicide and the exposure of his numerous immoralities, had cast, whether justly or not, a foul stigma on the whole Court and Aristocracy.

" The Spanish marriages, devised for family and selfish ends—prosecuted with an utter disregard of good feeling, ac · complished by the basest means, employed for base motives—

c

rendered the agents and the principals unpopular even in
France. The boast of M. Guizot from the tribune of the
Chambers—that by concealing truth he had cheated the British Minister—destroyed the influence that he had acquired
with moderate men, as the presumed representative of the
English alliance; and left himself with a character that,
though common to diplomatists, should not be avowed. The
political part of the Spanish transaction was less damaging
than the rumours regarding private services by the late Count
Bresson and the Queen-Mother of Spain; imposing on the
Queen a hateful arrangement, calculated to ensure the succession to the throne in the expected grandchildren of Louis
Philippe, or to leave material for impugning the character and
honour of Queen Isabella, if that should seem to be a convenient course, and their anticipations be disappointed. The
suicide of Count Bresson at Naples, confirmed the popular
feeling that his conscience was uneasy under the remembrance
of dishonourable actions insufficiently rewarded. The unfortunate insanity of Count Mortier manifesting itself publicly at
the same time, confirmed the general impression that Louis
Philippe chose singular agents to foreign courts, and subjected
them to strange discipline. Amongst the intelligent classes
of Paris who accounted for these calamities from ordinary
causes, the painful impression remained that Louis Philippe
would sacrifice the happiness, the freedom, the interests, and
the independence of nations, for the aggrandisement of an individual—if that individual were his son—and that M. Guizot
was his flexible instrument in the most disgraceful jobs. The
affair of Cracow confirmed the impression; and it was believed
in Paris, that the influence of France was sold to the Northern
Powers for the benefit of the Orleans family; that any inroad
on the independence of continental nations would be permitted
by the late rulers of France, or protested against in feeble and
undignified terms, never to be consolidated by acts.

" The effort made by the Queen of Spain to escape from the
surveillance of French agents, to assert her own and her king-

dom's independence, and to overthrow the unpopular and anti-national party planted by Louis Philippe, around not only her throne but her bedchamber—existing not merely in the shape of statesmen, but also in the form of waiting-maids and girls of all-work—excited admiration amongst the informed and chivalric portion of the Parisians.   The despatch of Narvaez from Paris to assume the functions of Premier—the return of the Queen-Mother to Madrid—the expenditure of half a million sterling in accomplishing anew the revolution of the bedchambers in the Escurial—disgusted all sound and proper feeling; and men said, Why is half a million of our money expended to endow an unborn child with a throne? while women added, A child that never may be born; although it has not been proved, but suspected only, that the great bribery fund was national money, and not taken from the private estate.

"The Napoleon of Peace, heedless, or ignorant of these complaints, followed the example of the Napoleon of War, in consulting family interests and placing the members of his house.   Algiers needed a Viceroy, and Bugeaud was recalled, that a young and inexperienced Prince might be installed on the shadow of a throne.   The incident of Abd-el-Kader's surrender followed, and the conditions made by the Arab priest and warrior, accepted by the Viceroy of Algiers—broken by the Government of France—clung to the minds of honourable men in that nation; and they said, Are disgrace and falsehood to be heaped over avarice and oppression in our name?

"The affair of Switzerland arose.   France sympathised with the Diet.   The Court and the Cabinet aided the Sonderbund.   France would have helped the Swiss to independence and nationality.   The Court or the Cabinet sold muskets to the Seven Cantons, and encouraged their attitude of defiance. Intervention was proposed; and the firmness of Viscount Palmerston alone saved Switzerland from degradation, after the Diet had vindicated its authority and restored order. The fact was known in France; and Frenchmen felt their country and themselves humiliated by the fact.   They saw the progress of transactions which made them the tools of the arbitrary powers, who, in repayment of these services, were to tolerate the new family in the regal circles of Europe. Jealous of England, they felt, notwithstanding, that constitutional freedom in Europe leant on her arm alone for its support, and that France had become a broken reed, with sharp and rugged ends. Italy followed Switzerland—Italy, that should have turned in difficulty to France for support, avoided the snare. * * * The French people * * * were grossly incensed to find their nation distrusted even by the Pope, when he needed some friendly help in accomplishing particles of reform. The demand by the Sicilians for an English guarantee of their constitution was still more humiliating. The people of France feel a greater interest in foreign politics than those of Britain; and they found out that their Government was higgling and bargaining with despotism, when it should have been, on their principles, generously aiding freedom : but the Government of Guizot was despotic." *

The worst wrong inflicted on France by the late Government was the moral depravity it engendered in a very numerous portion of the upper and middle classes, by the system of patronage we have already described. The effect of that system was to divide the nation into two hostile camps ; on the one side, a dominant caste of 600,000 single men, or heads of families ; on the other, nearly 34,000,000 of helots. It was a system essentially the same as that of Russia, with all its loathsome baseness, knavery, and rapacity ; and it has bequeathed to the Republic the most perilous evil against which the young constitution has to wrestle. Under the Orleans *régime*, all who were not employed by the Government, whether they were nobles or plebeians, were equally crushed under the administrative despotism, and equally helpless in defending either public or private rights against the encroachments of the Government. The holders of office, on the other hand,

* Tait's Magazine, March 1848.

were the virtual aristocracy of the country, and had good pay for doing little or nothing. The consequence was, that all the heads of families paying yearly in direct taxes 200 francs (8*l*.), and who were thereby constituted electors, instead of directing the studies and inclinations of their sons towards the exercise of an independent but laborious calling, thought of nothing but enabling them to fill some office under Government. Great as was the number of *employés*, that of the candidates for place was many times greater, and hence the depraved morality of the former class became the standard of excellence for a large portion of the youth of France. Injuries to men's material interests are the least of the evils wrought by despotism ; its deadliest curse is that which it lays on the souls of its victims. Never was degradation more rapid and complete than which was accomplished in the character of the influential classes of France under the monarchy of July. Sordid self-interest was their only motive ; boundless, unscrupulous subserviency to power usurped the place of conscience ; and lying, cheating, bullying, and eavesdropping were the arts most sedulously cultivated, as infallibly conducting their accomplished votaries to fortune and honours.

" Most of the *employés* of the several administrations," says the author of " France "—himself a Frenchman, and long the confidential friend of Louis Philippe—" most of the *employés* were compelled to perform the office of spies, and to report to their superiors on the conduct, principles, opinions, and connexions, not only of their colleagues, but also of their own relatives and friends ; and for that purpose they were allowed, and even induced to frequent, the company of either Legitimatists or Liberals, to profess apparently the same opinions, and to be of some service to them, if necessary to gain their confidence." The police were, of course, engaged even more assiduously upon the same dirty work ; and even ladies were not exempt from their vile scrutiny. Besides the general police, there was also a secret police surveillance, which was exercised over the higher classes in the departments by confidential agents of the Ministry of the Interior, who corresponded with the Minister himself. Indeed, the chief business of the latter was to direct all the ramifications of this organised rascality, and apply its results. " In order," says our authority, " to shew in all its turpitude the working of this secret police, I translate one of the accounts transmitted during the administration of Thiers, and which was kindly communicated to me, as I happened to be a friend of the party alluded to.

" ' M. de * * * persists in his sarcastic opposition, and, as a leader, is the more dangerous, as he possesses a large fortune, and an uncontrollable spirit. He has long patronised the Canal of —— : let him sink there his property, while the coquetry of Madame de * * *, skilfully managed, will soon bring about a *fracas*, and turn the laughers on our side. Her lover has chosen me for his confidant : he has not succeeded, but I give him hopes, and he assiduously continues his courtship. You shall know the results.'

" Thanks to the benevolent indiscretion of an *employé*, the results were the flight of the ministerial spy, after a sound castigation ; but how many others have succeeded in their plans? One principle of the Government of July, proclaimed and put in practice immediately after its establishment, was to ruin or dishonour those who declared against it ; and the revelations of the police, on the affairs of men in business, have reduced many to bankruptcy and beggary. The men who had taken the principal part in the Revolution, Audrey de Puyraveau and Laffitte, when they would no longer lend themselves to the anti-national system of the King, were reduced to sell all their property and wind up their concerns. The King himself set the example of slander. Benjamin Constant was poor, and had debts : his lady had prevailed on him to accept about 6000*l*. offered to her by the Queen, in the name of the King, as a mark of respect for his disinterestedness and patriotism. Benjamin Constant was the first to oppose the political direction of the new dynasty ; and, notwithstanding the assurance of secrecy which had accompanied the gift, the King, incensed at his opposition, divulged the fact, and represented it as a bargain. The poor patriot could not bear up under the feeling of degradation, and died five weeks afterwards, saying to his friends, ' That bad man has killed me.' "

Well might the abashed and contrite Laffitte publicly and solemnly beg pardon of God and his country for the sin he had committed in raising such a man as Louis Philippe to the throne of France !

The personal character of the ex-King is curiously illustrated in a letter to the " Atlas," dated Paris, Feb. 3, 1848. " Public anxiety," says the writer, " is beginning to be appeased concerning the health of the King. During the early part of the week, the various reports which were afloat became of serious injury to commerce, no business being done for several days anywhere except at the Bourse. ' The King is ill ;' ' He is better;' ' He is worse ;' ' He is dying,' were all so many magic words which had power to raise or depress the funds at pleasure, occasioning in some instances the greatest confusion and loss. For several days, those who had money invested in the public securities scarcely knew for an hour together the value of their fortunes. None could tell for a while whence sprang these contradictory rumours. It was only known too well, that if they were productive of loss to some, they must occasion enormous gains to others ; but who the gainers were remained a mystery for some time, until it was perceived that the agent of a high personage always managed to be on the safe side, buying and selling *à propos*, and realising enormous profits. No sooner was this discovered, than a report spread like wildfire that the rumours originated at the Tuileries, and sprang from the fertile brain of the high personage himself. ' Here is scandal !—here is base invention, indeed ! Who can believe such calumny as this ? How does party spirit blind us, to be sure ! An enemy has surely done this thing !' said I to myself, as, weary and disgusted with such baseness, I resolved to listen no more, to read no more newspapers, but to fly to books for relief, resolving that even these should not be modern ones, for I felt disgusted at our own times, and thoroughly ashamed of the vile detraction of the age we live in. Chance, fortunately, threw in my way a volume of the ' Espion Anglais,' or correspondence between two friends— Milor All-Eye and Milor All-Ear; an amusing book enough, and which has become of late years rather rare. I turned it over with indifference, when my eye fell upon an interesting chapter, which I thought might be likely to illustrate the case, and serve to refute the calumnies which have crept abroad. Milor All-Eye dates his letter August 3, 1782 :—

" ' I have just returned,' says he, ' from Passy, where I have been paying a visit to the Duke of Orleans, and was introduced by him to his family. His Royal Highness himself is a vulgar, good-natured man, something like an English farmer in manners and appearance, and received me with a cordial greeting in the garden. We entered a saloon on the ground-floor, where the Duchess, who had been informed of my visit, hastened to join us. She is a most remarkable woman, combining the lofty manners of the court with the liberal notions fast gaining ground among us. After awhile, as I had expressed a wish to pay my respects to the young Duc de Chartres, we repaired together to his apartment. He is a fine lad, just about thirteen. We found him busily employed in practising various tricks of sleight-of-hand which he had learnt from a juggler—one Lecamus—a pastime of which he is passionately fond. Some of them are marvellous, indeed, and he played them for our amusement with great delight to himself. The Duke of Orleans laughed heartily at his son's dexterity, but the Duchess looked grave, and condemned the amusement as suspicious and unworthy.'

" Somehow the chapter gave me subject of reflection, and I flung the book aside to follow the advice of Lindley Murray —' When you meet in reading with an observation that strikes you, digest it well and *examine it in all its bearings.*' "

This "cutpurse of the empire and the rule" has verified the prediction of his governess, Madame de Genlis, that the qualities for which he would be most conspicuous through life were avarice and perfidy. In the spirit of insatiable avarice, and with all the artifices of consummate perfidy, he reared the colossal fortunes of his house on the shame and woe of millions. His avarice and perfidy have undone him, and smitten down in sudden and irretrievable ruin the laborious work of four-and-thirty years. The good-natured world has been pleased to ascribe all sorts of virtues to this man. Their actual sum is soon told, and makes but a poor set-off against his monstrous wickedness. He was thrifty and frugal, except in disposing of what was not his own; wary and sagacious, until unparalelled prosperity, and the absorbing passions of his old age, extinguished his wonted prudence. He was a good family-man, and he wheedled and cheated, begged, filched, and robbed, with exemplary diligence, for the benefit of his young ones. He was not conspicuous for moral courage, but he had more personal intrepidity than his father. He was not a libertine, like Philippe Egalité or the Régent Orléans, but he was as unscrupulous as either — nay, even more so than the latter — where his own interests were concerned. Money was the standard by which he estimated alike things physical, moral, and spiritual; and he knew too well the money value of a fair reputation to risk it upon any light grounds. No wayward caprice could ever have tempted him to perpetrate any unprofitable villany; but from the pursuit of a lucrative object he was not to be diverted by any sense of honour or honesty, any touch of pity or remorse. The Régent Orléans patronised Law's prodigious swindle, partly because he was duped by the gorgeous promises of the Scotch financier, partly because he was delighted with a scheme that so well aided his favourite plan of stifling in universal corruption all opposition to his government. But Philippe was too proud to dabble in the filthy flood with which he deluged his country; his own hands remained clean, and not a sou found its way from the Rue

Quincampoix to his private coffers. In his place, Louis Philippe would have been too knowing for the Scotchman; but he would have used him up to a certain point, as he did the St. Simonians, and then turned him over to the attorney-general : meanwhile he would have swept half the fortunes in France into his own bags. He loved corruption as much as the Regent, but money more. The latter, blackguard as he was, would have shrunk with abhorrence from the nameless abomination practised upon the unhappy Queen of Spain. He was nobly true to his trust as guardian of the young King, and tenderly cherished the frail life interposed between himself and the throne. Louis Philippe conspired for selfish ends against his confiding kindred, and repaid every trust reposed in him with treachery.

Oh, what a model of decorum and domestic virtue was that King, in whose family Christina and her guardsman, and Sophy Dawes, were welcome and honoured guests ! We will lay before our readers the history of those foul transactions, in which the interests of the last-named of these wretches were mixed up with those of the house of Orleans. Our narrative is a condensation of that which Louis Blanc has founded on a careful scrutiny of official and other authentic documents.

La Baronne de Feuchères was by birth an Englishwoman, one Sophy Dawes. She appeared at Covent Garden, which she quitted to become the mistress of an opulent foreigner, with whom she lived at Turnham Green. The Baron de Feuchères subsequently married her, and his name served for some time to cover the scandal of her adulterous amours with the Duc de Bourbon, last of the Condés. Her power over the Duke was omnipotent ; he loved and dreaded her. Gifted with rare beauty and grace, fascinating and imperious, tender and haughty, by turns, she had considerable cleverness and no principle. The Duke had settled on her the domains of St. Leu and Boissy and about a million of francs (40,000l.) in money. She desired more, and was presented with the forest of Enghien. But a secret uneasiness tormented her ; she dreaded lest the Prince's heirs should take legal proceedings and despoil her of all she had so dexterously acquired. She, therefore, conceived the bold plan of making the Duke adopt the Duc d'Aumale, son of Louis Philippe, as his heir. The proof of this is in the following letter, of the year 1827, from the Duchess of Orleans to the Baroness de Feuchères :—

" I am very much touched, madame, by your solicitude to bring about that result which you regard as likely to fulfil the wishes of M. le Duc de Bourbon ; and believe me, if I have the happiness to find my son become his adopted child, you will receive from us at all times, and in all circumstances, that protection for you and yours which you demand, of which a mother's gratitude will be for you a sure guarantee."

It must have been a sore trial for such a woman as the Duchesse d'Orléans to associate her maternal hopes with such very equivocal advocacy. The Duc d'Orléans, on the 2d of May, 1829, learned from Madame de Feuchères that she had, in an urgent and impassioned letter, proposed to her lover to adopt the Duc d'Aumale ; on this information he addressed himself directly to the Duc de Bourbon, giving him to understand how grateful he was to Madame de Feuchères, and how proud he should be to see one of his sons bear the glorious name of Condé. At this unexpected blow, the Duc de Bourbon was overwhelmed with anxiety. He had never liked the Duc d'Orléans. He had stood godfather to the Duc d'Aumale, but never thought of him as his heir. Yet how could he, without insult, now refuse that which they assumed him to be so anxious to bestow ? Above all, how resist the entreaties and violent importunities of Madame de Feuchères ? Harassed and terrified, the Duc de Bourbon consented to an interview with the Duc d'Orléans. Nothing positive was concluded ; but the latter believed his hopes so well founded that he ordered M. Dupin to prepare a will in favour of the Duc d'Aumale.

The Baroness became more and more urgent, and the Prince gave vent to his anger in bitter reproaches. He had had no rest since this fatal plan was proposed to him ; he could not sleep at night, and the day was embittered by vio-lent quarrels. More than once incautious expressions betrayed the agitation' of his mind: " My death is all they have in view," he exclaimed one day in a fit of despair. Another time he forgot himself so far as to say to M. de Surval, "Once let them obtain what they desire, and my days are numbered." At last, in a desperate attempt to escape from Madame de Feuchères, he threw himself on the generosity of the Duc d'Orléans himself. "The affair which now occupies us," he wrote, on the 20th of August, 1829, "begun unknown to me and somewhat thoughtlessly by Madame de Feuchères, is in-finitely distressing to me, as you may have observed;" and he entreated the Duke to interfere and prevail on Madame to re-linquish her projects, promising at the same time a certain public testimony of his affection for the Duc d'Aumale. Re-sponding to this singular appeal, Orléans went to Madame, and, in presence of a witness specially provided for the occa-sion, he begged her to abandon her project. She was inflex-ible; and so the Duc d'Orléans, without at all compromising his son's prospects, had the credit of making an honourable and disinterested attempt.

This state of things was too forced not to end in some violent explosion. On the 29th August, 1829, the Duc de Bourbon was at Paris, and in the billiard-room of the palace: M. de Surval, who was in the passage, heard loud cries for help; he rushed in, and beheld the Prince in a frightful pas-sion. "Only see in what a passion Monseigneur puts him-self!" said Madame de Feuchères; "and without a cause! Try and calm him." "Yes, madame," cried the old man, "it is horrible, atrocious, thus to put a knife to my throat to make me consent to a deed you know I so abhor!" and seizing her hand he added, with a significant gesture, "Well, then, plunge the knife in at once—plunge it!" The next day the Prince signed the deed, which made the Duc d'Aumale his heir and secured the Baroness a legacy of 40,000*l.*

The Revolution of July burst forth; the Duc d'Orléans

became Louis Philippe. The Prince de Condé was intensely alarmed, but the restoration of tranquillity and the safe embarkation of his exiled kinsmen put an end to his fears. Still his melancholy remained, and a remarkable change was observed in his demeanour with regard to Madame de Feuchères. Her name uttered in his presence sometimes brought a cloud over his face; his fondness for her, though always prodigal in anticipating her least wishes, yet seemed mixed with terror. He communicated in confidence to M. de Choulot, and Manoury his valet, his intention of making a long journey, which was to be kept a profound secret from Madame de Feuchères; at the same time dark rumours circulated about the château. On the morning of the 11th of August the Prince was found with his eye bleeding, which he accounted for to Manoury by saying he had struck it against the night-table. The valet venturing to reply, "The table is not so high as the bed," the Duke remained silent and embarrassed. Some minutes afterwards, as Manoury was spreading a carpet in the dressing-room, he found a letter under the door next the back staircase and brought it to the Prince. The latter was exceedingly disturbed on reading it, and said, "I am not a good story-teller; I said I hurt myself in my sleep. The truth is, that on opening the door I fell, and struck my temple against the corner." It is worthy of remark, that the Prince afterwards wished Manoury to sleep by the door of his bedchamber, and that when the latter suggested that this would look strange, and that it would be more in course for Lecomte, his *ralet-de-chambre de service*, to do this, the Prince replied, "Oh, no! that must not be." Lecomte had been introduced into the château by Madame de Feuchères.

The preparations for the journey were nearly completed. For three days the Prince had resumed his usual amusements. After a cheerful dinner, at which M. de Cossé Brissac was present, they played at whist. The Prince was gayer than usual, lost some money, and abstained from paying it, saying, "To-morrow." He rose, and crossed the ante-room to pro-

cried to his bedchamber, and in passing made a friendly gesture to his servants, which seemed like an adieu.   Was this
one of those farewell tokens in which the thought of approaching death betrays itself?   Or had it reference to his projected
journey and exile?

He ordered them to call him at eight o'clock next morning, and they left him for the night.   It is necessary to understand distinctly the situation of the Prince's bedroom.   It
was connected by a short passage with a waiting-room, which
opened on one side into a dressing-room, having issue upon
the great corridor of the château; on the other side the waiting-room opened upon a back staircase, ending at the landing-
place, where were the apartments of Madame de Feuchères
and of Madame de Flassans, her niece.   The back staircase
led from this landing-place to the vestibule; and by an inter-
mediate landing, on the *entresol*, it communicated with a second corridor, along which were the chambers of l'Abbé Briant,
of Lachassine, the femme-de-chambre of the Baroness, and of
the Duprés, husband and wife, attached to her service.   The
room of the latter was immediately under that of the Prince,
so that they could hear when there was talking above their
heads.

This night (the 26th) the park-rangers went their accustomed rounds.   Lecomte had locked the door of the dressing-
room and taken away the key.   Why was this precaution
taken?   The Prince constantly left the door of his room un-
bolted.   Madame de Flassans sat up till two in the morning,
occupied with writing: she heard no noise, neither did the
Duprés.   All night the château was perfectly still.

At eight the next morning Lecomte knocked at the
Prince's door.   It was bolted: the Prince made no reply.
Lecomte retired, and returned afterwards with M. Bonnie:
both knocked without receiving a reply.   In much alarm, they
went down to Madame de Feuchères.   " I will come at once,"
she said; " when he hears my voice, he will answer."   She
hurried from her room but half-dressed, and reaching that of

the Prince, knocked, and called out, "Open, open! Monseigneur, it is I." No answer. The alarm spread. Manoury, Leclerc, l'Abbé Briant, Méry-Lafontaine, ran to the spot. The room was burst open: the shutters were closed, and the room dark. A single waxlight was burning on the mantelpiece, but behind a screen, which sent the light upwards towards the ceiling. By this feeble light the head of the Prince was seen close to the shutter of the north window. He seemed like a man in the act of listening intently to something outside. The east window being opened, the light fell upon a horrible spectacle. The Duc de Bourbon was hanging, or rather hooked on, to the fastening of the window-sash. Every one rushed in except Madame de Feuchères, who sank groaning and shuddering on a fauteuil in the dressing-room; and the cry, "Monseigneur is dead!" resounded throughout the château.

The Duke was attached to the window-bolt by means of two handkerchiefs, passed one within the other: one of these formed a flattened and elongated ring; the other an oval, the base of which *supported the lower jaw*, whilst the apex lay against the upper and back part of the head. This handkerchief was *not* tied with a slip-knot, *nor did it press upon the windpipe;* it left the nape of the neck uncovered, and was found so loose that several of the persons present could easily pass their fingers betwixt it and the neck. The head of the deceased drooped upon his breast; the face was pale; the tongue was not thrust out of the mouth, it only pushed up the lips; the hands were closed, the knees bent, and the points of the toes touched the carpet; so that in the acute sufferings which accompany the last efforts of life, the Prince would only have had to stand upright upon his feet, leaning against the window, to have escaped death. All these obvious circumstances were strongly at variance with the supposition of suicide: they struck most of the beholders with surprise.

The authorities arrived; the state and position of the corpse were noted down; an inquest was held, in which it was concluded that the Duke had strangled himself.   Indeed, the fact that the door was bolted on the inside seemed to put the idea of assassination out of the question.   In spite of many contradictions, it was believed that the Duke had committed suicide.

Nevertheless, this belief gradually died away in every mind, and even before it was ascertained that the bolt could be very easily moved backwards and forwards from outside. The age of the Prince, his want of energy, his well-known religious sentiments, the horror he had always testified at death, his known opinion of suicide as cowardly, the serenity of his latter days, and his project of flight,—these all tended to throw a doubt on his suicide.   His watch was found on the mantel-piece, wound up as usual; and under the bolster there was a handkerchief, with a knot on it—his custom when he wished to remind himself of any thing on the morrow.   Besides, the body was not in a state of suspension.   The *valet de pied*, Ro-manzo, who had travelled in Turkey and Egypt, and his companion, Fife, an Irishman, had both seen many people hanged. They declared that the faces of the hanged were blackish, and not of a dull white; that their eyes were open and bloodshot; and the tongue protruding from the mouth : all which signs were quite contrary to those observed in the corpse of the Prince.   When they detached the body, Romanzo undid the knot of the handkerchief fastened to the window-bolt ; and it was with very great difficulty he did so, so skilfully and strongly was it tied.   Now, there was not one of the Prince's servants but knew that his awkwardness was extreme ; that he could not even tie the strings of his shoes ; that although, indeed, he could tie the bow of his cravat, he was obliged to have the two ends brought round from behind by his valet; that he had received a sabre cut in his right hand, and had had his left collar-bone broken ; so that he could not lift his left hand above his head, and that he could only ascend the stairs with the double assistance of his cane and the banisters.

Certain other suspicious circumstances began to be commented on. The slippers, which the Prince rarely used, were always at the foot of the chair in which he was undressed; was it the old man's hand that on that fatal night had placed them at the foot of the bed? The Prince could only get out of bed by turning in a manner upon himself; and he pressed so on the edge of the bed as he slept, that they were obliged to double the covering four times to prevent his falling out. How was it that they found the middle of the bed pressed down, and the sides, on the contrary, raised up? It was the custom of those who made the bed to push it to the bottom of the alcove; this custom had not been departed from on the 26th. Who, then, had moved the bed a foot and a half from its usual place? There were two wax lights extinguished, but not burnt out, on the chimneypiece: who could have extinguished them? The Prince? Had he then voluntarily left himself in the dark when setting about such complicated arrangements for self-destruction?

Madame de Feuchères supported the hypothesis of suicide, and seemed to think that the accident of the 11th had been but an abortive attempt of the sort. She trembled when the Duke's travelling project was spoken of; and hearing Manoury talk freely on the subject, "Take care," she said; "such language may seriously compromise you with the King." But it seemed strange to all the attendants of the Prince that, when on the point of accomplishing so awful a deed, he had left no written intimation of his design, no mark of affection for those to whom he always had been so kind, and whose zeal he had always recognised and recompensed. This was a moral suicide, less explicable than the other. An unexpected discovery put a climax to all these uncertainties.

Towards evening on the 27th, M. Guillaume, secretary to the King, perceived, on passing by the chimney, some scraps of paper which lay scattered on the dark ground of the grate. Stooping down, he saw on these fragments, which lay on the remains of others burnt to ashes, the words,—" Roi . . . Vincennes . . . infortuné fils." The Procureur-Général,

D

M. Bernand, having arrived at St. Leu, the pieces of paper were put into his hands, along with others which Lecomte, the valet, had picked up. " The truth is here," he exclaimed, and having put the fragments together, he made out the two following sets of line :—

" Saint-Leu appartient au roi

Philippe
ne pillés, ni ne brûlés
le château ni le village
ne faites de mal à personne
ni à mes amis, ni à mes
gens.   On vous a egarés
sur mon compte, je n'ai

urir en aiant
cœur le peuple
et l'espoir du,
bonheur de ma patrie."

" Saint-Leu et ses depend
appartiennent à votre roi
Philippe : ne pillés, ni ne brûlés

le	le village
ne	mal à personne
ni	es amis, ni à mes gens.

On vous a égarés sur mon compte. Je n'ai qu'à mourir en souhaitant bonheur et prosperité au peuple Français et à ma patrie. Adieu pour toujours.

" L. H. J. DE BOURBON, Prince de Condé.

" P.S. Je demande à être enterré à Vincennes, près de mon infortuné fils."*

---

* The second document, of which the first would seem to be a rough draft, is to this effect :—" St. Leu and its depend . . . belong to your king, Philippe : do not pillage nor burn the . . . the village nor . . . harm to any one, neither . . . y friends, nor to my people. You have been misled with regard to me. I have only to die wishing happiness and prosperity to the French people and to my country. Adieu for ever.

" L. H. J. DE BOURBON, Prince de Condé.

" P.S. I request that I may be buried at Vincennes, near my unfortunate son."

In these strange admonitions, many thought they saw a proof of suicide. Others, more suspicious, could not conceive that these were the farewell words of a prince about to quit life. The fear of a pillage of St. Leu seemed incompatible with that disgust of all things which precedes suicide. It was, moreover, little likely that the Prince should have experienced such a fear on the night of the 26th, the night after the fête of St. Louis, wherein he had received very flattering testimonies of affection on the part of the surrounding population. It was also inexplicable how the Prince could write down Louis Philippe as the proprietor of St. Leu, which he knew did not belong to him. There was great surprise felt, that, having taken up his pen in the midst of preparations for suicide, he had said nothing precise respecting his design, and thus saved his faithful servants from a frightful suspicion. The very mode in which the papers were discovered was inconceivable. *How came it that these papers, so easily perceived on the evening of the 27th, escaped the diligent search of Romanzo, Choulot, and Manoury, and all those who that day visited every corner of the room, chimney included?* Was it not very likely they were thrown there by some hand interested in corroborating the belief of suicide? These things led to a conjecture that the document was of some anterior date, and that it was no more than a proclamation of the Prince during the first days of the month of August, when the revolutionary storm was still muttering. This hypothesis was strengthened by some who remembered that the Prince had, indeed, conceived the idea of a proclamation. For our own part, we incline to look upon the paper as a forgery. It could hardly have been a proclamation, from the very form of it; and the same objection before advanced, of the Prince's attributing St. Leu to the King, when in reality it belonged to the Prince, applies also to this case. Besides, a critical inspection of the words remaining, and of their arrangement, leads to a suspicion of forgery: they are too consecutive for a burnt letter.

Two parties formed opposite opinions, and maintained them with equal warmth. Those who believed in the Duke's suicide, alleged in favour of their opinion the inquest; the melancholy of the Prince since 1830; his Royalist terrors; the act of charity which he had confided, on the 26th, to the care of Manoury, for fear of not being able to accomplish it himself; his mute adieu to his attendants; the state of the body, which presented no traces of violence except some excoriations quite compatible with the supposition of suicide; the condition of his clothes, on which no soil had been observed; the bolt closed from within; the physical presumptions against the notion of assassination; and the impossibility of saying, with any degree of certainty,—There are the murderers!

To these arguments, the defenders of the dead man's memory replied by words and acts of powerful effect. One of them, M. Méry Lafontaine, suspended himself at the fatal window-sash in a manner precisely the same as that in which the Prince had been found, and the experiment was perfectly harmless! Another endeavoured, by means of a small riband, to shoot the bolt into its staple from the outside, and the trial was completely successful. It was related that Lecomte, when in the chapel where the body was exposed, cried out in anguish, " I have a weight upon my heart." M. Bonnie, contradicting the formal assertions of Lecomte, affirmed that, on the morning of the 27th, the bolt of the back staircase was *not* closed; and that, in order to hide this fatal circumstance, Madame de Feuchères, instead of taking the shorter route, had gone to the chamber of death by the longer way, that of the grand staircase!

On the 4th of September, the Prince's heart was carried to Chantilly. L'Abbé Pélier, almoner to the Prince, directed the funeral service. He carried the heart of the victim in a silver casket, and opened his lips to utter the last farewell. Deep silence prevailed, and prodigious was the impression when the sacred orator solemnly pronounced these words,—

" The Prince is innocent of his death in the sight of God!"
Thus ended the great race of Condé.

Madame de Feuchères hastily quitted St. Leu, and went
to the Palais Bourbon. For a fortnight she made l'Abbé
Briant sleep in her library, and Madame Flassans in her bedroom, as if dreading to be alone. But soon mastering her
emotion, she seemed as bold and unembarrassed as ever. She
resumed her speculations at the Bourse, gained considerable
sums, and laughed at her enemies. But she could not stifle
the murmurs which arose on all sides. The Prince de Rohan
made every preparation both for a civil and a criminal suit.
At Chantilly and St. Leu there were few who believed in the
suicide; at Paris, the boldest conjectures found vent; the
highest names in the kingdom were not spared. The King's
name was coupled with that of Madame de Feuchères, and
furnished political enemies with a weapon they were not
scrupulous in using. With malicious sagacity they remarked
that, from the 27th, the Court had by its trusty agents taken
possession of the theatre of the catastrophe; that the Almoner
of the Prince, although on the spot, had not been called on to
take part in drawing up the *procès-verbaux;* and that the
Prince's physician, M. Geurin, was not called in to the *post
mortem* examination, which was entrusted to three physicians,
two of whom, MM. Marc and Pasquier, were on terms of the
closest intimacy with the Court. It was asked, with a sarcastic show of surprise, Why had the Duc de Broglie prevented the insertion in the "Moniteur" of the oration of
M. Pélier at Chantilly?

A decisive and honourable means was open to the King,
to stifle rumours that did not spare even the throne. To
repudiate a succession so clouded with black suspicions, would
have silenced his enemies and done honour to himself. But
the head of the Orleans family had early shewn that indifference to money was not the virtue he aspired to. On the eve
of passing to a throne he hastily consigned his personal pro
perty to his children, in order that he might not unite it with

the State property, in accordance with the ancient law of the monarchy. Instead, therefore, of relinquishing his son's claim to the heritage of the Prince de Condé, he invited Madame de Feuchères to Court, where she met with a reception that immediately became the talk and the amazement of all Paris. The loud voice of public opinion rendered an inquiry inevitable; but nothing was left untried to hush up the affair. The *conseilleur-rapporteur*, M. de la Huproie, shewed a determination to get at the truth; he was suddenly superannuated, and the place of judge, which he had long desired for his son-in-law, was at once accorded to him. The depositions passed into other hands.

At length, however, the action brought by the family of the Rohans to invalidate the will of the Duc de Bourbon in favour of the Duc d'Aumale, was tried. The proceedings excited intense interest. M. Hennequin, in a speech full of striking facts and inferences, presented a picture of the violences and artifices by which the old Duc de Bourbon had been hurried into a consent to the will. From the well-known sentiments of the Prince, M. Hennequin argued that the will was not his voluntary act, but had been extorted from him; and in the impossibility of suicide, he saw proof of assassination. The younger M. Dupin replied with great dexterity. But it was a matter of general remark, that he parried precise facts and specific accusations with vague recriminations and tortuous explanations. He pretended that this action was nothing but a plot laid by the Legitimatists—an attempt at vengeance, which he called upon all friends of the Revolution of 1830 to resent. The interest of the Legitimatists in the affair was evident; but to combat an imposing mass of testimony, something more was necessary than a brawling appeal to the popular recollections of July. The Rohans lost their cause before the jury, but they gained it before the tribunal of public opinion.

Whatever may be the conclusion arrived at by the reader respecting this mysterious affair, there can be but one sentiment as regards a part of the conduct of Louis Philippe. Decency would have suggested that such a woman as the Baronne de Feuchères should not be welcomed at the Court, especially when such terrible suspicions were hanging over her. Decency would have suggested that the public should have full and ample conviction of the sincerity with which the causes of the Prince's death were investigated. Our own belief is this: The Prince de Condé was murdered, and Louis Philippe might have brought the murderer to justice, but would not. And there are Englishmen who deem it an honour to press the hand polluted by a booty so won,—the hand that has been held out in venal friendship to Sophy Dawes!!

TO A TRAITOR.

Thy lying heart, and not thy vanquisht arms,
   Degrade thee, vilest of earth's vilest race!
On France descends her glory with fresh charms,
   On thee thy infamy with fresh disgrace.

'Twas not enough to seat beside thy queen
   A harlot reeking with thy kinsman's blood;
'Twas not enough to lick the spoil obscene
   Which that low lozel cast before thy brood;

But thou must pilfer the poor pittance thrown
   To those who carved for thee the royal feast.
Off! off! let France stand upright, stand alone,
   From Austria, Guizot, Philippe, fraud, release.

                    WALTER SAVAGE LANDOR.

CHAPTER II.

THE BATTLE FOR REFORM.

WE have seen what abundant reason there was to justify the
cry for Parliamentary Reform that rang throughout France in
the summer and autumn of 1847.   The general feeling was
illustrated and enforced by no fewer than sixty-two Reform
Banquets, which were held in different towns, and attended by
the leading Oppositionists in and out of the Chambers.   The
omission of the King's health from the list of toasts, on
almost all these occasions, was a circumstance that gave
peculiar poignancy to the irritation with which such displays
were regarded by the Government.   But what put the climax
to its indignation was the announcement, that soon after the
opening of the session the Opposition would crown their
audacity by holding a Monster Banquet in the capital itself.
The King and his Ministers forthwith resolved to put down
these insolent contemners of royalty, these " everlasting foes
of order."   Military preparations were made on a most extensive scale; guns were mounted on all the fortresses round
Paris; large stores of ammunition were provided, and nothing
seemed wanting to enable the Government to crush any chimerical attempt at insurrection on the part of the Parisians.
These arrangements being made, the King prepared to meet
the Chambers with a bold front, in the full assurance that he
was once more about to signalise the triumph of might over
right.   The appearance of the old man on the last occasion
he was ever to meet his parliament is worth recording, and

again we have recourse to our clever friend of the "Atlas," who thus writes on the 30th of December, 1847 : —

"The political year is closed at length, and the new one began yesterday with the King's Speech and the opening of the Chambers. Hope is once more taking the place of disappointment and despair, in those whose memories serve them not with faith. The whole ceremony of yesterday reminded us, indeed, most strangely, of the same exhibition under the expiring Bourbons. The same pomp and circumstance — the same red velvet cushions — and the same gilded chair — the same old broken promises to sustain the same old tottering throne — nay, one could really have imagined that the very actors in that scene were all the same. The Queen personified 'Madame,' the Duchess of Orleans seemed the younger hope, 'Madame' de Berri—nay, the very 'child of miracle' was not wanting, and looked out from the front of the royal box with the same fair young face I so well remember in former days breathing hope and peace to all — hope which we know to have been false and treacherous — peace which exists nowhere, save in his own pure and childish bosom. The King looked not ill, but wearied and dispirited; and his voice, which on former occasions has ever been remarked for the richness of its modulation, was weak and inaudible. His 'most hearty congratulations' upon the happiness and prosperity of the nation were uttered in a low tone, and received in silence. It was like the voice of the dying discoursing to the *dead*. Louis Philippe, as he stood trembling before his stern judges, reminded me of the man in one of Hoffman's wildest phantasies, who was condemned to hold up the falling rock with his grandmother's knitting needle, which bends and bends in spite of the old man's frantic efforts until he stands *beneath* the mass, and knows that it must crush him in another moment.

"The whole scene was sad, and it caused a painful emotion to hear his Majesty talk of congratulation upon the prosperous events of the past year, when he knows, as well as as we, that it has been marked by a singular and ominous fatality. It is the year of Teste and Cubières, of Beauvallon, of Praslin, and Mortier, and will be recorded in our annals as anything but prosperous. It was curious to listen to these self-hugging felicitations, when we had just been dismissed from Michelet's lecture at the College de France, wherein he said with conviction, 'This year has been the most fatal to our country since the reign of Napoleon; it may be called the *moral Waterloo* of France; and the only consolation amid so much disgrace is the certainty of being already at the bottom of the abyss—we can sink no lower. A sentiment new to France, and unrecorded in her history, has been traced upon its pages by the hands of Louis Philippe and his Minister. It is that of fear—from fear of license we have submitted to the forfeit of our liberty—from fear of anarchy we have submitted to despotism—and from fear of an *impossible* war, we have allowed our national flag to be insulted in every quarter of the globe.'

"This discourse of Michelet made an immense sensation in Paris, and yet on the very morrow of its utterance an event occurred which has filled with consternation every well-wisher to peace and order—every one, in short, whose memory is long enough to remember dates prior to the year of our Lord one thousand eight hundred and thirty. The annual dinner given by the Poles in Paris, upon the occasion of the *fête* of Prince Adam Czartoryski, was announced to take place according to custom at the restaurateur Lemardelay's, and con-sequently, at the day and hour appointed numbers of Poles, having purchased tickets, were seen hurrying towards the restaurateur's in question, intent upon sustaining both mind and body at the same time—the one with goodly cheer, the other with hope and courage. But, lo! at Lemardelay's door, instead of the smiling *garçon*, with napkin beneath his arm, and silver spoons peering from each pocket, they were greeted by the rough welcome of two gendarmes, who sternly bade them withdraw, unless they were inclined to be driven! The

greeting was matter of some surprise, as was also the information that the dinner must be regarded as a political demonstration, and must henceforth be prevented accordingly."

This little go, in the way of banquet stopping, was a
prelude on the part of Ministers to their intended discomfiture
of a more formidable set of dinner eaters.   The paragraph in
the King's Speech, in which he alluded to the Reform question, was as follows :—

" Gentlemen,—The more I advance in life, the more I dedicate with
devotedness to the service of France, to the care of her interests, dignity,
and happiness, all the activity and strength which God has given, and still
vouchsafes me.   Amidst the agitation that hostile and blind passions
foment, a conviction animates and supports me, which is, that we possess
in the constitutional monarchy — in the union of the great powers of the
State—sure means of overcoming all those obstacles, and of satisfying all
interests, moral and material.   Let us firmly maintain, according to the
Charter, social order, and all its conditions.   Let us guarantee, according
to the Charter, the public liberties and all their developements.   We shall
transmit unimpaired to the generations that may come after us the trust
confided to us, and they will bless us for having founded and defended the
edifice under shelter of which they will live happy and free."

The debate on the Address, in reply to the royal speech,
was protracted through no fewer than nineteen sittings.   The
Ministers declared their intention to prohibit the Reform
Banquet.   The Opposition members announced their determination to attend it, notwithstanding ; and both parties
appealed to the law in justification of their respective views.
The 291st article of the Penal Code enacts, that—

" No association of more than twenty persons, the object of which is
to meet every day, or on certain fixed days, to occupy itself with religious,
literary, political objects, or others, can be formed without the assent of
the Government, and under the conditions which the public authority may
impose on the society."

This enactment was reconsidered and extended subsequently to the Revolution of July, in the year 1834, when
another law was passed providing that this article of the
Penal Code might be applied though such associations were

divided into sections of less than twenty members, and although they should not meet at fixed times.   At the same time the penalties for violating this law were augmented.   The question, therefore, between the late Government and the Opposition was, in the first place, one of law—Was, or was not, this legal prohibition applicable to the political meetings which had been held last autumn in various parts of the kingdom, at irregular intervals, by the agents of a political party avowedly acting under the direction of a central electoral committee sitting in Paris?   Did the term *association*, which alone occurs in the law, include political meetings of a more uncertain and occasional character ?

These questions did not escape the notice of the legislature in 1834, when the law itself was under discussion.   On that occasion M. Martin, the reporter of the bill, who afterwards himself filled the office of Minister of Justice, expressly stated that " Every one knew the difference between an association and a meeting (*réunion*).   Meetings are caused by unforeseen, temporary occurrences, and cease when the motive ceases.   Associations have a determined and permanent object. There exists a tie between the members of an association. *Nobody has yet supposed that meetings* (réunions) *are affected by Article* 291 *of the Penal Code.   Do not fear that they will be so affected by the law under discussion.*"   In the same debate, the then Minister of Justice himself declared that this law was proposed " against associations, and not against those accidental and temporary meetings which have for their object the exercise of a constitutional right."   These declarations, which are recorded in the " Moniteur" of the 22d of March, 1834, are certainly at variance with the construction put upon the law by the late Government; and it was evident that only by a trial in a court of law could this disputed point of jurisprudence be settled.

The Government seemed at last to admit this, and they even condescended to a sort of compromise with the Opposition : they gave it to be understood that they would allow the banquet to take place, but under protest. A single Commissary of Police was to be stationed at the door of the banqueting-hall, to warn those attending of the illegality of their proceedings, and then withdraw. Furthermore, in order in some degree to disarm the Opposition, the Ministry declared by their official organ, the "Débats," that the question about Reform was merely one of time, for that the principle was already agreed on by the Cabinet. "The question of Parliamentary Reform will be discussed in all its bearings during the present parliament. Not only will it be solved, but the solution will be what is already known," &c. The Reformists treated with contempt this delusive promise, which was to be fulfilled some time or other in the course of a parliament that had five years to run.

On Saturday, February 12th, the several paragraphs of the Address having been voted, a division took place on the whole collectively. The Opposition in a body abstained from voting, and of 244 votes given there were 241 for Ministers. The Opposition Deputies assembled next day, and resolved unanimously that they would all attend the proposed banquet, and that no member of their party, even if drawn by lot to present the Address to the King, should participate in that ceremony. Subsequently the banquet was fixed to take place on Tuesday the 22d of February, as announced in the following manifesto of the Committee : —

"The General Committee appointed to organise the banquet of the twelfth arrondissement, thinks it right to state that the object of the demonstration fixed for Tuesday is the legal and pacific exercise of a constitutional right, the right of holding political meetings, without which, representative government would only be a derision. The Ministry having declared and maintained at the tribune that this right is subjected to the good pleasure of the police, Deputies of the Opposition, Peers of France, ex-Deputies, Members of the Conseil General, Magistrates, Officers, sub-Officers, and Soldiers of the National Guard, Members of the Central Committee of Electors of the Opposition, and Editors of Newspapers of Paris, have accepted the invitation which was made to take part in the demonstration, in order to protest, in virtue of the law, against an illegal and arbitrary pretension. As it is natural to foresee that this public protest may attract a considerable gathering of citizens; as it may be assumed also that the National Guards of Paris, faithful to their motto, ' Liberté, Ordre public,' will desire, on this occasion, 'to accomplish the double duty of defending liberty by joining the demonstration, and protecting order, and preventing all collision by their presence; and as, in the expectation of a numerous meeting of National Guards and of citizens, it seems right to take measures for preventing every cause of trouble and tumult, the Committee has thought that the demonstration should take place in that quarter of the capital in which the width of the streets and squares enables the population to assemble without excessive crowding; accordingly, the Deputies, Peers of France, and other persons invited to the banquet, will assemble on Tuesday next, at eleven o'clock, in the ordinary place of the meeting of the Parliamentary Opposition, Place de la Madeleine 2: the subscribers to the banquet, who belong to the National Guard, are requested to meet before the Church of the Madeleine, and to form two parallel lines, between which the persons invited will place themselves; the cortège will be headed by the superior officers of the National Guard who may present themselves to join the demonstration; immediately after the persons invited and the guests, will be placed a rank of officers of the National Guard; behind the latter, the National Guards formed in columns, according to the number of the legions; between the third and fourth columns, the young men of the schools, headed by persons chosen by themselves; next, the other National Guards of Paris and the suburbs, in the order set forth above. The cortège will leave at half-past eleven o'clock, and will proceed by the Place de la Concorde and the Champs Elysées, to the place in which the banquet is to take place. The Committee, convinced that this demonstration will be the more efficacious the more it be calm, and the more imposing the more it shall avoid even all pretext of conflict, requests the citizens to utter no cry, to carry neither flag nor exterior sign; it requests the National Guards, who may take part in the demonstration, to present themselves without arms; for it is desired to make a legal and pacific protest, which must be especially powerful by the number, and the firm and tranquil attitude, of the citizens. The Committee hopes that on this occasion every man present will consider himself as a functionary charged to cause order to be respected; it trusts in the presence of the National Guard; it trusts in the sentiments of the Parisian population, which desires public peace with liberty, and which knows that, to secure the maintenance of its rights, it has only need of a peaceable demonstration, as becomes an intelligent and enlightened nation, which has the consciousness of the irresistible authority of its moral power, and is assured that it will cause its legitimate wishes to prevail by the legal and calm expression of its opinion.''

Availing themselves of a specious pretext afforded by this manifesto, the Government now resolved absolutely to prohibit the banquet. Three proclamations to that effect were issued on Monday. The first was addressed to the National Guard by their Commander in Chief, General Jacqueminot. The second was from the Préfecture of Police, and was as follows :—

"Inhabitants of Paris,—A disquietude injurious to labour and business has reigned for some time in the public mind. This arises from manifestations in preparation. The Government, from motives of public order but too well justified, and exercising the right invested in it by the laws, and which has been constantly brought into use without dispute, has interdicted the banquet of the twelfth arrondissement. Nevertheless, as it has declared in the Chamber of Deputies, as this question was of a nature to admit of a judicial solution, instead of opposing by force the projected meeting, it came to a resolution to suffer the contravention to be established, by permitting the guests to enter the banquet-room, hoping that they would have the prudence to retire at the first summons, in order not to convert a simple contravention into an act of rebellion. This was the only means of bringing the question before the Supreme Court of Cassation. The Government persists in this determination, but the manifesto published this morning by the journals of the Opposition announces another object, and other intentions. It sets up a Government against the true Government of the country, that which is instituted by the Charter, and which rests upon the majority of the Chambers. It calls for a public manifestation which is dangerous to the peace of the city. It convokes, in violation of the law of 1831, the National Guards, whom it arranges beforehand in regular line, by number of legion, with the officers at their head. Here no doubt is longer possible. The clearest and best established laws are violated. The Government will cause them to be respected; they are the foundation and the guarantee of public order. I invite all good citizens to conform to these laws, and not join in any assemblage, for fear it may give rise to disturbances that may be regretted. I make this appeal to their patriotism and their right reason, in the name of our institutions, of public peace, and the dearest interests of the city.

"G. DELESSERT, Peer of France,
"Préfect of Police."

"*Paris, this 21st of February.*"

And, lastly, the Government issued the subjoined:—

"Parisians,—T e Government had interdicted the banquet of the 12th arrondissement. It was within its right in doing this, being authorised by the letter and spirit of the law. Nevertheless, in consequence of the discussion which took place in the Chamber on this subject, thinking that the Opposition was acting with good faith, it resolved to afford it an opportunity for submitting the question of the legality of banquets to the appreciation of the tribunals and the High Court of Cassation. To do this, it had resolved to authorise for to-morrow the entrance into the banquet-room, hoping that the persons present at the manifestation would have the wisdom to retire at the first summons. But after the manifesto published this morning, calling the public to a manifestation, convoking the National Guards, and assigning them a place ranked by the legions, and ranging them in line, a Government is raised in opposition to the real Government, usurps the public power, and openly violates the Charter. These are acts which the Government cannot tolerate. In consequence, the banquet of the twelfth arrondissement will not take place. Parisians! remain deaf to every excitement to disorder. Do not, by tumultuous assemblages, afford grounds for a repression which the Government would deplore."

Even before the issuing of these orders, the partisans of the Government persisted in maintaining that ministers were resolved upon preventing the banquet, and indeed there were many circumstances tending to corroborate this opinion. It had long been rumoured that the ferocious and blood-thirsty Marshal Bugeaud had been secretly appointed Military Governor of Paris, and that he had declared his intention "to give it handsomely to the rabble with grape shot" (*mitrailler la canaille de bonne manière*). The "National" of the 10th made the following announcement :—" We have already stated that the Minister of War had placed the whole garrison of Paris on a war footing, and ordered axes, pickaxes, shovels, and provisions for four days, to be delivered to them, as if on the eve of taking the field. We learn to-day that directions have been given at Vincennes to manufacture ball cartridges day and night, and to send artillery, caissons, and waggons laden with ammunition, to the military school in the Champ de Mars. All those orders ought, in reality, to have naturally emanated from the Minister of War; but matters have been simplified, and at a critical moment like that in which we live it is the future Grand Master of the Artillery, the Duc de

THIERS.

ODILLON BARROT.

Montpensier, who gives and signs the orders. The following is one of those orders, of which we have obtained a copy :—

'Deliver immediately, from the artillery stores of Vincennes, to be forwarded, without delay, to the military school in Paris, the following articles and ammunition :—2 batteries of field-pieces, with their caissons laden ; 20 infantry caissons, also laden ; 300 grape-shot canisters ; 400 rockets and torches for night service.

'A. D'ORLEANS.' "

The authenticity of this statement was denied in equivocal terms by the Government organ, but subsequent events confirmed its accuracy.

It was not until a late hour on Monday that the determination of the Government not to allow the banquet was made known in the Chamber. The debate, which was on the Bordeaux Bank Bill, had attracted but few members, when suddenly, at a little before five o'clock, the doors were thrown open, and 250 Deputies rushed to their places. In five minutes the Chamber, almost empty before, was filled in every part. Odillon Barrot then rose and said,—The Chamber must remember that, when the Address was under consideration here, a discussion took place relative to the right insisted on by us, and denied by the Government, of meeting together, on condition of previously informing the authorities, and of assembling without tumult and without arms. That question was not decided. My opinion is, that it ought to have been settled by the Chambers, for when a constitutional question of such great importance is brought forward, the duty of parliament is not to leave it in doubt—for to it belongs the task of regulating the political rights of citizens. This question ought therefore to have been decided, but it was not so. However, an imperative duty remained for those who maintain that the right of meeting is one of those liberties which a citizen cannot allow himself to be despoiled of without compromising all the others ; and that was, to set forth, in presence of the pretensions of the Government, a solemn protest,—in fact, to exercise that

E.

right in such a manner, as that on their part, at least, there should be no concession ; that is, with the firm resolution not to stop short, except before some invincible obstacle. That arrangement had been accepted. We thought that the Government, believing itself armed with sufficient laws, intended to carry before the tribunals such persons as should persist in claiming the right of meeting, and of having the legality of that right in that manner decided; matters would so have passed over with calm, and without disturbance. The public, no doubt, was exceedingly occupied with the matter, as it could not remain indifferent to a dispute, on the issue of which depended the most precious of its rights, since from it flowed all the rest. Yet, notwithstanding this profound and most natural emotion of the public, I do not hesitate to declare that the contest would have been in every respect according to law, and exempt from all trouble and disturbance. (Denial from the centres.) I am convinced that, however severe a blow the policy of the Government might have received from the manifestation, public order would never have been a moment troubled. But it now appears, that to counsels of wisdom and prudence have succeeded other suggestions; that acts of authority relative to a disturbance which may be called into existence, appear to establish that force is to be opposed to the peaceful exercise of an evident right. It does not belong to me at present to remark on the opportuneness of the measures taken by the authorities. I fear that these measures, though said to be dictated by a care for order, may, on the contrary, become the cause of disturbance. The mani-festation, peaceably effected, would have calmed down men's minds ; but now the very opposite effect will be produced, and an indefinite germ of perturbation and disorder will be left behind. If my voice could exercise any influence on the country, I would say to it,—" The first necessity, the first duty of all, is to employ every possible means to prevent the evils which imprudent measures may produce." It is that thought, gentlemen, which I have considered it necessary to express before this grave assembly—if it depended on me to appease the agitation which I foresee, I should do so with all the energy of my patriotism. (Hear, hear.) But there my powers cease,—I cannot say any thing farther. It is to the Ministry that belongs the care of watching over public order, and it is to it that belongs the responsibility of what may happen. (Loud approbation from the left: great agitation.)

The Minister of the Interior (Duchatel) replied.—The responsibility of which the honourable Deputy speaks does not fall on the Government alone,—it applies to every one (hear, hear); and we have a manifest proof of the fact in the highly creditable care which M. O. Barrot himself has exhibited, in expressing the sentiments which the Chamber has just heard. I shall very frankly and very clearly declare what is the present attitude of the Government, and on what ground it has taken up its stand. (Hear hear.) M. O. Barrot has told you that the question of an unlimited right of meeting has been discussed in this Chamber, but not decided—that he had been anxious for a solution, and that it was in order that such a result might be come to that a banquet was announced and prepared; he added, that the Government itself had appeared disposed, as much as it depended on it, within the limit of its opinion, which is opposed to that of M. O. Barrot, to lead to the judicial solution which could settle the dispute. All that is true : we could, reckoning on the right which we consider as incontestable, and on the practice which has never been called in question—we could, I say, have prevented, by the employment of force, the banquet announced for several days, and which has disturbed and agitated the capital. We were struck, like the honourable gentleman, with the advantage which would accrue to every one from obtaining a decision in a court of law ; and whilst we maintained the principles expressed in this tribune by the Government, we were ready to permit matters to arrive at the point when, a contravention having evidently taken place, a case for decision in a court of law could follow. (Hear, hear.) But, gentlemen, the matter

has changed.   I believe that there is not a single person in
this Chamber who has not this morning read a manifesto published by a Committee (the members of which are not mentioned), and inserted in all the Opposition journals.   What is
the purport of that manifesto ?   It does not confine itself to
speaking of the banquet, and preparing the judicial solution of
the question—no, it makes an appeal to all those who profess
Opposition principles, and invites them to a manifestation which
I have no hesitation in declaring would compromise the tranquillity of the capital.   Nor is that all : the manifesto, in contempt of every law—in contempt, in particular, of that of 1831
—calls on the National Guards to assemble ; and not only that,
but invites the students of the schools, young men under age,
to join the *cortège*, which is to be defended, as it were, by the
National Guards of the 12th Legion ; it announces that the
National Guards are to be placed in the order of their legions,
and under the conduct of their officers.   Such a manifesto
violates all the laws of the country, on which tranquillity and
public order depend.   (Hear, hear.)   The law relative to mob
assemblages is clearly violated by it, as is that relative to the
National Guard.   (Hear, hear.)   I appeal to the impartiality
of this Chamber, and I ask, What else is this manifesto but the
proclamation of a government wishing to place itself by the
side of the regular one of the country ?   A government emanating from a Committee, of which I know nothing, taking the
place of the constitutional Government founded by the Charter,
and supported by the majority of the two Chambers, takes on
itself to speak to the citizens, to call out the National Guard,
to provoke assemblages of the people in the public streets.
That cannot be permitted ; it is our duty not to allow such
things to exist ! (Hear, hear.)   We are responsible for the
maintenance of public order.   I hope, like M. O. Barrot, that
it will not be troubled ; but I should not answer for its not
being so if the Government did not take all the precautions
that it deems necessary, since I have not the same faith as the
honourable Deputy in those who might take part in the mani-

festation. (Hear, hear, from the centres; disapprobation from the left.) I now sum up what I meant to say,—We have on this occasion acted a just part by every one. Until the manifesto of this morning, we maintained the situation which the Government had taken on the discussion of the Address : we were inclined to allow the question to be decided judicially, but cannot permit a government suddenly got up to exist in the face of the legal and constitutional Government of the country. (Loud approbation from the centre.)

M. O. Barrot.—I fear that the honourable Minister is designedly exaggerating matters. (Murmurs, and cries of Yes, yes, from the left.) If the honourable Minister had merely declared that a solemn manifestation, in which a great part of the population was to take part, could disquiet the Government, and disquiet it the more that all would be regular and peaceful (No, no!), I think that he would be nearer the truth. But, I may ask, whilst leaving aside some expressions in the document, and which I neither avow nor disavow (Great interruption)—I avow most loudly the intention of the document, but I disavow the language used—When men summon a great concourse of citizens together, would they not fail in their duty if they did not adopt every possible means to preserve order? If, in our country, great meetings cannot take place unless when regulated by the official authorities, why, I suppose, they must even submit to such regulations; but, in free countries, it is usual for such meetings to lay down their own rules for preserving order : and, on the occasion of the present manifestation, the men who took part in the matter were anxious that as great a number as possible of respectable citizens — of the National Guards—should be present, to impose on those who could have any idea of disorder, and hence they were invited. You say that the National Guards were invited to join with arms (Denial from the centres), but that was not the case : you are fighting against a mere chimerical supposition (Denial from the centres). Thanks to the progress of our political habits, thanks to the intelligence of the country, I can give you the utmost assurance that order would not have been troubled. You, by an unexpected compression, by a state of siege which you do not even pretend to dissemble, you add to the difficulties of a position already too much strained. Now, on you, and on you alone, be the responsibility of such con-duct. (Exclamations from the centre.) You are not willing to have order with and by means of liberty: undergo, then, the consequences of what you have done. (Great agitation.)

The Minister of the Interior. — Had I any occasion for proofs to justify the determination come to by the Govern-ment, I should find them in the very words of the honourable gentleman. This manifesto, which he accuses us of having grossly exaggerated, he neither avows nor disavows. (Move-ment.) When the manifesto is neither avowed nor disavowed, can it be considered a subject of security by us who are charged to maintain public order? Is it a subject of security to see a manifesto published which provokes a violation of the law, and which M. O. Barrot dares not venture to say he avows? (Agitation.) But the honourable gentleman declares that what is complained of are mere matters of police regulations, adopted spontaneously to prevent any disturbances that might take place: consequently, there existed the elements of dis-turbance, or else why adopt such regulations? (Denial on the left.) Disorder was therefore nearer than was supposed, (Hear, hear.) I ask, When were self-constituted committees admitted to have the mission of calling out the National Guards in order to maintain order? (Loud denial on the left, and disapprobation.)

M. de Courtais. — Will you dare to call out the National Guard? Only try it! (Exclamations from the centre.)

The Minister of the Interior. — I listened to M. O. Barrot with great attention, and I declare to him that I regard most seriously the responsibility which weighs on us. The Cham-ber will do me this justice, that I have not, in this discussion, employed any irritating expression. (Hear, hear.) I might have deemed myself authorised to make use of recriminatory language, for it appeared to me that it was intimated that we wanted to conceal behind a question of public order the question of Ministerial existence, and that we were anxious to exaggerate the proportions of an incident exceedingly grave in itself, in order to advance our own interest; but I have not considered it fit to employ any recrimination: being, above all, the guardian of public order and of the law, I shall content myself with merely saying that we cannot admit the system which the honourable Deputy has advocated in this tribune, nor can we admit either that there is any just cause to complain of that pretended compression which is really destined only to prevent acts evidently contrary to the law. I maintain what I said just now. We are willing to allow matters to reach a point at which the judicial question may intervene. That situation we had taken up, and we still maintain it. Call that, if you please, violence and compression, but it is not so: it is the only thing that can be reasonably called for by every one — it is the performance of the duties of the Government, the maintenance of order, and the respect for the laws, on which the tranquillity of the country and safety of our institutions depend. (Approbation; great agitation.)

Here the matter dropped, and the Chamber adjourned at six o'clock, in a perfect tumult.

Immediately after the adjournment of the Chamber on Monday, the Opposition Deputies held a meeting and drew up the following manifesto, which appeared in the Opposition journals of Tuesday:—

"A grand and solemn manifestation was to have taken place this day in favour of the right of meeting contested by the Government. All measures had been taken to ensure order, and to prevent all kind of trouble. The Government had for several days been made acquainted with these measures, and knew what would be the form of this protestation. It was not ignorant that the Deputies would go in a body to the place of meeting, accompanied by a great number of citizens and National Guards without arms. It had announced its intention of not throwing any obstacle in the way of this demonstration, so long as order should not be troubled, and to confine its proceedings to a *procès-verbal*, sufficient to note that it considered what the Opposition regard as the exercise of a right in the light of a contravention.   Suddenly the Government, seizing for pretext a publication whose only object was to prevent disorders such as might have been occasioned by the affluence of a vast number of citizens, intimated its resolution to prevent by force all assemblages upon the public paths, and to interdict the population and National Guards from all participation in the projected manifestation.   This tardy resolution of the Government did not allow the Opposition time to change the character of the demonstration; the Opposition was then placed in the alternative of provoking a collision between citizens and the public force, or of abandoning the legal and pacific protest it had resolved upon.   In this situation the members of the Opposition, personally protected by their character of Deputy, could not voluntarily expose the citizens to the consequences of a struggle as fatal to order as to liberty.   The Opposition has then deemed it to be its duty to abstain on its own account, and to leave to Government the whole responsibility of its measures.   All good citizens are called upon to follow the example.

"In thus adjourning the exercise of a right, the Opposition engages, in the face of the country, to make this right prevail by all constitutional means.   It will not be wanting in its duty; it will pursue, with perseverance and more energy than ever, the struggle it has undertaken against a corrupting, violent, and anti-national policy.   In not going to the banquet, the Opposition performs an act of moderation and humanity.   The Opposition knows that it has yet to fulfil a grand act of firmness and justice."

The above manifesto was not the unanimous act of the Opposition.   Several Peers of France and eighteen Deputies were opposed to the banquet being abandoned.   M. de Lamartine strongly urged that the Opposition should continue its act of legal protestation by exercising the right of assembling. A conference took place at his house in the evening, and the resolution of going to the banquet had been already adopted, when it was announced that it had been countermanded by the Commissioners.

The Banquet Committee also published a manifesto, assigning reasons why it had been decided that the banquet should not take place,—" having full confidence that the act of accusation against a Ministry which had led the population of Paris to the threshold of civil war will be presented to the Chamber, and that France, forthwith consulted, will know how, by the weight of her opinion, to do justice to a policy which has so long excited the contempt and indignation of the country."

The Electoral Committee of the second arrondissement also published on Tuesday a manifesto, in which it expressed its astonishment and regret that the Deputies of the Opposition should have given up the banquet without at the same time laying down their commission as Deputies, and entreated them to do so without delay. This document bore the signatures of the twenty-five members of the Committee.

The Parisians were greatly dissatisfied with the want of firmness displayed by Odillon Barrot, and many abused him in the most unmeasured terms, whilst those who were more moderate in their censure declared that he was "too timid and too rich" to be a fit popular leader at such a crisis; at night, some of the populace treated him to a *charivari* under his windows.

The proclamations of the Government authorities were placarded at the place of meeting in the course of Monday evening, where crowds had been assembling all day; but the fact of the suppression of the banquet, with all the attendant circumstances, was not generally known throughout Paris until the appearance of the evening journals. The excitement then displayed was most extraordinary. It was by main struggle that a paper could be procured, and so soon as the fortunate purchaser had fought back his way, with the paper crushed in his hand to save it from being snatched away, he was surrounded by a number of anxious listeners, to whom he read the contents by the light of the nearest lamp or shop window, or of torches held aloft by the crowd. In a time incredibly short the papers had disappeared, and not one was to be had at all. After a long interval, more papers were printed, and the boys who carried them to the stands at which the evening journals are sold were continually intercepted, and the papers forced from them by competitors, who seemed ready to pay any price. Add to this the spectacle of cannon

and ammunition waggons occasionally arriving from Vincennes. Yet, strange to say, the funds rose at the Passage
de l'Opéra 30 centimes. " Do not mind that," said a shrewd
observer ; " those speculators deal with immediate effects, and
do not trouble their heads about distant contingencies. As
they come, the speculators will deal with them as marketable
commodities."

During the night, between Monday and Tuesday, military
waggons and artillery caissons, escorted by cavalry, were incessantly passing along the line of Boulevards which connects
Vincennes with the quarter of the Tuileries and Palais
Bourbon ; and orders had been issued to concentrate troops
around the Chamber of Deputies on Tuesday morning. Orders
to pass had been delivered to all those whose business or
offices called them to the Chamber. The garrison had been
increased to 100,000 men. Each company of infantry carried,
besides their usual arms, a collection of implements for cutting down barricades, such as hatchets, pickaxes, adzes, &c.
These were tied upon the knapsack, each soldier carrying
one.

The public excitement on Tuesday morning did not shew
itself by any violent demonstration, but at an early hour
considerable numbers, chiefly of the working classes and
respectable shopkeepers, were to be seen moving along the
Boulevards and all the avenues leading to the Champs
Elysées, and at noon the vast area between the Chamber of
Deputies and the Church of the Madeleine was thronged with
a dense multitude, which at one time could not have amounted
to less than thirty thousand persons. A little before twelve
o'clock, a procession of labouring men, consisting of several
hundred, attired chiefly in blouses, arrived by the Rue St.
Honoré, and the Rue Duphot, at the Place de la Madeleine,
and halted at the hôtel where the meeting of the Opposition
Deputies had been usually held. Until this moment no
display of military force took place at this point. Soon afterwards, however, a regiment of infantry, accompanied by a

civil magistrate wearing the tricolour sash, arrived on the spot, and drew up in front of the hôtel. The usual summons to disperse being read, the persons forming the procession submitted without any resistance, and marched away, taking the route towards the eastern faubourgs.

About this time the Boulevards Italiens and the Rue Lepelletier were filled with a deputation of students, who had arrived at the office of the "National" with a copy of a petition to the Chamber for the impeachment of Ministers. The attitude of the crowd which followed them was harmless, and nothing had yet occurred of a really alarming character. Nevertheless, the money-changers in the Boulevard began to close their shops, and were imitated by all other shopkeepers as the day advanced.

As early as half-past ten the populace had collected round the front of the Chamber of Deputies, on the river side, to the amount of 5000 or 6000, and escaladed the railing and walls of the garden. Some succeeded in gaining the interior, and rushed into the reserved parts of the gallery. The troops soon came up and succeeded in dispersing the populace, who retired quietly before the troops, singing the "Marseillaise," and crying, *Vive la Réforme! A bas Guizot, l'Homme de Gand!*

The multitude around the Church of the Madeleine, whence the banquet procession was to have set out. now became most formidable in numbers, though manifesting no symptoms of disorder or violence. The regiment which had arrived was drawn up in line along the railing of the church. Soon after several squadrons of the municipal cavalry arrived, and the populace was desired to disperse. This order being disregarded, the charge was sounded, and the dragoons rushed on the people. A first effort was made to disperse the crowd by the mere force of the horses, without the use of arms, and the dragoons did not draw. This, however, proving ineffectual, several charges with drawn swords were made, the flat of the sword only being used. By these means the multitude was at length dispersed, without any loss of life or other serious casualties. At one o'clock the main thoroughfares were clear.

Throughout these operations the good temper, forbearance, discipline, and intelligence of the troops of every class were especially remarkable. The same good humour was observable generally on the part of the people, who were seen shaking hands with the cavalry commanded to disperse them, and saluting the infantry regiments with *Vive la Ligne!* This was ominous. The lull did not last long. By half-past two o'clock alarm and agitation every where prevailed. All the shops in the northern portion of the metropolis were now closed. At the Hôtel des Affaires Etrangères there was a strong military force, half a troop of Municipal Guards *à cheval* patrolliug in front of it. Along the wall of the garden of the Boulevard a body of soldiers of the line (the 21st Regiment), who would not allow the passengers to walk on the flagging. At the great entrance was a body of Municipal Guards *à pied.* Stones were thrown at the windows; a mock window being, curiously enough, the object of the principal attack. The residence of the hated Minister was the chief point of attraction for the crowd throughout the day; and as often as they were repulsed they still returned to shout, " Down with Guizot! " " Down with the Ghentman! " " Guizot's head going for twenty-five francs! "

It was singular to observe, in most respects, the perfectly similar appearance of that quarter to-day and at the same hour of the 27th July, 1830. The same species of attack on the Hôtel des Affaires Etrangères, then inhabited by Prince Polignac — the same measures of repression — the same expression of hatred towards the Minister on the part of the people — the same air of severity on the countenances of the gendarmes. Near to the gate occurred an incident exactly like one that was witnessed on nearly the same spot on the former occasion :—A horse-soldier ordered a man to move on, telling him that if he did not he would cut him down. The man, folding his arms, and looking sternly at the soldier, replied, " Would you, coward ?" The trooper rode off.

The Municipal Guards of the post at the corner of the Place de la Concorde, near the Turkish Embassy, sallied out and attempted to drive the crowd before them, but were obliged to retreat into their fortified guard-house, to avoid being disarmed ; for not only did the people not give way, but absolutely pressed upon them. The soldiers had scarcely secured themselves within, when the people ran off in their turn, fearing that they would be fired upon.

Immediately afterwards the people stopped a carriage, in which was a Ministerial Deputy on his way to the Chambers, which is only separated from the Place de la Concorde by the bridge. They made him alight, and then shook him for several minutes. Ultimately they allowed him to proceed. A different process was adopted towards, it was said, M. Marrast, principal editor of the " National," whom they cheered, and all but ' chaired.' Thus the proceedings of the day displayed the same mixture of the grave and the gay, of tragedy and farce, that a French assemblage always exhibits. All that has been described was done in the presence of an immense force of Municipal Guards by a perfectly unarmed crowd. They were charged scores of times by the cavalry, who inflicted some very serious wounds with their sabres ; but the people scampered off laughing, and subsequently returned to their previous position, and provoked new assaults by mockeries and execrations of the Municipal Guards and their employers. The charges made upon the people were not always attended with impunity to the assailants. Several of the Municipal Guards were severely wounded with stones ; one of them, a trumpeter, was knocked off his horse.

In the Faubourg St. Honoré the pavement of the new street, the Rue de Joinville, was dug up ; and there also a regular barricade was thrown up, but was abandoned when the constructors of it found there was no opposition to them.

From thence they proceeded to the Avenue des Champs
Elysées, when they destroyed the superb metal lamp-posts
with which it is adorned.   They were about to smash the
Jardin d'Hiver, when a body of Chasseurs arrived *au grand
galop*, when they took to their heels.   At the Place du
Châtelet a formidable barricade was also formed, and a gun-
smith's shop in the adjoining street (La Mégisserie) was
plundered.   Attacks were also made on the premises of two
other armourers, and about thirty or forty guns and pistols
were obtained by the assailants.   A few barricades, formed of
overturned carts and omnibuses, were surrendered with little
show of resistance to the soldiery.

All the avenues leading to the Palais Bourbon (the Parliament House) were occupied by horse and foot Municipal Guards
and troops of the line.   A squadron of dragoons was stationed
in front of the edifice along the quay, whilst another kept
constantly moving to clear the bridge of La Concorde.   In
advance of the bridge, on the side of the Place de la Révo-
lution, was a numerous body of horse-chasseurs employed in
dispersing a multitude of about 5000 or 6000 individuals,
who quietly retired before them, singing the "Marseillaise," and
crying, *Vive la Réforme! A bas Guizot, l'Homme de Gand!*
The passage through the adjoining streets, and the Place de
Bourgogne, was intercepted by troops of the line, and none
but Deputies and persons provided with tickets were permitted
to enter the palace.   General Perrault was on horseback in
the court, ready to take the command of the troops; and a
Commissary of Police was stationed at the foot of the bridge,
to address the legal summonses to the people.

The Chamber presented a gloomy aspect.   Few Deputies
were in attendance; the benches of the Opposition were completely vacant.   M. Guizot arrived at an early hour; he
looked pale, but confident.   He was shortly afterwards followed by the Ministers of Finance, Public Instruction, and
Commerce.   Marshal Bugeaud, who was believed to have
accepted the military command of Paris in the event of a

revolt, took his seat close to the Ministerial bench. The Chamber then resumed the adjourned discussion on the bill relative to the renewal of the privilege of the Bank of Bordeaux. At three o'clock Odillon Barrot entered the hall, accompanied by Messrs. Duvergier, de Hauranne, Marie, Thiers, Garnier Pagès, &c. Their appearance produced some sensation. Shortly afterwards M. de Hauranne went up to the President and handed him a paper, supposed to be a proposition for the impeachment of Ministers. This paper having been communicated by the President to M. Guizot, the latter, after perusing it, laughed immoderately. MM. Thiers, Dupin, Lamartine, Billault, Crémieux, and the Minister of the Interior and Justice, next made their appearance; but the discussion on the Bank Bill continued until five o'clock, and no incident of interest occurred. When the discussion terminated, M. Odillon Barrot ascended the tribune, and deposited on the table a formal proposition, to the effect of impeaching Ministers. The President, however, adjourned the Chambers without reading it, to the great disappointment of the Opposition, but announced that it should be submitted to the approbation of the bureaux on Thursday.

The following are the articles of impeachment against the French Ministers, laid on the table of the Chamber by Odillon Barrot:—

" We propose to place the Ministers in accusation as guilty,—1. Of having betrayed abroad the honour and the interests of France. 2. Of having falsified the principles of the constitution, violated the guarantees of liberty, and attacked the rights of the people. 3. Of having, by a systematic corruption, attempted to substitute, for the free expression of public opinion, the calculations of private interest, and thus perverted the representative government. 4. Of having trafficked for ministerial purposes in public offices, as well as in all the prerogatives and privileges of power. 5. Of having, in the same interest, wasted the finances of the state, and thus compromised the forces and grandeur of the kingdom. 6. Of having violently despoiled the citizens of a right inherent in every free constitution, and the exercise of which had been guaranteed to them by the charter, by the laws, and by former precedents. 7. Of having, in fine, by a policy overtly counter-revolutionary, placed in question all the conquests of our two revolutions, and thrown the country into a profound agitation.''

[Here follow fifty-three signatures—M. Odillon Barrot at the head.]

The Chamber adjourned soon after five o'clock. Up to this time no very serious apprehensions appear to have been entertained as to the result of the day's proceedings. It was a troublesome riot, and that was all. The people were un-armed, and their attempts to cope with 100,000 soldiers was a melancholy absurdity! The funds even rose 10 centimes, and maintained that advance until the close of the Bourse. Late in the afternoon the Government took heart of grace and ven-tured to call out the National Guard. The *rappel* was beaten at five o'clock, and the manner in which this was done was curious and significant. The drummers, who were preceded and followed by two sections of National Guards, were accom-panied by some hundreds of young fellows in blouses, armed with long sticks, and roaring out the favourite cries and songs of the day.

The skirmishing continued until a late hour in the Fau-bourg St. Antoine; but by midnight all the barricades, erected in the course of the day, had been thrown down, and Paris was throughout the night in the entire possession of the troops, who bivouacked in the streets and market-places.

On Wednesday morning all hackney-coaches, cabs, omni-buses, and every description of public carriage, had disap-peared from the streets and the public stands, their owners being warned by the fate of the vehicles which were seized by the populace on Tuesday evening to form barricades, and some of which were burned. The iron railings in several parts the town were torn down to supply weapons to the populace. This took place at the hôtel of the Minister of Marine, in the Place de la Concorde, at the Churches of the Assumption and of St. Roque, in the Rue St. Honoré, and elsewhere.

By nine o'clock, the people assembled in considerable

numbers in the quarters St. Denis and St. Martin; and at ten
o'clock they had succeeded in erecting barricades at the Porte
St. Denis, in the Rue de Clery, in the Rue Neuve St.
Eustache, the Rue du Cadran, and the Rue du Petit-Carreau.
Conflicts took place at some of these barricades between the
populace and the Municipal Guards, and two young men were
killed. Several Municipal Guards were pursued to the Place
du Caire, by young men armed with sticks. The guards fired,
and wounded several persons. A woman was killed on the
spot. The officer of a platoon of the National Guard, who was
on the place, was so indignant, that he cried,—" To arms ! "
whereupon the Municipal Guard beat a retreat. Two hours
later, the Place du Caire was perfectly calm; in fact, not a
soul was to be seen except three National Guards in the
Passage du Caire.

At the Porte St. Denis the troops charged the people, and
the barricade in the Rue Cadran, at the entrance to the Rue
Montmartre, was attacked by the Municipal Guards, who fired
on the mob, killing a child, and seriously wounding two men
and three women.

At twelve o'clock, all the quarter of the markets was fully
occupied. There was a battalion of the 21st Regiment on the
Marché des Innocens, besides detachments of the Municipal
Guard, horse and foot, and two detachments of Cuirassiers.
Two pieces of cannon were on the spot, one of which was
directed towards the Rue Montmartre, the other towards the
Rue de la Ferronnerie. They were ready to be employed at
a moment's notice. The fish-market was occupied by a battalion of the 1st Regiment.

On the Place du Carrousel, the Horse Municipal Guard
made repeated charges; but the people, after dispersing on
one spot, immediately re-assembled on another. At the barricade in the Rue de Clery, which was half destroyed, the
Municipal Guard fired, and several persons were wounded.

The National Guards of the Second Legion began to assemble
at an early hour in the Rue Lepelletier, in front of the Opera-

F

house.   At half-past eleven there were about one hundred and
fifty of them collected, and they formed in two lines across
the street, one division at each extremity of the theatre.   In
the centre were the officers ; outside, the people frantic with
joy.   A National Guard being asked what had happened,—
" We have declared for Reform," said he : " that is, some of
us differ about Reform, but we are all agreed about Guizot.
Down with Guizot ! "   *Vive la Réforme! Vive la Garde Nationale !* cried the people incessantly.   An hour afterwards the
National Guards proceeded, with their *sappeurs* at their head,
in full uniform, to the Tuileries, to declare their sentiments.

They returned about one o'clock, and occupied the Rue
Lepelletier again.   A platoon closed the street on the Boulevard, and was hailed with shouts of *Vive la Garde Nationale!*   A squadron of Cuirassiers, supported by half a
squadron of Chasseurs *à cheval*, arrived.   The *chef d'escadron*
gave orders to draw swords.   The ranks of the National Guards
closed.   The shouts of the people redoubled, although not a
man of them was armed.   The squadron made a half movement on the Rue Lepelletier, when the officer in command of
the National Guards drew his sword, advanced, and saluted
him.   A few words were exchanged.   They separated.   The
one placed himself at the head of his soldiers, and gave the
word to " wheel and forward," and they resumed their march,
accompanied by the cheers and clapping of hands of the multitude.   The officer of the National Guards returned very
quietly to his post, and sheathed his sword.

It is said the words exchanged between the officers were
these,—" Who are these men ? "   " They are the people."
" And those in uniform ? "   " They are the Second Legion of
the National Guard of Paris."   " The people must disperse."
" They will not."   " I shall use force."   " Sir, the National
Guards sympathise with the people, the people who demand
Reform."   " They must disperse."   " They will not."   " I
must use force."   " Sir, we, the National Guards, sympathise
in the desire for Reform, and will defend them."

By half-past two o'clock three more scenes of the same kind had occurred. The Municipal Guards, who occupied the unpopular position of the gendarmes of 1830, were now, by order of the Government, mixed up with the troops of the line, on whom the people were lavish of their compliments and caresses. A column of cavalry and infantry, Municipal Guards *à cheval*, Cuirassiers, and Municipal Guards *à pied*, and infantry of the line, arrived by the Boulevard at the end of the Rue Lepelletier. They made a move like the others as if to wheel into that street, but the attitude of the National Guard made them pause, and immediately the word was given to continue their march, the people rending the air with cries of *Vive la Réforme! Vive la Garde Nationale!* and *Vive la Ligne!* Again a precisely similar occurrence took place, but this time it ended with the absolute retreat of the troops, for they turned round and retired up the Boulevard.

Such was the conduct of the Second Legion of the National Guard. The initiative, however, appears to have been taken by the Third Legion, who this morning, at the *mairie* of the third arrondissement — Place des Petits Pères — declared for Reform. The Municipal Guards, whose barracks adjoin the Church of the Petits Pères, were ordered to disarm them, and advanced to the charge with bayonets levelled; but the movement was imitated by the National Guard, the bayonets crossed; blood was about to flow, when the Colonel of the National Guard, M. Textorix, cried out, " Hold, soldiers ! these are the people ; respect the people." The effect was electric. The Municipal Guards raised their bayonets, shouldered arms, and marched off.

This incident had a powerful influence on the rest of the National Guards of that legion. They almost to a man joined their comrades, and attained the number of 3000 by one o'clock. Their officers having then held a council, agreed to depute their Colonel to the King, to acquaint his Majesty with the wishes of the National Guard,—in other words, Reform and the dismissal of the Cabinet. That officer immediately pro-

ceeded to the palace, but was not admitted into the royal presence; he only saw General Jacqueminot, the Commander-in-
Chief of the National Guard, who promised that he would that
instant carry himself the memorial to the King. The National
Guards remained assembled on the square awaiting the return
of the Colonel, their determination being to march upon the
Tuileries if the reply was negative. Occasionally strong pa-
trols were sent out to interpose, if necessary, between the
combatants; but no hostilities took place in the neighbourhood, the troops quietly remaining on the adjoining Place des
Victoires, without giving the least provocation. The Nationals
filed by them shouting for Reform and the dismissal of Ministers, surrounded and followed by an immense mass of people
uttering the same cries, and the soldiers of the line by their
countenances testified that they concurred in the popular feeling. In one of the by-streets a detachment of troops, stationed
there to intercept the passage, were helped to bread and wine
by the people, and their officers looked on, nay, encouraged
them to accept the provisions offered to them.

The Fourth Legion also took arms, and stationed detachments in different directions to maintain order and prevent the
effusion of blood.

The National Guards of the first arrondissement, which had
shewn a better disposition towards the Government than those
of the other arrondissements, were drawn up at three o'clock
in the Rue Rivoli, and had ten additional rounds of cartridges
served out to them. The other legions were by no means
treated with the same liberality in this respect. " I was in a
certain house," says the correspondent of the " Times," " at
nine o'clock on Wednesday night, February 23. There were
scores of men arriving momentarily with news or seeking
orders. Two men, less respectably dressed than the others,
after several efforts, made known the object of their visit. One
was a decent mechanic, aged about thirty-five; the other a
poorer looking man, of at least sixty. ' I come, gentlemen,'
said the former, ' to prevent mistakes about an occurrence at

our barricade in the Rue Vieille du Temple.' It was a beautiful one, and having completed it we placed ourselves before it,
unarmed.   The — Regiment of the Line advanced and halted.
A general officer (whose name I suppress) gave a sign to the
troops, who fired upon us unarmed as we were.   Just at that
moment a portion of the Sixth Legion of National Guards
debouched from the Rue ———, and seeing the troops prepare
again to fire placed themselves before us.   The same General
made a sign like the former to the soldiers, who poured a volley
on the National Guard.   Several of them fell—three dead.   I
stooped down and took up the musket of one of them, and
' covering ' the General, pulled the trigger.   The musket was
unloaded, and there was not a ball-cartridge in the *giberne* of
poor Rousselot, for that was the name of the owner of the gun.
I thought it might be useful to prove that the crime of commencing the civil war was not ours ; and having done so, for I
have brought my comrade to corroborate me, I shall go back
to our barricade.' "

Ten of the people made prisoners by the troops were confined in the guard-house of the Boulevard des Bonnes Nou-
velles, which has uniformly been taken by the people in every
émeute.   The people attacked it at five o'clock, disarmed the
soldiers, discharged the muskets, returned them to their owners,
and liberated the prisoners.   They carried off the flag that
adorned the entrance, and presented it as a trophy to the
Third Legion of the National Guards.   The 5th Regiment,
which joined the people in July 1830, was there during this
affair, and again fraternised with the people.   The people were,
at five o'clock, proceeding to the Préfecture of the Police to
liberate the prisoners confined there.   On their way they
called at the " Réforme " newspaper office, and were told that
all was not over ; that the banquet must take place ; and that
good care would be taken to secure their liberties.

The members of the Left mustered strong in the Chamber
of Deputies this day.   M. Vavin, one of the Deputies for Paris,
rose amidst profound silence, and said that he had a solemn duty

to accomplish, which was to call the Minister of the Interior to account for the scenes then passing in the capital. During twenty-four hours serious disturbances had taken place in Paris, and the population remarked with astonishment the absence of the National Guard. On Monday, orders had been given for its attendance. Why had they been countermanded ? Why was it only after a first collision that the drummers were permitted to beat to arms ? If from the beginning the National Guard had been called out, fatal misfortunes would have been avoided.

M. Guizot, who had shortly before entered the Chamber, immediately rose and said,—I have nothing to say at the present moment to the questions of the honourable member. The King has sent for Count Molé, who is empowered to form a ministry." (Loud cries of Bravo! and cheers followed this announcement, which appeared to annoy M. Guizot. He then continued.) We are not to be prevented by such manifestations as those I now hear, as long as we remain in office, which will be till our successors are appointed, from doing our duty. We shall consider ourselves answerable for all that may happen. We shall act in every thing we do according to our best judgment and our consciences, and according to what we consider the interests of the country.

After some interruption created by this announcement, M. Odillon Barrot rose and said,—In consequence of the situation of the Cabinet, I demand the adjournment of the proposition which I made yesterday (the impeachment). (Loud cries of Yes, yes, and No, no.) I will submit to the decision of the Chamber on the point. (No, no.)

M. Dupin then rose and said,—The first thing necessary for the capital is peace. It must be relieved from anarchy. Every one knows that the spirit of July exists yet. Homage has been done to the will of the nation. But the people must know that its deliberations must not be on the public way. The assemblages must cease. I do not see how the Ministry, who are provisionally charged with the public affairs, can occupy themselves at the same time in re-establishing order and with the care of their own safety. I demand the adjournment of the proposition presented yesterday. (Loud cries of No, no.)

M. Guizot.—As long as the Cabinet shall be entrusted with public affairs, it will make the law be respected. The Cabinet sees no reason why the Chamber should suspend its labours. The Crown, at the present moment, is using its prerogative. That prerogative must be respected. As long as the Cabinet is upon these benches, no business need remain suspended.

The President then put the question as to the adjournment of M. Odillon Barrot's proposition. About one hundred members of the Opposition supported the adjournment; and the whole of the Conservatives were against it. The Chamber immediately rose in great agitation.

So ended the political life of a man in whom was most signally manifested how impotent, how fatal to their owner, are all the resources of a great and daring intellect, and knowledge most varied and profound, when not united with the wisdom of the heart. To M. Guizot, above all other men, may be applied the saying of the late Lord Holland, that " God had given him great talents, but the devil had taught him the use of them." Self-love was in him as intense as in the master with whom he was so fitly mated, only the form of its display was different. Louis Philippe's ambition resolved itself into love of lucre; Guizot coveted power for its own sake, and for the indulgence of an imperious and indomitable will. Both master and man were alike indifferent as to the means by which they advanced, so they did but accomplish their ends. Neither of them had a conscience; the substitute for it with the one was self-interest, with the other, pride. The same unconquerable disdain of all opposition that gave a semblance of dignity to Guizot's fall, was the primary cause of all his political guilt. " His soul," says De Cormenin, " is too full of pride to leave room for any other sentiment. He

might be thrust head foremost into the ocean, and he would
not admit that he was drowning; and he believes in his own
infallibility with a violent and desperate faith." Great has
been the wonder expressed that Louis Philippe should have
succeeded in making a pliant tool of Guizot, a man so greatly
his own intellectual superior. But the wonder is misplaced;
in Guizot the ex-King did not make a tool, but found one.
The Minister's system happened to accord with the Monarch's
schemes, and it was pursued by its inventor with a boundless
fanaticism that needed no prompting.

As we shall hardly have occasion to mention this man
again, we will here introduce a remarkable illustration of his
character, which was first disclosed in England on the day this
sheet went to press, The facts are related by the correspondent of the "Morning Chronicle," under date Paris, March 20.
"In the 'Moniteur' of yesterday," he says, "a document is published. which was found among the papers left by M. Génie,
the Secretary of M. Guizot, at the office of Foreign Affairs.
It is a Report from M. Bouchy, the Procureur du Roi, to the
Minister of Justice, with respect to some charges brought
against M. Libri, a well-known member of the Institute, and
a professor of the University, for stealing books from the
public libraries. M. Libri was in the confidence of M. Guizot
and M. Duchatel. He was frequently employed by these two
ministers to make researches in the public libraries, and he
had consequently access to all the most valuable collections in
France; and he took the opportunity thus afforded him of
abstracting valuable works from the libraries in Paris, Car-
pentras, Montpellier, the Chartreuse at Grenoble, and other
places, to the amount, it is calculated, of between three or
four hundred thousand francs. The Report is dated as late as
the 4th of February last. Several of the works have been
sold by public auction in Paris, and some of them have found
their way to the British Museum. A manuscript Psalter,
belonging to the Chartreuse at Grenoble, was part of the
stolen goods, and was purchased by an eminent collector in

London for 280*l.* What makes the affair still more curious
is, that M. Libri was the intimate friend, visitor, and confidant of M. Guizot up to the very last; although M. Guizot
must have been fully aware of the suspicions against him, for
the Government was in possession of information on the
subject more than two years ago. It has always been said of
M. Guizot by his friends, with a degree of pride which they
were entitled to feel, that he was pure, that he was indifferent
to money, and that he would leave office as poor as he entered
it. I believe that M. Guizot is entitled to all the credit in
that respect which has been claimed for him. I hear that he
has left France a poor man. But if M. Guizot was indifferent
about money himself, he was equally so as to the purity of
those about him. It is well known of M. Guizot, that he did
not care what a man's conduct was, provided that he was a fit
instrument for his purpose. There never was a minister who
had more corrupt or more unscrupulous agents about him.
As long as delinquencies were kept from the knowledge of
the public, the private conduct of an agent made no difference
in the eyes of M. Guizot. His relations with M. Libri
shew that he did not feel contaminated by coming into daily
intercourse with one more than suspected of a disgraceful theft.
Up to the 24th of February, M. Libri was in daily communication with M. Guizot. It was he who wrote the articles in the
'Journal des Débats,' in which M. Guizot's Italian policy was
defended, and in order to write them he had the whole of
the most private correspondence placed at his disposal. It
was he, also, who wrote the articles in the 'Revue des Deux
Mondes,' in defence of M. Guizot's administration. The
exposé of this affair has created a very painful sensation here,
and the sensation is almost as much that of regret for the
injury it does to the reputation of M. Guizot, as for the
disgrace with which it stamps M. Libri himself. M. Libri
got a hint of the discovery from an acquaintance of his, who
now holds a high office in the department of Foreign Affairs.
He immediately effected his escape from France, and is now

in England." With such evidence as this before them, our readers will not accuse us of having exaggerated the moral obliquity of M. Guizot's character, or of having depicted in too dark colours the wide-spread depravity engendered and fostered by his system. But to return from this digression,—

When M. Guizot was entering the Chamber before announcing his resignation, the Tenth Legion of the National Guard on duty saluted him with, *A bas Guizot! Vive Louis Philippe!* M. Guizot looked annoyed, and passed on without making any remark. A minute afterwards, M. Muret (de Bort) came out of the Chamber, and announced that M. Guizot and his colleagues were out of office. The announcement was received with loud cheers, and immediately spread like wildfire. In less than half an hour it was known all over Paris, that the Guizot Cabinet was dissolved and that the King had sent for Count Molé; and the report was followed by an immediate cessation of hostilities, except in the districts between the Portes St. Martin and St. Denis, where the people could not be persuaded of its truth. Elsewhere the populace were in the highest state of exultation. Victory disposed them to good humour, and every one was delighted with the prospect of returning order and tranquillity. But these hopes were soon destroyed. About ten p.m. large bodies of insurgents came up the Boulevards from the quarter St. Martin, to celebrate their triumph by hooting M. Guizot. In other respects their conduct was quite pacific. They sang and shouted to their hearts' content, crying out, *A bas Guizot!* and *Vive Louis Philippe!* and even forced the inhabitants to illuminate their houses; but none of them shewed the least inclination to outrage, or seemed to contemplate anything like revolution. But it unfortunately occurred to some of them that M. Guizot's hôtel ought to be illuminated as well as the houses of his neighbours, and a proposition to that effect was made to the soldiers on guard. While the parley was going on—the street excessively crowded, not only with insurgents, but a vast number of respectable persons drawn to the spot by curiosity—the whole line of troops fired without warning along the Boulevards, making frightful carnage among the inoffensive throng. Fifty-two victims fell dead or wounded. The people fled in consternation, but fear soon gave way to indignation and thirst for vengeance. The cry then burst forth from every lip,—"To arms! Down with the assassins! Down with Louis Philippe! Down with all his race! Barricades! barricades!" and these cries were speedily re-echoed through all the streets of Paris. That volley decided the fate of Louis Philippe's dynasty. The feeling of the people was completely changed, and those who three minutes before were perfectly satisfied with having succeeded in effecting a change of Ministry, now demanded a new form of Government, and declared they would take nothing less. The sequel is told by the "National:"—

"Soon afterwards we saw a large cart, full of corpses, come back to the 'National;' the cart was lighted by torches, surrounded by those brave men whose tears were stopped by their indignation, and who, uncovering the bleeding wounds, and pointing to those men, but a short time back singing and joyful, now inanimate and still warm, cried with fury,—"They have been struck by assassins! We will avenge them! Give us arms!—arms!" And the torches throwing their fearful light upon the dead bodies, and upon the men who had borne them hither, still added to the violent emotions caused by this dismal *convoi*. M. Garnier Pagès, who was at that moment in our bureaux, addressed the citizens. It is easy to conceive what he and we felt in presence of such just exasperation. This Deputy gave his word that he would do his utmost to obtain for the people, thus attacked and fired at, the satisfaction they demanded upon the impious, atrocious Ministers. The cart then departed, drawn and lighted on its way in the same manner. As they bore the dead to distant quarters of the city, the men who accompanied them uttered the same accents of manly grief and terrible indignation, and on all sides public indignation responded to theirs. M. de Courtais, a Deputy of the Opposition, hastened to the Boulevard des Capucines, to inquire the cause of the infamous butchery which took place in the evening. We add the account he gives :—He found the Colonel of the regiment which had fired quite concerned at what had taken place, and this officer gives the following explanation of the manner in which, what he himself calls a deplorable event, took place. At the very moment the crowd arrived, a musket, which went off by some mischance in the garden of the hôtel, broke the leg of the Lieutenant-Colonel's horse. The officer commanding the detachment thought it was an attack, and immediately, with the most culpable irreflection, commanded his men to fire. The officer was immediately sent to prison. Such is the explanation given to M. de Courtais. But what is a private explanation in presence of so great a catastrophe ?"

The decisive shot which changed the fate of the realm was no chance one, as at first supposed. It was fired by Lagrange, the condemned Lyons conspirator of 1832, who, by his own confession, finding that affairs were likely after all to take a favourable turn for royalty, determined to risk this last step, in order to rouse the angry passions of the multitude. A few minutes afterwards another murderous volley was discharged on the crowd in the Rue de la Paix, which still further increased the indignation of the people. They returned to the barricades, at which they worked without interruption all night, and next morning there was not a single leading street in the capital which was not a fortress.

A significant occurrence took place at night in the Boulevards Italiens : three regiments of the line, armed to the teeth, preceded by five hundred National Guards, a regiment of Cuirassiers, three field pieces and three caissons of ammunition, appeared. The people coolly stopped and unharnessed the horses, opened the caissons and distributed the ammunition. Numbers then mounted astride the guns, and were dragged off by their comrades in derisive triumph; the line troops, the Guards, and the people fraternising with enthusiasm.

THE SLAUGHTER OF THE POPULACE AT THE HOTEL DES ETRANGERS.

The drums of the National Guard calling them out were heard without ceasing the whole night; all the posts of the Municipal Guards were attacked, taken, and every thing in them burnt by the people,—even the sacks of money, *all* was cast to the flames.   Many of the Guards escaped with nothing but their shirts, some by changing their clothes, and many were killed or burnt to death.   The people went to every house and demanded arms; every person gave them willingly, and to avoid a second call, wrote on their doors, "The arms are given."   An Englishwoman, wife of an officer of the Municipal Guards, was alarmed by the bursting open of her door by the infuriated people; she thought her last hour was come: fortunately she did not lose her presence of mind, but went boldly up to them, saying, "You know, doubtless, that I am the wife of one of the officers of the Municipal Guard; my husband is on duty: what do you want with a poor defenceless woman?"   "Do not be alarmed," said the people, "we do not war with women; on the contrary, we will protect you: all we want is the arms you may have in the house."   "I have none," she replied; "but you are at liberty to look."   "No, madam, we take your word."   They retired, assuring her that no harm should come to her.

The attempt to establish a Molé Administration having failed, the King sent late at night for M. Thiers to the Palace of the Tuileries, and asked him to form a Ministry.   M. Thiers undertook to do so, provided that he might be permitted to join with him, as one of his colleagues, M. Odillon Barrot.   To this the King acceded.   Marshal Bugeaud was during the night appointed Commander-in-Chief of the National Guard, but finding he was not to have *carte blanche*, he resigned almost as soon as appointed, and was replaced by General Lamoricière.

CHAPTER III.

THE BATTLE FOR A REPUBLIC.—VICTORY.

SUCH was the state of Paris on Thursday morning at daybreak; and with every successive hour the situation of the Government grew more critical. From all sides accounts arrived of the union of the National Guard with the people, and (what was still more alarming) of the regiments of the Line with the National Guard. The National Guard would not fire on the people; the Line would not fire on the National Guard. The force of the Government was paralysed. About nine o'clock, the 45th Regiment of the Line fraternised with the National Guard bodily. The 30th Regiment gave up their arms to the people at the first summons. At eleven, the quarters of the five companies of Pompiers of Paris were assailed; the whole of their arms and ammunition were given up to the insurgents. Reports of similar defalcations were every moment brought to the Tuileries; and at length it became evident that if something were not done, and that speedily, the whole body of the troops would desert the Sovereign. At length the following proclamation was issued, and posted at the Bourse and in every street :—

First Proclamation, at Eleven o' Clock.

" Citizens of Paris!—Orders have been given to suspend the firing. We have just been charged by the King to compose a Ministry. The

Chamber will be dissolved immediately. General Lamoricière has been nominated Commander-in-Chief of the National Guard of Paris.

"MM. O. Barrot, Thiers, Lamoricière, and Duvergier de Hauranne are Ministers.

"LIBERTY! ORDER! UNION! REFORM!

(Signed) "ODILLON BARROT and THIERS."

This proclamation came too late, and was torn down as fast as it was posted! By the time it was issued the people felt that they were the victors, for not only had the whole of the National Guard of Paris taken their part, but a large portion of the soldiers of the Line had openly joined them, while many more had refused to fire upon them. A piece of duplicity on the part of the authorities, which was discovered, had also an exasperating effect. On the orders being given to suspend the firing at the barricades, the troops were withdrawn, and the people were informed that they had been ordered back to their barracks; but they soon learned that they had been drawn round the Tuileries, for its defence.

There was an immediate cry of *Aux Tuileries!* and from all parts of the capital immense bodies of the insurgents, now well armed, and marching along with the National Guards, were to be seen directing their way towards the Palais Royal and the Palace of the Tuileries. By twelve o'clock the whole of that quarter of the town was invested. The new Ministers had in vain gone among the people, and exerted all their personal influence to allay the popular fury. They were coldly received. "We have been too often deluded. This time we will make all sure," was the universal cry. The alarm in the palace may be guessed at by the fact, that before one o'clock the following proclamation was to be seen at the Bourse and in several of the streets:—

Second Proclamation, One o'Clock.

"Citizens of Paris!—The King has abdicated in favour of the Count de Paris, with the Duchess of Orleans as Regent.

"A General Amnesty. Dissolution of the Chamber. Appeal to the Country."

But it was again too late. The tardy concession could not

save the dynasty or even its palace. It was about this time
that red flags began to appear, with the words "Republic!"
rudely traced upon them, and the terrible cry became frequent, — *A la potence Louis Philippe!* — "To the gallows
with Louis Philippe!" At half-past twelve the attack on the
Palais Royal commenced, and from that moment till half-past
one the firing was incessant. The Palais Royal was taken by
storm after a battle which lasted nearly an hour. The Palace
of the Tuileries made no resistance. At half-past one it surrendered, and the people entered at one side, just as the
King and his family were escaping at the other. As the
people arrived at the Place du Palais Royal they were received by a discharge of musketry from a post called the
Château d'Eau. The coolest act of this day was the manner
in which these men in blouses dislodged the troops and set
fire to their barracks. They were headed by the National
Guard; all at once the guard opened its ranks, and out stepped
some 500 to 1000 of the people, who coolly walked without
flinching (their comrades falling at their sides) till they arrived directly under the walls of the barracks. They then
laid hold of some citadines, filled them with straw, set fire to
them, and thus smoked them out. Some of the soldiers
escaped by the back way; the captain and a few others attempted to cut their way out, but were immediately shot or
bayoneted. The remains of twenty burned bodies were
found in the ruins.

Some partial conflicts had previously taken place in various
parts of the town, and several striking incidents had occurred. An officer, thinking to be safer in another station, or
wishing to assist it, had moved with his detachment of
soldiers a few steps from the post he occupied; when a mass
of people, whom he had not seen crowding down a side street,
interposed between him and the station he had left. As he
looked ahead, slackening pace, other troops of people passed
shouting in the distance before him. He called a halt, and
seemed doubtful and hesitating, looking back at his inter-

THE ATTACK ON THE PALAIS ROYAL.

cepted post as if he would be glad to return to it. The people set up a shout, and the soldiers looked downhearted, and by no means inclined to act. A *gamin*, having watched the scene, and perceiving instinctively the moment favourable for an audacious step, marched up alone, pistol in hand, to the officer. Presenting it, "Deliver yourself prisoner," said he. "Will you take us through the people to our post, then?" said the officer. "To be sure," said the *gamin;* "never fear." And the officer, giving up his sword, to the great delight of the audacious lad, signed to the troop to reverse their arms. Then taking the arm of the youth of the people they marched through the crowd, the *gamin* strutting gloriously with the sword till he had seen them all into the post; then mounting guard, he kept possession till a detachment of National Guards passed, and invested the place.

In another part, a score of unarmed people, dashing recklessly upon an almost impregnable military post, before the officer had time to say, "Present—fire," surrounded him, drew his sword from his hand, pushed in among the soldiers, putting them into confusion, snatched or wheedled their muskets from them, and then led them prisoners through the streets to the Mayoralty.

A band of insurgents in search of arms visited the residence of the Duke d'Elchingen (Prince de la Moskowa). The Duke was absent, and the Duchess was alone. "We come for arms," cried the group. "Take them," said her grace, pointing to some swords and fire-arms. "And that one?" said a citizen, pointing to a sword left suspended on the wall. "That sword," she replied, "belonged to my father-in-law. 'Tis the sword of Marshal Ney. Do not, pray, deprive me of that. The people always respected it." The men were moved, and taking down the weapon, they all kissed it with emotion, and placing it in the hands of Madame d'Elchingen they bowed and withdrew.

One of the most affecting incidents of the day of the 24th was the following:—In the quarter of the Panthéon the people demanded arms with loud cries. A lieutenant of the 12th Legion penetrated, at the head of some National Guards followed by an immense crowd, into the barracks situated in the Rue du Foin, and occupied by the 7th-Regiment of the Line ; the Colonel of the regiment advancede to persuade the people to withdraw ; they attempted to disarm him ; and the old soldier, who had gained his position by his sword, shed tears of mortification at seeing himself under the necessity either of submitting to an insult or of giving orders to fire on the people. The Lieutenant of the National Guard, touched with his grief, cried, " No, you shall not be disarmed if I can prevent it ; but, Colonel, give us some muskets and ammunition, they are massacring our brethren, and we desire to help them." He hesitated a moment, and then ordered that twelve muskets and some packets of cartridges should be given to the crowd. No sooner had he given the order than the old soldier, owing to the great emotion he had suddenly felt, fell to the ground as stricken by apoplexy. He was immediately raised, and after being twice bled, recovered. ·

A young girl was present at the last massacre of the Municipal Guard of the post of the Place de la Concorde, which fired on the 5th Legion. There remained only one of these unfortunate men. "Mdlle." cried M. de V———, commandant of the firemen, "you may save this man!" "What must I do? I am ready!" "Throw yourself into his arms and claim him as your father!" The young girl threw herself at the same moment into the arms of the Municipal Guard, and weeping, cried, "Gentlemen, in the name of God, spare my father, or kill me with him!" At the same moment the muskets of the assailants were lowered, and the Municipal Guard, protected by his liberatress, was saved.

The correspondent of the "Morning Chronicle" describes a visit he made to the Palais Royal, as soon as the firing had ceased. With great difficulty he wended his way over some half-dozen barricades in the Rue Vivienne to the Palais Royal. The *grilles* had been opened, and the garden was nearly empty. The fighting having been outside, but few of the slain were to be seen, but some of the wounded were in the Galerie d'Orléans, where they were attended to by lads in blouses, and armed with muskets, pikes, and cutlasses, but with a degree of care and attention that surprised the Englishman, and convinced him that they were not the heartless ruffians they looked. Proceeding to the garden court, gilt chairs, splendid pictures, canopies, tables, and all the other etceteras of a splendidly furnished palace, were to be seen every second emerging from the windows of the palace, which were forthwith thrust into the fire. At length a very splendid chair appeared, which must be known to many of our readers ; it was the throne upon which Louis Philippe sat for the first time as King, before he went to the Palace of the Tuileries, and has ever since been pointed out at the palace, on that account, as a relic. It was, however, on this occasion, mercilessly thrown into the fire, amidst thunders of applause, and in a few minutes the real throne of Louis Philippe crumbled into dust, like the power of which it was the symbol. The splendid silk velvet draperies, with the magnificent gold trimmings, soon followed, and one of them shared the fate of the throne, while the other, at the suggestion of a humane, or perhaps avaricious personage, was carried away to solace the wounded. Whilst this was going on, numerous blouses and bayonets were to be seen occasionally at the windows of the palace, and the loud crash of the magnificent mirrors was from time to time to be heard, as they shivered under the relentless blows of their destroyers. In short, the Palais Royal was sacked as completely as it was in 1789, and in a much shorter space of time.

When the Revolutionists had forced their way into the Palais Royal and had reached the apartments of General Athalin, one of Louis Philippe's aides-de-camp, they encountered the General's lady, a woman of dignified deportment and stature, whom the General had espoused for her rare beauty, being but the daughter of a poor fisherman of Gran-

ville. "My friends," she exclaimed, "I trust you have not
come here to offer any injury to myself or my husband. I am
not one of your fine ladies, but a daughter of the people: I
throw myself then confidently on your protection. But I will
not leave my husband; he is confined to his bed by illness."
The band were struck with the boldness of the appeal. They
repaired to the General's chamber, placed him in an arm-chair,
and, headed by this daughter of the people, they conveyed
him to a friend's house in the neighbourhood. On reaching
his destination, the General recollected leaving a sum of
130,000 francs (£5200) in notes and gold in his desk. He
handed the key of the desk to a working-man in a blouse,
whom he did not know. An hour after the man returned
with every sous of the money.

After the retreat of the royal forces from the Tuileries,
the palace was entered by some of the National Guard, who
marched in with their muskets shouldered, but-end upwards,
and were soon afterwards followed by thousands of the people,
all astonished to find themselves masters of the place. They
immediately began to ransack the royal apartments, but there
was method and moderation even in their way of doing mischief. A few of their leaders laid down rules of conduct for
them, which were willingly obeyed. One unfortunate man
ventured to steal a silver spoon; his companions ordered him
to kneel, and saying they disavowed him and thus treated
robbers, they shot him dead. After tearing the covering of
the throne into shreds, which were distributed as relics
among the invaders, they carried the disgraced remains in
triumph through the streets, then smashed them to atoms, and
burned them at the foot of the Column of July. The King's
private property was ruthlessly demolished; but it is gratify-
ing to know that, with this exception, the treasures of art
accumulated, both in the Tuileries and the Palais Royal,
generally remained uninjured. It is certain, however, that
attempts were made to burn the Tuileries and the Louvre,
which were found to be on fire in three places on Thursday

THE ATTACK ON THE TUILERIES.

night. Had this been effected, the consequences would have been terrific; for the populace, gorging in emotions of all kinds, would have carried the work of devastation further, and varied the scene of horrors.

A sum of 331,000 francs, which was found in the strong box of the Civil List, was conveyed in safety to the Bank of France. The crown diamonds were also saved, and other articles of value were borne to the *garde-meuble* with the greatest care. A workman, who was among the first to enter the palace, found a large quantity of plate and jewels, with which he hastily filled the Duchess of Orleans' bath; then throwing a sheet over the top, he lay down on it, until he was able to deliver the treasure into safe hands. The bath, still covered with the sheet, was carried to the Mayoralty, the bearers crying out as they passed along, " Make way for the wounded."

" We passed quickly through the crowded public rooms " (says a correspondent of the " Manchester Times ") " into the Duchess of Orleans' apartments. The first thing that struck us was a half-finished picture, full length, of the unfortunate Princess and her two sons, standing beside the *fauteuil* arranged for *posing*, and all as if abandoned only ten minutes ago. We were pleased at the respect shewn even to this image. While one man was throwing out at the window a bust of Louis Philippe, from which another had cut off and pocketed the nose with great *sang froid*, the people passing before the picture raised their caps, saying, *Vive la Duchesse d'Orléans!* while immediately one or two stationed themselves before the picture and two small oval ones on the chair, to preserve them from damage. A little further on was a breakfast set out on a table, and half eaten, from which the Duchess and perhaps the whole family had been obliged to fly, and which the people, ferociously hungry, sat down to on the very chairs still round the table, and soon made clear work of with great glee."

A deaf lady, living in apartments at the Tuileries, heard

nothing of the *émeute*, when she was surprised reading by the entry of the people.   When she recovered herself, they told her she must quit the palace, but should be escorted whither she pleased, and might take her clothes and jewels with her, and, leaving her to pack up her things, they locked her door and placed a guard before it.   Three hours later they returned to take her away, when one of her large boxes, badly corded, came open, and all her things fell out; they packed it again for her, and marched away with three drums in front and a strong guard, and deposited her and her property at the house of one of her relations.

There is a mystery still hanging over the invasion of the Tuileries, which time alone can clear up.   It is evident that the suggestion, " Burn all the papers," which was responded to by immediate execution, must have emanated from a *friend* and not an enemy.   All the papers and documents were burnt on the spot—and many persons doubtless saved thereby from dishonour.   A gentleman is said to have picked up in the court-yard of the palace, amid a mass of blackened matter, seven pages of manuscript merely scorched and perfectly legible.   They are written, we are told, in the King's own hand, and seem to have formed part of the journal which he had been in the habit of keeping all his life.   The last phrase written therein is curious—" *The storm is gathering around us, but will not be*———." The writer must have been called suddenly away, for the words are followed by a long dash of the pen, and an ominous blot.   The conclusion of the sentence would have been, no doubt, expressive of the delusion which seems to haunt every monarch even on the very brink of perdition.

The appearance of the Tuileries, the Palais Royal, and their environs, after the battle, is thus described by the correspondent of the " Morning Herald :"—"The Tuileries presents a sad, and I would say, shabby, rather than ruined appearance. The windows are smashed, and sheets of torn paper flying about, with rags and scarves hanging out, according to some notion of mockery or tomfoolery not plainly discernible. So far the works of art have been respected—the pictures and statues uninjured—and robbery forbidden on pain of death. They may smash, but not pocket—such is the received maxim of mob law. I have heard, that while they were tearing and breaking a widow's bonnet arrested their violence, and they respected the symbol of mourning. As you pass by the Carrousel, out through the angular streets into the Rue St. Honoré, adjoining the Palais Royal, you cannot doubt that you are on the field of a real battle. The large building which used to be occupied by the Municipal Guard, exactly facing the palace, looked battered all over, and the conflagration had not quite ended. The square without, as well as the court within, and the streets flanking the Palais Royal, were all black with the embers of the burned furniture and carriages. The handsome glass gallery has been turned into an ambulance for the wounded."

Another spectator visited the Tuileries about half-past five, the garden was then literally strewed with dresses, bonnets, music-books, and other ladies' gear. The furniture and other solids had been already nearly all burnt, but there was still enough to furnish fuel for three huge fires, the one in the Rue Rivoli, and the others on the quay. The cellars were filled with drunken rioters, and sounds were heard which left no doubt that, after having satiated themselves, they were breaking up the puncheons, to prevent others from following their bad example. In the Place du Carrousel there were some thousands of bloused and armed citizens, in all the stages of drunkenness, from the muzzy to the dead. They had almost all some trophy from the palace, mostly of a warlike order. One thing was particularly striking. Every person, man and woman, was searched as he came out at the gate, lest by any chance any of the patriots should be tempted to pillage. The guards and searchers were all *des gens du peuple*, and mostly boys of eighteen or twenty years of age, and the strictness with which the search was made was very minute. No one seemed to object to the search, and, to the credit of all, the very few things found were almost, without exception, in point of money value utterly worthless.

Farce, of course, mingled, as usual, with the tragic sights and emotions of the day. A bill was stuck upon the Tuileries with this inscription:—*Maison à louer, en totalité à cause de non payement.*—"The whole of this house to be let, by reason of default of payment." Soon after the work of devastation was done, and the crowd began to withdraw from the Tuileries, a working man with a musket on his shoulder was going along the Boulevards to the Madeleine: he suddenly stopped before two gentlemen and a lady, who had ventured down to their *porte-cochère* to get a peep at what was going on. "Who do you suppose," said he, addressing the group, "will be most put out by this *charivari?* Why Abd-el-Kader, to be sure; for what now becomes of the famous promise made at his capitulation? *Enfoncé l'Arabe!*" (We have done the Arab!) And so saying, quite satisfied at having unburthened his mind to some one, he passed on his way.

THE DUCHESS OF ORLEANS AND HER CHILDREN AT THE CHAMBER OF DEPUTIES.

CHAPTER IV.

REJECTION OF THE ORLEANS DYNASTY.—PROCLAMATION OF THE
REPUBLIC.—FLIGHT OF THE ROYAL FAMILY.

THE scene in the Chamber of Deputies on Thursday was
one of the most extraordinary ever beheld. It was, in fact, a
combined repetition of what occurred in the Constituent
Assembly on the 10th of August, 1792, and of the decisive
blow struck by Buonaparte on the 18th Brumaire, when he
turned the legislative body out of doors with his grenadiers.
The dynasty and the legislature were alike deposed by the
armed people on the memorable 24th of February, 1848.

At one o'clock the President took the chair; upwards of
300 members were present. In half an hour afterwards the
Duchess of Orleans entered with her two sons and the Dukes de
Nemours and Montpensier. The young Comte de Paris came
first, led by one of the Deputies. It was with great difficulty
that way could be made for him amidst the crowd of officers
and soldiers of the National Guard. His presence at the
door caused a strong sensation, which broke forth in murmurs
that soon rose to loud exclamations of, "You cannot enter!
You have no right here!" Several of the people, however,
rushed into the chamber with the young Count, and placed
him under the tribune. A moment afterwards the Duchess
of Orleans entered and seated herself in a chair, with her two
sons beside her. Immediately the passages, and every vacant
space, was filled with such of the populace as had succeeded
in squeezing themselves in with the National Guards. The

Princess soon after quitted the semicircle, and retired to one of the upper benches of the centre, and opposite to the President's bureau. The Chamber was agitated in every part. The first to speak was M. Dupin, who said, that in the present situation of the capital it had been found necessary to re-assemble the Chamber without loss of time. The King had abdicated the crown in favour of his grandson, and devolved the regency on the Duchess of Orleans. At this announcement cries of Bravo! resounded from the centre, and from some of the public galleries. Disapprobation was expressed on the benches of the left, and one voice was heard above the rest exclaiming, " It is too late!" A scene of confusion it is impossible to describe ensued. The Duchess and her children now appeared in the midst of a group of Deputies. The National Guards hastened to surround the royal family. The Dukes of Nemours and Montpensier were seated behind the two young princes and their mother.

M. Marie all this while endeavoured in vain to make himself heard; but at length succeeded in obtaining silence. He said,—In the critical condition of Paris, it is our urgent duty to take measures which will have some authority with the people. Since this morning the evil has made great progress. (Cries of, Good!) Which part will you take? But an instant since the Duchess of Orleans was proclaimed Regent. But there is a law which gives the regency to the Duke of Nemours, and you have not the power at this moment to make a new law. What you have to do is to name a Provisional Government. Not to create new institutions, but to advise with the two Chambers on the necessity of satisfying the voice of the country.

M. Crémieux.—Some great measure is necessary for the safety of the public. It is important that every one should agree in proclaiming a great principle, and in assuring to the conquering people a solemn guarantee. Let us not do as we did in 1830. Let us not re-enact in 1848 what was done then. (Applause from the public gallery.) Let us form a Provisional Government, not to regulate the future, but to establish order. (Cries of Good, very good!) We cannot do more now. (No, no.) I have a great respect for Madame the Duchess of Orleans. (Bravo!) And it was I who conducted the royal family to the carriage which bore them away. (A voice: *Bon voyage!*) The population of Paris has shewn the most profound respect for the misfortune of the King; but we who are sent here to make laws must not break them. Now one law, already voted, disposes of the regency, and I cannot admit that its potency can be abrogated at the present moment. Since we have arrived at the point of undergoing a revolution, let us confide in the country. I propose a Provisional Government of five members. Several voices seconded the proposal.

M. de Genoude then rose, but at that moment M. O. Barrot entered the hall, upon which there was a general call for him to speak. M. de Genoude demanded that he should be heard. M. O. Barrot made a gesture of assent, and retired behind the President's bureau.

M. de Genoude.—Nothing practical can be done, nothing stable, amidst the excitement of a crowd. This was attempted in 1830, and you see the consequence.

M. O. Barrot.—Never were firmness and patriotism so much needed as now. We must all unite in the same sentiment: that of saving our country from that detestable scourge—a civil war. (Applause.) Nations do not die, I know, but they may be weakened by internal dissensions, and never did France stand so much in need of that greatest of strength, the unanimity of her children. Our duty is plainly marked out. It invites us to rally round that which is most generous in the heart of the country. The crown rests on the heads of a child and of a woman. (Strong marks of assent in the greater part of the Chamber; dissent in the galleries.) This is a solemn appeal! (At this point the Duchess of Orleans rose and uttered some words, the purport of which the reporters were unable to catch. The persons who surrounded her recommended her to sit down again.)

It is in the name of political liberty, of order, of that union
which must predominate in the wishes of all good citizens, that
I demand of all my colleagues to rally round this double representative of the Revolution of July. (Fresh marks of dissent
and approbation.) I would lay down my life a thousand times
to ensure the triumph of this cause—that of my country's
liberty.   Can it possibly be supposed that what has been
decided by the Revolution of July can be again placed in question? (Sensation.)   The task is a difficult one, I know; but
there are in this country such elements of greatness, generosity, and good sense, that an appeal is only necessary to
rally the whole population under that standard.   By these are
reconciled the means of assuring liberty and the rights of the
country with the necessities of order.   Let us rally all our
forces to work for this great end.   Our duty is simple, and
traced out by the laws and by honour.   If we do not perform
it with force and courage, I cannot say what will be the consequences.   Be convinced, that the man who would have the
courage to take on himself the responsibility of a civil war
would be in the highest degree culpable and criminal towards
his country.   (Very good!)   For my part, I will not bear
such a weight.   The regency of the Duchess of Orleans—a
Ministry chosen amongst the men of the most tried opinions
in the country—and an appeal to the country, which will pronounce itself with all its liberty and in the limits of legality—
these are opportune to the situation.   Such is my opinion,
and I will not take the responsibility of any other situation.

A person not belonging to the Chamber, M. Chevalier,
editor of the "Bibliothèque Historique," ascended the tribune,
amid a tumult of confusion ; but at last he made himself
heard.   Beware, he cried, of proclaiming the Count de Paris
without being authorised to do so.   But if the Duchess of
Orleans and the young Count have sufficient courage to go
along the Boulevards in the midst of the people and the
National Guards, I answer for their safety.   If the people will
not consent to confer on him the crown——

Voices in the crowd—Vive la République!

M. Chevalier: What you have now to do is to give us a Government, and to give it at once; you cannot leave a whole population without magistrates, without directing heads. (The noise prevented the voice of the speaker from being heard.)

M. de Larochejaquelin then rose to speak, but had only uttered a few words when a great crowd rushed into the chamber, composed of National Guards in arms, and citizens, some unarmed, in blouses, or with casques, shakos, and others armed with sabres, guns, swords, and flags. The tribune being thus filled with people not members of the Chamber, the President put on his hat; and this act was received with cries of, Down with the hat! An indescribable tumult then ensued, in the midst of which the tribune was occupied by National Guards and pupils of the Ecole Politechnique. The Deputies began to retire, and the crowd occupied the benches of the Chambers. The noise was at its height, when M. Ledru Rollin made himself heard: In the name of the people I protest against the kind of Government which has now been proposed to us. You have been told of the constitution of 1789. I am afraid that constitution, as well as that of 1791, has been forgotten. It is not the first time I have protested. In 1842, I demanded the constitution of 1791. (Good, very good!) This constitution enacted that an appeal should be made to the people for a law of regency. (Yes, yes, and loud applause.) I protest against the Government which is proposed, and I do so in the names of the citizens who are here now, who have fought for the last two days, and will fight again this evening. (Shouts from all sides, Yes, yes, and brandishing of weapons.) I demand, in the name of the people, that a Provisional Government be named. (Yes, yes.)

M. de Lamartine.—I have shared in the sentiments of grief which a short time ago agitated this assembly, when it saw the saddest sight that has been offered in human

annals—that of a Princess presenting herself with her innocent son, and leaving her palace to seek the protection of
the Chamber. But if I shared in this respect for a great
misfortune, I also share in the solicitude and in the admiration which must be excited at the sight of a people which has
been fighting for the last two days against a perfidious
Government, in order to re-establish the empire of order and
liberty. (Cries of Bravo!) Let there be no illusion. (A
voice : We must no longer have any.)   Do not think
that an acclamation in this Chamber can replace the united
will of 35,000,000 of men. Another kind of acclamation
must be heard, and whatever may be the government which
this country will adopt, it must be cemented by solid and
definite guarantees. How will you do it? How will you find
the conditions necessary for such a Government in the floating
elements which surround us? By descending into the very
depth of the country itself, boldly sounding the great mystery
of the right of nations. (Very good!) Instead of having
recourse to subterfuges to maintain one of those fictions
which have nothing durable, I ask you, first, to form a Provisional Government, whose duty it would be to stop the flow
of blood and put a stop to the civil war—(Acclamations from
all parts of the Chamber)—a Government which we institute
without giving up the rights for our anger, or that of the great
mission of establishing peace between citizens—a Government
on which we will impose the duty of convoking the whole of
the people.

At this moment a loud knocking was heard in one of the
tribunes, which was immediately filled by a crowd of men
bearing muskets. Several of them forced their way to the
front seats, and pointed their muskets at the Deputies below.
Some of these weapons were also turned in the direction of
the royal party.   Immediately the persons near the Duchess
of Orleans seemed to address her energetically, and a moment
after she rose, and, with her sons and the two princes, quitted
the chamber by a door on the extreme left   M. Sauzet left

the chair, and a great number of Deputies also rose from their places. The greatest disorder was now visible. Immediately after this, M. Dupont (de l'Eure) mounted on the President's chair. M. de Lamartine and M. Ledru Rollin appeared simultaneously at the tribune, but their voices were drowned by the noise. Some National Guards and other persons tried in vain at the same time to get a hearing. Cries of "To the Hôtel de Ville!" here arose, followed by a cry of "No Civil List!" and another of "No King!" Some one having directed the attention of the crowd·to the picture of Louis Philippe swearing obedience to the Charter, cries of "Tear it down!" arose. A workman armed with a double-barrelled fowling-piece, who was standing in the semicircle, cried out, "Just wait till I have shot at Louis Philippe!" and at the same moment both barrels were discharged. Great confusion ensued, in the midst of which two men jumped on the chairs behind the President's seat, and prepared to cut the picture to pieces with their sabres. Another workman ran up the steps of the tribune, and exclaimed, "Respect public monuments! respect property!" Cries were then made from all quarters, of "Lamartine! Let Lamartine speak."

M. de Lamartine.—A Provisional Government is about to be proclaimed. (Cries of *Vive Lamartine!* Names—names!)

The noise not ceasing, the names were written on a slip of paper, and carried round the chamber on the top of a musket. In the midst of shouts, M. Ledru Rollin read the names. The tumult was at its height, and all the Deputies left; the chamber no longer contained any but National Guards and the people. M. Rollin continued,—We are obliged to raise the sitting in order to go to the seat of government. (Shouts from all parts, "To the Hôtel de Ville!" "Vive la République!") The crowd then dispersed at four o'clock.

Another terrible scene now took place at the Hôtel de

Ville, where, on adjourning from the chamber, the members of the Provisional Government sat to decide upon the course to be adopted. Suddenly the doors of the Salle du Conseil were violently shaken, and the people demanded aloud to have the first act of the Provisional Government communicated to them. Individually the great majority of the members were opposed to the establishment of an unmitigated democracy. The populace, however, filled the hall, and completely overpowered them by demonstration of their inflexible purpose of seeing a Republic in its most democratic form resolved on. In vain it was attempted to adjourn the question till minds should become calm. Every proposition of that nature was met by menacing shouts, directed even against the most popular of the members of the Government. M. Dupont (de l'Eure), who made many attempts to defend the proposition of a Republic in its less democratic shape, was compelled to silence by the most deafening shouts of *Dupont à la fenêtre!* and was so exhausted by fatigue and excitement that he twice fainted. M. Marie met with no better success. The anxieties he underwent had such an effect on his countenance, that in leaving the meeting his own son could not recognise him. The populace willed that a pure democratic Republic should be formed, and that every male above a certain age should be eligible to the National Guard, and empowered to carry arms. Every attempt to oppose this, in however mitigated a form, was the signal of renewed shouts of *Dupont à la fenêtre! Marie à la fenêtre!* The popular will prevailed, and resolutions were passed in accordance with it.

The Provisional Government at once issued the following proclamation: —

" To the French People.

" A retrograde and oligarchic Government has been overturned by the heroism of the people of Paris. This Government has fled, leaving behind it traces of blood, which will for ever forbid its return. The blood of the people has flowed as in July, but happily it will not have been shed in vain. It has secured a national and popular Government, in accordance with the rights, the progress, and the will of this great, and generous people. A Provisional Government, chosen by the acclamation and at the call of the people and some of the Deputies of the departments in the sitting of the 24th of February, is for the moment invested with the care of organising and securing the national victory. It is composed of MM. Dupont (de l'Eure), Lamartine, Crémieux, Arago (de l'Institut), Ledru Rollin, and Garnier Pagès. The secretaries to this government are MM. Armand Marrast, editor of the ' National ;' Louis Blanc, Ferdinand Flocon, editor of the ' Réforme,' and Albert. These citizens have not hesitated for an instant to accept the patriotic mission which has been imposed on them by the urgency of the occasion. When the capital of France is under fire, the mission of the Provisional Government is that of public safety. All France will understand this, and will give the assistance of its patriotism. Under the popular government now proclaimed by the Provisional Government, every citizen is a magistrate. Frenchmen, give to the world the example which Paris has given to France. Prepare yourselves, by order and confidence in yourselves, for those strong institutions which you are about to be called upon to give yourselves. The Provisional Government desires a Republic, subject to the ratification of the French people, who are to be immediately consulted. Neither the people of Paris nor the Provisional Government desire to substitute their opinion for the opinions of the citizens at large, upon the definite form of government which the national sovereignty shall proclaim. The unity of the nation, formed henceforth of all classes of the people which compose it. The government of the nation by itself. Liberty, equality, and fraternity for its principles. The national device and pass-word to be ' The People.' Such is the democratic government which France owes to herself, and which our efforts will assure to her. Such are the first acts of the Provisional Government.

(Signed), " Dupont (de l'Eure), Lamartine, Ledru Rollin, Bédeau, Michel Goudechaux, Arago, Bethmont, Marie, Carnot, Cavaignac, Garnier Pagès.

" The Municipal Guard is disbanded. The protection of the city of Paris is confided to the National Guard, under the orders of M. Courtais."

This proclamation was followed by another, appointing a Provisional Ministry, as follows : — M. Dupont (de l'Eure), President of the Council, without portfolio; M. de Lamartine, Minister of Foreign Affairs; M. Crémieux, Minister of Justice; M. Ledru Rollin, Minister of the Interior; M. Michel Goudechaux, Minister of Finance; M. François Arago, Minister of Marine; General Bédeau, Minister of War; M. Carnot,

Minister of Public Instruction and Worship; M. Bethmont, Minister of Commerce; M. Marie, Minister of Public Works; General Cavaignac, Governor of Algeria. To these decrees succeeded :—

" The Municipal Guard is dissolved. M. Garnier Pagès is named Mayor of Paris, and to him are given as *adjoints*, MM. Guinard and Recurt. M. Flotard is named Secretary-general. All the other Mayors of Paris are provisionally maintained. The Préfecture of Police is under the dependence of the Mayor of Paris. In the name of France, the Provisional Government decides that the Chamber of Deputies is dissolved. The ex-Chamber of Peers is forbidden to meet. A National Assembly will be convoked as soon as the Provisional Government shall have regulated the necessary measures of order and police."

Further appointments followed in rapid succession. General Subervie was substituted for General Bédeau, as Minister of War; General Bédeau taking the command of the first military division; Admiral Baudin was appointed Commander of the Fleet; the Police department was entrusted to the citizens Caussidière and Sobrier ; and citizen Et. Arago was appointed to the Direction-General of the Post-office. A notice also advised the bakers, or furnishers of provisions of Paris, to keep their shops open to all those who might have occasion for them. The people were expressly recommended not to quit their arms, their positions, or their revolutionary attitude. It was further announced that the liberation of all who had been imprisoned on political grounds had been effected; but, at the same time, all who had been convicted of crimes against persons and property were detained.

The Revolution was now consummated ; Royalty had vanished like a dissolving view, and its place was already filled by a new and totally different spectacle; " a powerful monarchy, twelve hundred years old, which came in with the long-haired Pharamond and his slow ponderous bullock-cart, had departed with Louis Philippe, his frizzled *toupée* and one-horse brougham." Twelve hours before, no sober mind could have believed such a thing to be possible; but the inspired madness of a heroic populace put the logic of commonplace politicians to shame and confusion, and blazoned again to the world this old neglected truth, that there is nothing on earth so impossible as the perpetuation of injustice.

Several anecdotes are recorded as to the infatuation of the King and his Ministers, and their strange indifference to the roar and rush of the torrent that was soon to sweep them away. On the 22d, Louis Philippe's Minister of the Interior, M. Duchatel, sent a despatch to the several préfects, assuring them that disturbances had broken out in various parts of the capital, but that they were "*rien de sérieux.*" On the 23d he wrote that "tranquillity was completely restored." On the 24th, at half-past one, one of the new Ministers of half-an-hour's duration, probably M. O. Barrot, sent off telegraphic despatches, announcing that the King had abdicated, and the Duchess of Orleans had been appointed Regent; two hours after, the Provisional Government informed the provinces that the Court and Government were destroyed. On the night of the 21st the Duke de Montpensier was to have given a grand *soirée;* a sumptuous breakfast was to have been given at five in the morning, it not being doubted that the Parisians would promptly be put down. Among the papers in M. Guizot's office was found a letter from the Duke d'Aumale, complimenting the Minister on the energetic course he had adopted with respect to the banquet.

After the victory on Thursday, M. Léon de Maleville, a well-known Liberal Deputy, went along to the Ministry of the Interior, about half-past one o'clock, to assist in taking possession and guarding the documents. He opened the door of the private cabinet of the Minister, and was struck with astonishment to see—whom? The Minister himself, coolly standing before the fire, with his hands behind him. "In the name of Heaven, what are you doing there?" exclaimed the Deputy. "Why, to be sure," replied M. Duchatel, "I'm waiting for my successor in office, to deliver up to him." "A very different successor in office you will have immediately upon you, if you don't fly in an instant—a successor who may make you deliver up life as well as office keys; for we can't insure any one against the popular passion in such a moment as this." "Pooh! don't think to frighten me with shadows." "What do you mean?—are you mad? Why, I tell you it's not a change of Ministry—it's a *revolution.* You and your party are annihilated. The King himself has just abdicated, and then fled. The people are even now streaming into the palace; and if you don't take this moment to fly, we can't assure you your head a day—not perhaps an hour longer." "My God!" said the poor Minister, getting pale, "is it really so?" And in a minute the office of the Interior had seen the last of M. Duchatel.

And where, meanwhile, was the frizzled-wigged last representative of Pharamond's line? Where was that stout rider, who, on the preceding Tuesday, had declared that " he was so firmly seated in his saddle that nothing could throw him out of it?" He was flying in ludicrous alarm from imaginary pursuers, chased only by his own fears, and without wit enough left to know that he was secure from danger, being clothed, as in impenetrable mail, in the contempt of a magnanimous people!

It appears that the King, ever since the death of Madame Adelaide, had lost much of his energy, and given up in some degree his early habits and the punctuality in business for which he had always been distinguished. On the morning of Thursday he had risen somewhat later than usual; he said that he had passed a restless night, and that he was weary, both in mind and body, with the petitioning of the two royal Dukes (Nemours and Montpensier) for that which they knew he could not grant. He had been writing all the preceding evening in his own bedroom, and a sealed letter to the Queen of Belgium was amongst the papers found upon his writing-desk. It is understood that the seal was respected, and that the letter was religiously despatched to its destination. So little apprehension was felt as to the result of the day's debate, that the royal children were brought as usual to the King; and it being Thursday, his Majesty had examined, as was his wont on that day, all the copy-books of the Count de Paris, and expressed his satisfaction at the progress evinced by the royal pupil in his various studies.   At ten o'clock the children were dismissed, and at that hour the strife began by the announcement of M. Emile de Girardin.   "Nay, but I received him yesterday," exclaimed the King, much irritated, to the aide-de-camp in waiting.   "Pardon me, Sire, he says that his business is urgent, and that the safety of the empire depends upon your Majesty's reception of his message."   The King, now interested, but not yet alarmed, gave the order to admit the visitor. It appears by M. de Girardin's own account, that he was so overcome with emotion that for an instant he could not speak, and the King said abruptly, and in no measured tone of voice, "What more is now required by you and your fellows (*vous et vos pareils*)? have we not made enough concession in all conscience?"   "There is yet another one, your Majesty, which is become more necessary than all the rest."   "Then it cannot be granted," returned the King, peevishly; "indeed I have regret for that which is already done."   "And so have I, your Majesty: for it is not yet enough."   "*Qu'est-ce à-dire?*" exclaimed the King, interrupting him with great vehemence.   The haughtiness of the expression, which is untranslateable—the abruptness of the tone in which it was uttered, roused the fiery temper of Girardin, and he answered almost coarsely,—"The one concession more which is demanded by the people is your Majesty's abdication; on the instant too, and without any reservation."   The King started to his feet with such sudden movement that he upset the ink-stand which he had just been using, and the broad black stain may yet be seen upon the carpet.   He rushed to the window; Girardin followed him, and, pointing to the crowd, exclaimed, "Six battalions of National Guard surround the palace—all are of one mind, and those who sent me here are strong in their unanimity—blood has been shed, and now there is no retreat."   Louis Philippe grew deadly pale, and his hand shook violently as he took that of M. de Girardin, but his voice faltered not as he answered, " You are perhaps in the right, Monsieur—I will go down to the Chambers, not to plead for myself, but to protect my dynasty."

- It appears that the King now verbally intimated his intention to abdicate. De Girardin hurried away to report the fact to the insurgents, but the intelligence he brought was universally treated with disdain. *Nous ne voulons pas de ça*—" That won't do for us," cried the people. It was not until a later period in the day that the abdication was formally signed. The Queen is said to have earnestly dissuaded the King from an act which she conceived to be unworthy of him. Rather than submit to such disgrace, she was prepared to see him die before her eyes, and to perish with him.

Even after the rough lesson read to him by De Girardin, Louis Philippe was slow to learn how utter was his defeat. Not until the last moment that he could remain without peril to his life, did he reluctantly consent to quit the palace. Already was the Palais Royal taken and the people within a few steps of the Tuileries; already was fire set to the carriages in the royal stables within a gun-shot of the palace gate; already the Guards and people were drawing close round the Tuileries on all sides, and the troops in full retreat; when the King and royal family were still in the Salle des Maréchaux, and contemplating tranquilly from the balcony the mass of the troops before them in the Carrousel, ready to give the order to fire on the assailants. In this juncture, to save useless bloodshed, a National Guard, waving a white handkerchief, rode through all that mass of cavalry and infantry, right up to the balcony on which stood the royal family and the staff, and demanded the Duke of Nemours. He told him every post in Paris was taken, the troops disarmed and in full retreat, the National Guard and the people within a gun-shot of the palace, and that to seek to defend it longer, and give order to the troops in the Carrousel to fire, would only be needlessly shedding blood on both sides—blood which would never be forgiven. The whole party seemed astounded by the news. The closeness of the danger bewildered them. They retired a moment to deliberate. Already the assailants began to appear, defiling through several inlets upon the place. There was no time to be lost. At a sign from the Duke of Nemours, the troops began to dash rapidly out of the Place du Carrousel by the Quay, over the bridge, and into their barracks close at hand. The artillery caissons galloped rapidly down the river side, towards the Invalides. As the troops retreated, the people advanced; and already the foremost of them rushed shouting into the court and began to press into the palace, when the King and the staff fled out at the garden-door.

We are indebted to the correspondent of the "Weekly Chronicle" for the following graphic description of a part of this strange episode, from the first advance of the insurgents to the flight of the ruined dynasty :—

"The Place du Carrousel is a vast open square, encompassed on three sides by the bodies and wings of the Tuileries; while the fourth side is bounded by an irregular range of mean houses — birdshops, bookstalls, and *marchands de vin*. In the midst of the square stands a tall isolated house, painted all over with staring advertisements, and looking as if it had been left there by some strange oversight when the ground was cleared to build the palace. This house has some rough brick abutments at the corners.

"When the head of the advancing column reached the open square, its speed diminished considerably, and a curious movement took place in front. The few individuals forming the first rank kept coming round to the sides, so as to leave the second rank exposed. These did the same in their turn; and this instinctive motion—which looked like a sort of *boiling over*—had the effect of spreading the head of the column into a great cluster, which was continually urged forward, and at the same time thickened, by the pouring on of those in the rear. By this process I, from being in the fiftieth rank or so, soon found myself in front; and immediately, as you may sup-

pose, *boiled over* in my turn.   To say truth, as an unarmed
spectator, I did not feel called on to form a rampart for a
strong fellow with a pike, whom I perceived peeping over my
shoulder from behind.   Glancing hastily round the square for
a place of shelter, it occurred to me, that whatever movements
might take place, I might contrive to interpose one or other of
these abutments, before alluded to, between me and the bullets.   So I ran forward, and took up my station in that central
position.

"The square into which the insurgents were now swarm-
ing, was occupied by three or four thousand cavalry and infantry, with a battery of five or six cannon.   In front were several
groups of Generals and other officers on horseback; who appeared to me to be in great confusion—all talking together;
some galloping from group to group; some riding along the
ranks of soldiers; no one, so it struck me, in possession of
absolute command.   As for the soldiers, anxiety, indecision,
and extreme fatigue were painted on their pale visages.   The
Cuirassiers sat on their horses in motionless squadrons; the
infantry, drawn up in long lines, stood like statues; all gazing
silently at the roaring multitudes that kept advancing towards
them, urged on by the pressure of the vast columns behind.

"And truly there was something in the aspect of that
savage mob that might have appalled the stoutest heart.   The
wild, strange figures, I beheld among them recur to my memory
like the shapes of an incoherent dream.   Hideous faces, dis-
torted with rage, gaunt with want, inflamed with liquor, came
nearer and nearer; some blackened with soot—some red-
dened with ochre—hundreds crowned with the terrible RED
CAP.   The fiercest and most reckless were of course in front.
Amongst the motley crowd were figures that, under any other
circumstances, would have excited laughter.   I saw a great
blacksmith armed with a delicate rapier, having a costly hilt
of sparkling steel and jewels.   He eagerly besought a *gamin*
next him to take this weapon in exchange for a great cutlass
which the urchin carried, and which his strength was mani-

festly inadequate to wield; but the boy disdainfully refused. There was a miserable object, clad in rotten, loathsome rags (through which his flesh shewed in a dozen places), carrying a tall spear with a broad antique blade, richly damasked, springing from a great tassel of gold and silk, and having for cross-piece a twisted serpent curiously carved in steel. A ragged boy had a pair of pistols with ivory stocks, and set with a large ruby; and I saw him freely give one of these to an urchin as ragged as himself. There was a man who had lost his gun offering a hatful of cartridges for a sword—a bargain which was caught at in a moment. One had a butcher's hook —another a carpenter's adze—a third carried a heavy area spike, the tip of which shewed as if it had been lately on the grindstone. Many had bayonets or short pikes fixed on the ends of broomsticks. I saw one man with nothing but a long piece of wire, about as thick as a stair-rod, sharpened at the extremity. Sledge-hammers, crowbars, shapeless lengths of iron, gleamed amongst the weapons. I saw a man with a great scythe blade, another with a hoe, while a third carried in his hand a coil of rope with an iron weight at the end. One man toiled under a fluted iron column—a gas-post, probably, torn down to serve as a battering-ram. Amongst the boys I noticed several with their aprons full of stones.

" Suddenly a soldier's horse, richly caparisoned, broke loose, dashed into the middle of the Place, and after stopping and looking round him, began to kick furiously. He was caught and mounted by a beggar with ragged trousers and naked feet, who carried a plank with a piece of red carpet nailed to it by way of a flag, and brandished above the red cap on his head a butcher's chopper. Thus raised, he seemed to think himself the leader of the insurrection; but whilst he was bawling with violent gesticulations, the horse suddenly set off at full gallop, dashed through the infantry, who hastily opened their ranks to let him pass, and disappeared beneath the archway beyond—with his luckless rider, capless, flagless, hatchetless, clinging in terror to his mane. In the midst of this strange confusion two figures especially struck me :—one, that of a Turk in full costume, with his loose trousers, silk sashes, &c., who stood gravely, sword in hand, apparently well-disposed for the fray ;* the other, that of a young woman, elegantly dressed in a richly-coloured velvet *visite*, who kept close beside a handsome young fellow with long hair, armed to the teeth with pistols, sword, musket, and bayonet. I set them down for a student and his mistress ;— they both laughed and talked eagerly—evidently enjoying the scene, and apparently indifferent to the danger. I could not see the girl's face, but I pictured her with the features of an antique heroine, glowing with dauntless love.

" But I had little time for fanciful observations, the terrible conflict that seemed to be preparing soon engrossed my attention. From amidst the hesitating, leaderless mob, a hundred contradictory cries arose. Some young officers of the National Guard advanced towards the Tuileries, brandishing their swords and beckoning the others to advance. A few, chiefly of the populace, followed them, but the majority hung back. Some cried out to garrison the houses, and began to knock at the doors with their guns ; some cried to fire on the troops ; some cried, *Ne tirez pas!* some shouted, ' To the Palais Royal! they are slaughtering the people there by hundreds !' Some cried, ' No, no! stand firm—no retreat!' One of the Royalist Generals rode up to an officer of the National Guard, who was near me, and bitterly reproached him. ' What!' he said, ' we have fought for you and the country on a hundred battle-fields abroad, and you abandon us now and join the rabble ! Shame ! shame !' I did not hear the reply.

" Meanwhile the fusillade from the Palais Royal grew louder and more rollingly continuous ; and several hundreds of the fiercest insurgents marched off down the Rue de Chartres in the direction of the sound ; many others fell back

* This was perhaps Achmet Pasha, son of Mohammed Ali, who is known to have fought gallantly on the popular side.

(as it struck me) from an opposite motive, and in ten minutes or so after we had entered the Place, it was comparatively empty again.

" Taking advantage, as it seemed, of this lull, the officers in command of the troops wheeled them round in squadrons, and marched them through the marble arch into the court of the Tuileries, which is separated by tall iron railings from the open square. Here the regiments were spread in a long line, two or three ranks deep, close beneath the windows of the palace, along its whole façade. The cannons were also dragged rumbling into the court, and the great gates shut.

" These movements were hardly completed, when the square began to fill again with National Guards, armed populace, and fraternising soldiery, who advanced all the more boldly that the enemy was further off. The same confusion —the same contradictory cries, continued to prevail ; and amidst the uproar, about a hundred of the mob ran forward and discharged their muskets at the soldiers in front of the Tuileries. Immediately there was a general rush to get out of the square ; every one expecting a volley from the Royalists, and no one, it would seem, feeling prepared to be shot down. I placed myself as flat as a pancake behind the buttress, and shut my eyes — expecting to hear the thunder of three thousand muskets, and the whistling of as many bullets through the air. But not a shot was fired ; and a few minutes afterwards Marshal Bugeaud came out on foot, in full uniform, covered with orders and stars, crying out, *Le Roi abdique — le Roi abdique en faveur du Conte de Paris, avec Madame la Duchesse d'Orléans pour Régente.* He was immediately surrounded by a group of some fifty of the populace, who all shouted at once — some, *Vive le Conte de Paris!* some, *A bas les Bourbons!* some, *Une République — pas de Régence!* Amidst which clamour, the poor Marshal, hustled and gesticulating, strove in vain to make himself heard. That which struck me most in this strange scene was the *utter futility* of this concession, so tardily made and so inadequately published ;

announced to a little group at one point of Paris, while the whole population were in arms, fighting, devastating, advancing, in an immense circle, upon the doomed monarch.

" My belief is that the King and his Generals were at this moment smitten with a panic, and hardly knew what they did. It was, indeed, within ten minutes or half an hour afterwards, if not at the very same moment, that the monarch fled from the palace. I could not, however, but admire the intrepidity with which Marshal Bugeaud advanced alone into the midst of this raging populace, infuriated against him personally, as commander of the troops, quite as much as against the King himself. He looked pale as the mob closed angrily around him; but he held himself erect, and spoke with an unfaltering voice.

" Immediately afterwards my attention was attracted by another cluster of people, who hemmed in an unfortunate Lieutenant of the Municipal Guard, and with horrid yells were threatening to tear him to pieces. The poor fellow had left his regiment, with two of his men, to join the people, as it afterwards appeared; but the Municipal Guards having been, throughout the whole struggle, the chief object of the popular abhorrence, his mere uniform was the signal for a shout of vengeance, which prevented him from making himself heard. He stood amidst the throng, with his hands joined, great drops of sweat on his brow, all his features quivering, and his body swaying and reeling to and fro, as the mob thrust and plucked at him. Suddenly, a National Guard, a little thin man, plunged into the throng, dashing the armed rioters aside, right and left. He flung his arm round the trembling dragoon, and cried in a stentorian voice, — ' I take this man under the protection of the National Guard, and let me see who dares to molest him !' The people still murmured and hooted; but the little man drew his sword, and flourishing it over his head, dragged his *protégé* to the shelter of an adjacent stable. As he turned indignantly to reproach the mob for their cowardice — hundreds rushing on one — I recognised to my surprise (why should I conceal his name?) my friend Barral, the chemist—a pale, thin, studious man, whom you may find, day after day, bent over his retorts, with a great pair of green spectacles over his eyes, the last man in the world from whom you would expect any special daring in the field. Yet Barral, as I afterwards learned, had led the attack against two posts, which were taken during the night, besides rescuing this trooper and several others out of the hands of the furious mob. So fallacious are appearances—so often may a nervous, delicate frame, lodge the high-beating heart of a hero! Honour to the philosopher who exchanges, at his country's call, the laboratory for the battle-field, and the pen for the sword, enhancing the lustre of scientific attainments by the noble virtues of courage and clemency!

" Five minutes afterwards the people were passing into the palace, not a shot hardly being fired by the soldiers in defence. The Tuileries, in fact, were not taken, but yielded. There was no assault that I saw,—nothing resembling a capture—only an evacuation—a surrender. As the traveller pursued tosses his glove to the bear, and while the brute stays to examine it makes good his escape, so the royal fugitive tossed his sumptuous palace to the mob, and by the time the monster, dazzled and triumphant, had demolished his statue and ransacked his halls, the monarch himself was half way to the coast. The effigy was shattered, but the man was saved."

The departure of the King and Queen is thus described by an eye-witness, M. Maurice, editor of the " Courier des Spectacles :"—

" About one o'clock in the afternoon, whilst in conversation with the Colonel of the 21st Regiment of the Line, who appeared well disposed, and of which he gave proof in ordering his men to sheath their bayonets, a young man in plain clothes, who turned out to be the son of Admiral Baudin, on horseback, trotted past us at a quick pace, crying out that Louis Philippe had abdicated, and requesting that the news

might be circulated. A few instants after, at the Pont Tournant, we saw approach from the Tuileries a troop of cavalry
of the National Guards, at a walking pace, forming the head
of a procession, and by gestures and cries inviting the citizens
to abstain from every unfavourable demonstration. At this
moment the expression, ' A great misfortune ! ' (*une grande
infortune*), was heard, and the King Louis Philippe, his right
arm passed under the left arm of the Queen, on whom he
appeared to lean for support, was seen approaching from the
gate of the Tuileries, in the midst of the horsemen, and
followed by about thirty persons in different uniforms. The
Queen walked with a firm step, and cast around looks of
assurance and anger intermingled. The King wore a black
coat, with a common round hat, but wore no orders. The
Queen was in full mourning. A report was circulated that
they were going to the Chamber of Deputies to deliver the
act of abdication. Cries of *Vive la Réforme ! Vive la France !*
and even, by two or thee persons, *Vive le Roi !* were heard.
The procession had scarcely passed the Pont Tournant, and
arrived at the pavement surrounding the obelisk, when the
King, the Queen, and the whole party made a sudden halt,
apparently without any necessity. In a moment they were
surrounded by a crowd on foot and horseback, and so pressed
on that they could no longer move freely. Louis Philippe
appeared alarmed at this sudden approach. Indeed the spot,
chosen by an unhappy chance, produced a strange feeling. A
few paces off a Bourbon King, an innocent and resigned
victim, would have been happy to have experienced no other
treatment. Louis Philippe turned quickly round, let go the
Queen's arm, took off his hat, raised it in the air, and cried
out something which the noise prevented me hearing; in fact,
the cries and *pêle-mêle* were general. The Queen became
alarmed at no longer feeling the King's arm, and turned
round with extreme haste, saying something which I could
not catch. At this moment I said, *Madame, ne craignez rien;
continuez, les rangs vont s'ouvrir devant vous*—'Have no fear,

Madame; go on, the crowd will open and make way for you.'
Whether her anxiety gave a false interpretation to my intention or not I am ignorant, but pushing back my hand she
exclaimed, *Laissez moi!* in a tone of extreme irritation. She
seized hold of the King's arm, and they both turned their
steps towards two small black carriages with one horse each.
In the first were two young children. The King took the
left and the Queen the right, and the children with their
faces close to the windows of the vehicle, looking at the
crowd with the utmost curiosity; the coachman whipped his
horse violently, in fact with so much rapidity did it take
place that the coach appeared rather carried than driven
away: it passed before me, surrounded by the cavalry and
National Guards present, and Cuirassiers and Dragoons.
The second carriage, in which were two females, followed the
other at the same pace, and the escort, which amounted to
about two hundred men, set off at a full gallop, taking the
water side, towards St. Cloud."

"The flight of Louis Philippe," says the "National," "was
marked by an incident which does so much honour to the
feelings of our population, that we hasten to mention it. At
the moment the ex-King was escaping by the little low door-
way nearly opposite the bridge, and going into the little
voiture that waited for him, he found himself surrounded by
the people. Two Cuirassiers stationed in the Place de la
Concorde rushed to his protection, and this brave regiment,
without however using their arms, opened a passage. An
officer seeing the danger, cried out, ' Messieurs, spare the
King!' To which a stentorian voice replied, ' We are not
assassins—let him go.' ' Yes, yes; let him go—*qu'il parte,*'
became the general cry. ' The people have been too brave
during the combat not to be generous after the victory.' "

The family were strangely scattered in their flight. The
Duchess de Montpensier, the innocent cause of all the uproar,
scared from the palace by the inroads of the mob, wandered
about the streets of Paris until five o'clock that day, accom-

panied by an old Spanish servant, who knows not a word of French. She was met in the Rue du Havre, close to the railway station, by a gentleman who, knowing her by sight, took upon himself to protect her and conduct her to his house, where she remained for some days. How she managed to stray unmolested and unrecognised so far from home, is a mystery to this hour. She says that, seeking to avoid the crowd, she turned down the streets which seemed most free, without caring whither they might lead. She arrived in England on the 29th of February, accompanied by her husband's aide-de-camp.

The Duchess of Orleans, after leaving the Chamber of Deputies on Thursday, proceeded with her children to the Invalides, where they passed the night. At five o'clock next morning they left in a hackney-coach, accompanied by an aide-de-camp of the Governor of the Invalides, Marshal Molitor. She did not leave Paris until the following Wednesday, and was accompanied to the frontier by a distinguished member of the Provisional Government, M. Marrast. The Provisional Government sent the Duchess her jewels and a large sum of money.

The Duke de Nemours and the Duke de Montpensier were both separated from their wives in the flight. Nemours arrived in London on Sunday the 27th of February, accompanied by his sister, her husband the Duke of Saxe Coburg, and four children. So sudden had been the escape of the whole party, that not one of them came provided with a change of raiment. The Duchess de Nemours arrived at Portsmouth on the 4th of March, under the escort of the Duke de Montpensier.

When the Duke de Nemours went to the Chamber of Deputies, on the 24th of February, he was dressed in the uniform of a Lieutenant-General. In the midst of the tumult which terminated the sitting, the Prince leaped from a window to the garden in order to effect his escape. He was at this moment met by two of the combatants who were going towards the Chamber, and one of whom took off the uniform of the National Guard, which he wore, and exchanged clothes with the Prince. The Prince, when undressing himself, gave the citizens different valuable articles which he had about him, and amongst others a very valuable watch, a poniard-knife, a ring, a purse containing several pieces of gold, and two gold chains; he then ran off in the direction of the Rue de Bourgogne, where he got into a cab. The preceding details would have remained unknown had not the police, in its active researches after the property which had been taken from the palace, come on the trace of some of the articles belonging to the Duke de Nemours. A warrant was in consequence issued against a journeyman watchmaker residing near the Chaussée d'Antin, and the result of its execution was the finding of almost the whole of the objects. The party in whose possession they were found, and who has the character of being an honest and hard-working man, protested that it was his intention to send them to the Duke de Nemours whenever he had an opportunity. He declared that he never considered them as his property, although he might justly have done so, for the Prince, when he gave them to him, told him to keep them, as he had no pocket in his assumed dress to put them in, and was moreover afraid that his having them about him might prove an obstacle to his escape, should he be stopped, for they might cause him to be recognised. The young man was set at liberty on making this declaration, and a seal was set on the articles found. He also told the magistrate that, on the 25th of February, he had informed his master of the circumstances; and that, having had an intention of writing to Queen Marie-Amélie, he had prepared a rough copy of a letter, which he had not recopied, not knowing how to get it to its destination, but in which he informed her that he kept the articles given him by the Duke de Nemours at the disposal of the Prince, with the exception of some louis in the purse, which he had been compelled to spend when out of employment, but which he would replace when he should be again in work.

I

Though Nemours was in too great haste to look after his wife before he started for England, it chanced that the same train which conveyed the Duke carried the lady's-maid of the Duchess. On the arrival of the train at the station, which is six miles from Boulogne, the Duke and the lady's-maid accidentally entered the same omnibus; but so completely had the Duke contrived to disguise himself that his own servant rode opposite to him six miles and did not recognise her master till, on embarking in the packet which brought them to the English coast, he called her by name. The Duke's complexion is very light, and his hair, eyebrows, and moustache had all been died a jet black.

The Queen had no bonnet on when she quitted the palace, and was indebted to the kindness of a woman in the crowd for a handkerchief to wrap her head in. The hack-carriage in which the King and Queen left the Tuileries, drove off to St. Cloud at such a rate, that when they had crossed the bridge the horse was too exhausted to mount the hill leading to the château. Several men pushed the carriage up, however. After taking some papers, the King entered a hackney-coach at St. Cloud, and drove off to Versailles, and thence to Trianon, where he halted a short time, and then continued his route. But before leaving the park he saw at a distance, approaching towards him, six men on horseback, and became afraid that they were in search of him. He therefore ordered the coachman to stop, alighted, and ran into a guard-house at the gate of the park, near the railroad station (Montretout), and concealed himself behind a stove. The men having passed, an aide-de-camp informed him that there was no danger. He accordingly re-entered the carriage and drove off. The fugitives arrived at Dreux on Thursday the 24th, at half-past eleven in the evening. On his arrival at Versailles, Louis Philippe and his suite, not finding any post-horses, was obliged to ask for horses from a regiment of cavalry. His flight had been so rapid and unforeseen, that he was forced to make at Trianon a collection among the officers, which produced two hundred francs.

At Dreux, a faithful farmer afforded shelter to the whole party, now consisting of the ex-royal pair, Generals Dumas and Rumigny, M. Thuret the King's valet, and a German lady attending on the Queen. Here each person of the party assumed the most complete disguise: the King shaved his whiskers, discarded his wig, and donned an old cloak and cap—even his friends could not recognise him. Before break of day they started again, and came to La Ferté Vidame; where an English tenant and *protégé* of Louis Philippe, Mr. Packham, had been building great mills. Escorted by a trusty farmer, they went through byways to Evreux; thence by night, on Saturday, to the house of a gentleman at Honfleur; and on to Trouville, to embark for England. But the boisterous weather prevented them for two days, and they returned to Honfleur. A passage having been secretly secured for them in the Express steamer, on Thursday afternoon, March 2, they went in an open fishing-boat to Havre, the ex-King passing as an Englishman; and about eight o'clock that evening they cautiously embarked.

A correspondent of the "Presse" thus reports the last words uttered by the dethroned King of the Barricades, on quitting the French shore:—"M. R——, one of my friends, was present at the embarkation of the ex-King in a fishing-boat, on Thursday last. When on the point of quitting the French soil, Louis Philippe turned towards R—— and said, 'Join the Republic frankly and sincerely, for I carry with me the French monarchy, and I shall descend with it to the tomb. I have been the last King of France. Adieu.'" For once Louis Philippe appears to have spoken the truth with sincerity.

The events of the passage across the Channel are recorded in a letter to the "Hampshire Independent," by one who was on board the vessel in which the exiles made their escape. The Express, he says, had been lying off Havre for two days, when an old man, apparently lame, dressed in a large travelling cloak, and his face nearly covered with a shawl, a pair of green spectacles, and a travelling cap, came on board, assisted by the British consul and Captain Goodridge. " While coming on board, I heard the consul say to him, ' Take care, uncle,' as if he was speaking to a relative, and warning him to be careful how he stepped on the ladder. The passenger was immediately conducted to the engineer's room (a most unusual place for a passenger to be shewn into), but, owing to its small size, and a fire burning in it, he was unable to remain there, and was obliged to go into the saloon. As soon as the old gentleman was on board, Captain Goodridge handed an elderly lady down the gangway. I heard her say to him, ' I am obliged to you,' and from her pronunciation I knew she was not an Englishwoman. She was very plainly dressed. Her hair was as white as silver, and I thought I never saw a countenance in which anxiety, fatigue, and fear were so visibly depicted. As soon as she was in the saloon, I could perceive that she had been, and still was, weeping." [We need not say that it was the ex-King and Queen.] " About midnight we were nearly run down by a large brig. No vessel ever had a more narrow escape than ours. We were within three or four yards of the brig. Fortunately we were going at about half-speed. The noise and confusion on deck arising from this disaster aroused the passengers. Her Majesty rushed out from her cabin into the saloon, exclaiming, ' Oh, where is my dear gentleman?' The King endeavoured to console her. She embraced him affectionately, crying bitterly, and talked to him, lamenting that his dangers were not yet over, notwithstanding the many he had escaped. The King was much affected, and he wept and sobbed violently. Her Majesty was implored to return to her cabin, but she declared that she would not again leave the King, and she lay down by his side on the floor of the saloon during the remainder of the night."

The only luggage brought on board by the party consisted of a reticule and a bag which appeared to contain money, two or three cloaks of a rich and costly description, and, what was most important, a small but very heavy box, containing the exile's last mementoes of all he had held most dear in the land he was quitting for ever. The box was filled with five-franc pieces, shining newly, as if direct from the mint.* Fifty of these pieces were distributed after breakfast among the crew. The Express arrived off Newhaven at seven o'clock on the morning of the 3d March, but, owing to the state of the tide and the weather, could not safely enter the harbour. At noon the fugitives were landed from the steamer's boats at Newhaven-bridge.

Louis Philippe appeared extremely delighted at having reached the shores of England, and expressed his pleasure in very warm terms to those around. Though cheerful, he looked pale. In reply to a remark from one of the persons present, congratulating him on having reached this country, he exclaimed,—" Yes, yes, I know I am safe among you—a victim of great misfortune. I know the English people; they are kind to those in misfortune." He shook hands with all those who offered their hands, as did the Queen. Some one said his anxieties were now over; to which he answered,—" Yes, I have suffered much during the past week, but the country people were very kind to me;" meaning the peasantry in the neighbourhood of Honfleur, in whose houses he had been secreted in disguise. In this disguise he now appeared. It consisted of a green blouse, grey trousers, a red and white " comforter," and a *casquette*, or peasant's cap. Over the blouse was a pea-coat, which had been borrowed from the captain of the Express. His beard was apparently of a week's growth. The Queen was attired in mourning of the humblest kind; consisting of a black bonnet, a very thick veil, and a woollen cloak of black and white plaid with broad checks. She looked much careworn.

Among the crowd assembled on the pier one Mr. Thomas

---

* The Provisional Government was perfectly aware of Louis Philippe's place of concealment, and on Friday, the 25th, they sent him money to enable him to proceed on his journey.—PELLETAN, *Hist. des Trois Jours de Février*, 1848.

Stone signalised himself, by recognising the ex-King afar off in the boat which brought him ashore, and pledging to him the protection of the British nation. The reported colloquy on landing is serio-comic :—

Stone.—" Welcome to England, your Majesty."

Louis Philippe.—" I thank you, I thank you ; I have always felt pleasure in coming to England. Thank God I am in England once more !"

Stone.—" We will protect your Majesty."

Ex-King (much agitated).—" I thank you, I thank you."

The ex-King and Queen took up quarters in the Bridge Inn, kept by one widow Smith. The ex-King's first act was to pen an autograph letter to Queen Victoria, and give it to trusty hands for soonest possible delivery. This done, Mr. West was privileged to proffer successfully his dressing-case for the use of the ex-King. A lady also was desirous to place a chest of clothes at the disposal of the ex-Queen ; but the offer was respectfully declined. The village barber was summoned to the ex-King, to remove the week-old beard ; an operation which he was at first unequal to, from nervousness, but ultimately performed with commendable skill. In a short time the ex-King was perfectly at home under good hostess Smith's assiduities ; and declined the offered hospitalities of the gentry, who soon arrived in numbers. The ex-Queen busied herself in letter-writing, and seemed less open to impressions of the present. Mr. Packham was master of the ceremonies, and introduced the visitors ; among others, deputations who had come pilgrimages of compliment from Brighton and from Lewes. Three gentlemen were introduced ; one being the Reverend Theyre Smith, Rector of Newhaven. " Mr. Smith !" exclaimed the King ; " that is curious indeed ! and very remarkable that the first to welcome me should be a Mr. Smith, since the assumed name was ' Smith ' by which I escaped from France ; and, look, this is my passport, made out in the name of ' William Smith ' ! "

Among the memorabilia of the Bridge Inn have been preserved the two following passages from the ex-King's conversation. Talking of the Revolution, he clasped his hands and exclaimed,—" Charles the Tenth was destroyed for breaking the Charter, and I have been overthrown for defending it, and for keeping my oath. I wish this to be distinctly understood, and I hope it will be made known."—" Truly happy and thankful, indeed, am I," he said again, " that I have once more arrived in England, and which I will not leave again. The bullets were striking the windows and doors when I escaped from the Tuileries, but here I am, safe and unhurt. I have nothing to tax my conscience with, and nothing to reflect upon (laying his hand upon his heart), and I thank you very much."

The ex-King and Queen seemed gratified with the sympathy evinced towards them. On Saturday, the early breakfast was prolonged by calls from more visitors : Mr. Lawrence and Lady Jane Peel had a long and animated interview. On this day, too, M. Duchatel, the late Home Minister, had an interview with his fallen master.

At nine o'clock the ex-King and Queen proceeded on their journey, and, by the help of a special train, were soon at Croydon. Here they were met by their children, the Duke of Nemours and the Duchess Auguste of Saxe-Coburg, with the Duke of Saxe-Coburg. The recognition has been described by a witness. " At the moment the train was brought to a standstill, the Duke de Nemours rushed towards the window of the carriage in which his exiled parents were seated, and, grasping his father's hand, he covered it with kisses. The Queen, who was sitting on the right of her royal husband, and was consequently further from the platform, on observing the Duke, gave utterance to a scream, apparently from excessive joy, and then fell back in her seat. The door of the carriage having been opened, the ex-King alighted, and immediately embraced his son with great apparent fervency, kissing him again and again, while the tears poured down his furrowed cheeks. The next moment the ex-Monarch clasped in his arms the Princess

Clémentine, who was standing close to her brother. The Princess, who up to this moment had maintained an admirable self-possession, now gave vent to her stifled feelings, and sobbed convulsively. The ex-King kissed her unceasingly for some moments, and then, turning to her august husband, embraced and greeted him affectionately. The Queen recovering herself in a few moments, stepped out of the carriage after the King, and successively embraced, with intense feeling, her royal children. The whole party were for some time much agitated, and apparently altogether unconscious of the presence of strangers. The first burst of emotion over, the royal fugitives were conducted into the waiting-room, where they remained for some time in seclusion."

Claremont was reached by three o'clock. At five, Prince Albert arrived by a special train, to pay his respects. On Sunday, the Duke and Duchess of Montpensier arrived from East Sheen, where, under some mistake, they had been awaiting their parents.

The ex-King and Queen assumed the title of the Count and Countess of Neuilly after their arrival at Claremont. By whatever name she is called, all honour to Marie-Amélie! A less high-sounding appellation would better befit her ignoble husband.

" If," says a writer in the " Spectator," " Louis Philippe has a genius, or strong natural bent apart from the mere dictates of self-interest, we should say that it is for low comedy. His evasion has been marked throughout by a kind of dry humour. The French people put him out in his reckoning: his calculations, like most political mistakes, were based too much in a reliance on direct conventional motives: he thought that pay, discipline, and promotion, were alone to sway the army; views of peace and order, as sources of profit, the shopkeeping National Guard; prudence, and fear of degradation, the respectable political agitators: he did not take into account a love for the romantic, which he did not share— an enthusiasm for the theatrical, which he only used as an engine. He could not, in spite of experiences, imagine that men should risk social position, advancement, life, nay the shop itself, because they had some abstract ideas of political right, or because they could not resist the opportunity for performing a great drama. The people quite upset his calculations. But he had his revenge, by turning their heroic epic into a farce.

" The people would have set him aside in a cool and dignified manner, or have escorted him politely to the frontier. He preferred dodging the great nation in a chase without pursuers. The poet and minister Lamartine would have read him an exalted farewell lecture : but the poet was defeated in his high-tragedy vein by the ludicrous and gratuitous panic of the dispersion. France deposes her King, and proclaims the fact with majestic pomp : the successor to Charlemagne again inverts the national dignity by appearing on our shores in a Listonian costume. He comes for shelter, with his cajoling tongue in his cheek : he returns to us, even on deposition, 'with pleasure ;' he contrives to know all sorts of obscure gentlemen by name ; he shakes hands all round ; and addresses a knot of anonymous obtrusive sight-seers as 'the British nation.' There is not a puffing advertiser, nor a parliamentary candidate, not even a playhouse manager, that better understands the art of humbug. No one better knows that an Englishman's most esteemed delights are—to be known correctly by name, to shake hands with a king, and to be considered as 'the British nation.' Louis Philippe claims an old friendship with those respectable politicians the three tailors of Tooley Street. But he has flattered in still more touching manner that large section of the British people, the *gens* Smith : he took out his passport of escape and came over as 'William Smith.' He has fallen on his true social designation—he is properly one of the Smiths. His adventures, his crown, his French birth, his royal extraction, are but accidents : his nature is *bourgeois*, and eminently English : he is a respectable, 'warm,' bulky, alert old gentleman—a fundholder, a shareholder—prosaically, materially, and sceptically commonsensible—comfortably contemptuous of dandified appearances. ·He should stick to his new name, and for evermore be 'Mr. Smith.'"

CHAPTER V.

THE CLAREMONT VERSION OF THE FEBRUARY REVOLUTION.

The lesson taught by the great example of February, 1848, will gradually become clear to the minds of all men; but it has many stubborn prejudices to overcome before it can obtain full and free acceptation. A stout effort has been made by a portion of the English press to prove that the fall of Louis Philippe argues nothing more than the personal weakness of that unlucky monarch,—that, in fact, the revolution of February was only an accident, instead of being, as we suppose it, a normal result of an everlasting principle. The "Times" of March 6, had an article, from which the following is an extract :—

"When the late Government undertook to check and prohibit the Reform demonstration, it doubtless never crossed the mind of any Minister that it was possible to fail in th attempt; and though the danger became infinitely greater than had been anticipated, *we still think it probable, that if the Government had retained the full exercise of its powers it would not have failed. But the King thought fit to play another game.* Not dreaming that a few hours would suffice to turn the fury of the people of Paris against his own person and family, *he held in reserve the sacrifice of an unpopular Minister as a convenient concession, which might be made at a pinch to quell a popular tumult.* But he made this concession at the time and in the manner in which it was certain to prove indifferent to the people, and fatal to the maintenance of

authority.   On the afternoon of Wednesday, February 23,
Paris was greatly agitated, but no severe fighting had taken
place; a few barricades had been raised, and retaken by the
troops; *the plans of the Government were complete;* Marshal
Bugeaud had been named to the command of the forces in
Paris; *and M. Guizot informed the King that he was confident
that the Executive Government could put down the insurrection.
The Royal answer was—a dismissal.*   The King dismissed
M. Guizot, and dissolved the Cabinet, at that momentous
instant when all the energies of united power were required to
fight in the streets a battle which it had itself deliberately
provoked.   *Still, however, the mischief might yet have been
repaired if vigorous measures had been taken.*   But from that
hour nothing but the most extraordinary *blunders and pusil-
lanimity marked the conduct of the court."*

It is a doctrine as dangerous as it is false, that if kings
and ministers succumb to the combined enmity of both the
lower and the middle classes, it is only for want of sufficient
obstinacy in resisting.   No physical strength can, in civilised
lands, sustain a throne in opposition to the moral force of a
nation arrayed against it.   " Charles X.," says the " Examiner," " with 12,000 bayonets, sank before the Paris populace.   The discovery was soon complacently made, that
the failure was owing to his want of force.   Louis Philippe
has made a similar attempt with 100,000, with the same
result; and ' more powder more kill' is still the argument,
and his overthrow is ascribed to his want of resolution, not to
the resolution that was opposed to him.   If Louis Philippe
had not firmness enough for his evil enterprise, we suspect
the conclusion to be drawn is that no monarch can be found
possessed of the boldness necessary to putting down a
thoroughly malecontent and highly-spirited people.   But there
are some persons disposed to believe that the thing was
feasible; for there are minds that always read the lessons of
experience backwards, and that still fondly cling to the belief
that armed might could have prevailed.   Their faith in the

bullet and the bayonet is inexhaustible.   They would demon-
strate to you how Pharaoh would have succeeded in his pursuit by carrying a higher hand.   But somehow or other,
happily for the world, the saying of Euripides is everlastingly
applicable, that when Heaven dooms a man τον νουν εβλαψε
πρωτον.   And the talk of what might have been done if a
certain wanting quality had been present, is but tantamount
to calculating what the man might have done if the man had
not been the man he was ; in which case he would never have
made the attempt.   If Louis Philippe had had the high
courage necessary for his evil enterprise, the probability is
that he would not have had the heart for it; for the generous
qualities are in close affinity, and magnanimity is of near re·
lation to bravery and constancy.   The intense selfishness that
prompted Louis Philippe's faults was incompatible with resolution in the hour of danger.   As for seventeen years he had
thought of nothing but making himself great, so in the crisis
of his fate he thought of nothing but making himself safe.
Self was the uppermost, or rather the only, consideration.
He had never had any higher vocation than Self and Sons, a
sort of Dombey firm ; and with the first demand for a particle
of devotion, for an atom of chivalry as big as the pin's head
that serves him for a heart, the man was off, taking care of
Self, and shrouding the precious thing in a dirty blouse.   But
to complete and perfect the disguise, he assumed over all a
' fear-nought coat'—a *fear-nought!* disguise indeed!"

    When "The Times" and the "Chronicle" argued that
more boldness would have saved the King of the French and
his Minister, that theory had not yet been shaken by the
events in Vienna and Berlin.   There, at least, the troops
shewed no want of vigour or alacrity; nor were their efforts
enfeebled by the least aversion, on the part of the Governments, to put down insurrection at any cost of blood.   Nevertheless the insurgents were triumphant in both capitals, and
it was only by making unrestricted concessions that the respective sovereigns were fortunate enough to save their crowns,

which they had brought into extreme danger by their mis-
timed obstinacy.   But, even before the popular victories in
Vienna and Berlin, Europe afforded one striking example to
shew that a stubborn reliance on physical force is not the
safest policy for the defenders of thrones.   As the "Daily
News" well remarks :—

"There is, perhaps, no stronger contrast, no more complete opposition to the policy of Louis Philippe, than is presented by King Leopold of Belgium.   Whilst Louis Philippe sought to nail his throne to the ground, and himself to
the throne, King Leopold has sat as loosely as a sailor ba-
lancing on the deck of a tossing vessel.   Whenever there
came a change of parties, Leopold has bent in the right direction.   No matter what the sentiment prevailing, Catholic or
popular, Leopold lent it his royal ear.   During the late effer-
vescence of Republicanism, King Leopold is said to have addressed some of his Liberal servants with the observation that
he had no very deep or obstinate desire to remain their king
—that he had done his best for them, but that if he was in
the way, he would most willingly withdraw.   Every one was,
in consequence, most desirous to retain a monarch who obstructed no Liberal interest or progress, and who, in resigning,
would have left the state a prey to anarchy, commerce a victim
to bankruptcy and ruin, and contending parties no protection
against each other.   The middle and commercial class of
Belgium—all, in fact, that is influential in Belgium—prefer
King Leopold to any Republic.   So would this same class in
France have preferred Louis Philippe to any Republic, if he
would but have let them.

"But Louis Philippe's whole soul and activity were
directed to Madrid and to Vienna, and his anxiety was about
kings and tetrarchs; when, had he been wise, he would have
been reviewing and contenting his National Guards.   He gave
banquets to diplomacy, stars to foreign ministers, titles to his
courtiers, and bâtons to his generals.   He had far better have
turned his attention to the shopkeepers of the Rue St. Denis, .

and the manufacturing population of the Faubourg St. Marceaux.   His Majesty so obscured his horizon with crowds of courtiers in red ribands, that he forgot the mob and the paving-stones, on the very heaps of which he had mounted the throne, and which were as readily thrown up to scale it again.

" No, let it not be said that Louis Philippe perished from want of courage—he perished from want of common sense and common prudence; qualities which as a man he eminently possessed, but from which, as a king, he allowed himself to be secluded, till he lost their warning and their clue."

A condensed narrative of the Revolution of February has been put forth in a manner and under circumstances that im part to it something of the character of a state paper.   The " Standard," in which it first appeared, professes to have re ceived it from Paris ; but there is little doubt that it comes not from Paris, but from Claremont.   We copy the document :—

" Wearied by the prosperity which for nearly eighteen years France had enjoyed under the Constitutional Monarchy, the Republican party meditated a great trial of strength.   The Banquet of the 12th arrondissement of Paris was accordingly proposed by the Opposition as apparently a favourable occasion.   Already, through the agency of the press, of which it was absolute master, the party had wrought upon the population of Paris, had corrupted a portion of the National Guard, destroyed the popularity of the Chamber of Deputies, and alienated the affections of the people from Louis Philippe in his own capital.   It raised the standard of revolt, published its manifesto, challenged the Government to combat, named the day of battle, summoned the National Guards and the schools, and assigned to each their places in the warlike array.   The chiefs of the secret societies were not openly named, but a WORD OF ORDER was privately circulated ; and they were, at the proper time, to take their places at the head of their several sections.   The Conservative opposition (*Gauche dynastique*) shrunk from this audacious proclamation ; it did not desire the overthrow of the monarchy ; but, fancying itself in a condition to arrest the popular movement at its will, it was not displeased that a lesson should be given to power.   In its imprudence it flattered itself with the notion that it was in a position to command, when it could do nothing but obey.

" The sedition was not in the least discouraged by this defection.   It prosecuted ts movement on the morning of Tuesday, February 22, at first in appearance inoffensively. It proceeded by attempts to win over the troops of the line, and to seduce them by cries of ' Long live the Line!' All the regiments, however, preserved the attitude of respect to their duty. A like appeal was made to the National Guard, that armed representative of the city whose presence had always hitherto been so strong an encouragement to the army. This was, however, no longer the same National Guard which had contributed to establish the throne of 1830—no longer that National Guard which had so loyally defended the throne in 1832. Misled by perfidious counsels (we except, however, from this reproach the 1st Legion, which repaired to its post of duty), the guard forgot that its commission was to protect the capital from disorder and anarchy ; it forgot that the law forbade it every manifestation of political opinion while under arms ; and, finally, that the Charter had confided all the institutions of the state to its patriotism.

" On the morning of the 22d of February, the detachment of the 7th Legion on guard at the Chamber of Deputies had refused to clear the colonnade, lobby, and the avenues, crowded by the seditious. On the following day a company of the 4th Legion appeared in arms before the Chamber, upon the pretext of offering a petition in favour of reform ; detachments of the 2d, 3d, and 7th Legions raised shouts of ' Reform for ever!' ' Down with the Ministers!' everywhere, in a word, the uniform of the National Guard, in ordinary times the symbol of public order, might be seen between the troops and the insurgents protecting the seditious.

" On the 23d the King decided upon changing the ministry. He summoned Count Molé, who did not think it consistent with his duty to accept the charge of forming a government. In the course of the night the supreme command of the National Guards and of the troops of the line was confided to Marshal Bugeaud, and the King charged M. Thiers with the duty of forming a new Cabinet. M. Thiers accepted the trust, with authority to associate with him M. Odillon Barrot.

" On the morning of Thursday, the 24th of February, the new Ministers, accompanied by a great number of their friends, proceeded to the Tuileries. Doubtless they acted with good faith, but, dupes of a fancied popularity— as they had always been—and of a supposed ascendant influence over the masses, they imagined that, in order to calm every thing, it must be sufficient for them to shew themselves, and to cause a general cessation of firing—flattering themselves with the opinion that the National Guard would be adequate to the restoration of tranquillity. It was through the effect of this unhappy illusion that they issued the order *not to fire*, and that the defence of the throne and of the person of the King was paralysed. To the Almighty alone it belongs to say to the waves, ' So far shalt thou go, and no farther.' Vainly did M. Odillon Barrot endeavour to appease the billows—his voice was lost in the tempest. Hardly had the insurgents

heard of the order (not to fire) that had been given, before they learned
that they had no longer anything to fear from the armed force opposed to
them; besides that, they had found a stanch support in a part of the National Guard. They redoubled their confidence and audacity, and directed
their course to the Palace of the Tuileries, resolved to attempt another 10th
of August. Already were their hoarse clamours heard in the streets neighbouring to the Carrousel and the Palais Royal, when, at nearly eleven
o'clock, the King on horseback, followed by his sons, the Dukes de Nemours and Montpensier, traversed the ranks of the National Guard and
the troops of the line, stationed in the court of the Tuileries and the Place
du Carrousel. The troops of the line received Louis Philippe with enthusiasm, the National Guard mingled savage cries of ' Reform for ever!' with
the acclamations ' Long live the King.'

" Returned to his apartments, the King found them invaded by an immense crowd, and then commenced the scene of the abdication.

" The troops of the line, paralysed by the order not on any account to
fire, presented but a weak rampart against the insurgents—they fell back
within the court of the Tuileries. The National Guard had wholly disappeared, the insurgent crowd continued to advance; already were heard the
discharges of their fire-arms. The Ministers, in a state of consternation,
lost all hope. Amid the terrible confusion which reigned round Louis
Philippe, some exclaimed, ' Will you permit your whole family to be
butchered?' Others, ' The Regency of the Duchess of Orleans will save
all!' The King signed his abdication, and withdrew from the Palace of
the Tuileries to retire to St. Cloud.

" Meanwhile the Duke de Nemours, doubtless with the design of protecting the King's retreat, was still on horseback in the court of the Tuileries, with two regiments of infantry. The position could, however, be
defended no longer. The Duke gave directions to abstain from firing, in
order to spare useless bloodshed. He also, though in vain, sought to repel
the seditious rabble by a weak detachment of National Guards that had
just re-entered the court. While these events were taking place, he learned
that the Duchess of Orleans, with her two sons, had quitted the Tuileries
by the garden. It was in good time: an instant later and she must have
been unable to save herself or her infant children, for armed bands were
already making their way into the gardens through the railing of the Rue
Rivoli. The Prince ran to join her. On his arrival at the Place de la
Concorde he gave orders for the troops to be drawn up along the Champs
Elysées, with a view to conducting the Duchess of Orleans safely to the
Palace of St. Cloud. In the meantime he posted guards at all the exits of
the Place, and at the Pont Tournant. While the Prince was superintend-
ing the execution of these different measures of precaution, the Duchess of
Orleans was with her children conducted into the Chamber of Deputies, in

K

the midst of a group, in which were many members of the Chamber, and officers in attendance upon the Count of Paris.

" The Duke de Nemours, apprised of this, rejoined the Duchess with a resolution which involved more than one description of courage ; for he went to see broken before his eyes the law that had named him as the future Regent, and exposed his head to an imminent peril.

" The Chamber received the Duchess with acclamations, which were redoubled after the speech of M. Dupin. On the benches of the Deputies and in the tribune, ' Long live the Regent!' ' Long live the Count of Paris!' were loudly shouted. The sitting, however, was prolonged. The Radical opposition drowned the voice of M. Odillon Barrot, who spoke in support of the Regency. Finally, several orators insisted upon an appeal to the people. At this moment the headstrong rabble, armed with sabres, pikes, and fire-arms, preceded by persons in the uniform of the National Guard who bore a tricolour flag, threw itself into the hall. A young madman in a blouse, from the height of the tribune, levelled a gun with direct aim at the President. Another stared with ferocious earnestness upon the group in which were the members of the Royal Family. The national represent- ation was contemptuously disregarded, profaned, outraged, and dissolved ; the Regency was trampled under foot ; the Republic proclaimed ; and the Duchess of Orleans and her two sons, with the Duke de Nemours, had to make their escape through a frightful tumult and the greatest dangers.

" Thus the insurrection was at the same time mistress of the Palace of the Tuileries and of the Chamber of Deputies. The National Guard, whose duty it was to repress the sedition, had become its auxiliary. The army, reduced to inactivity, had lost its moral force ; what remained then to do ? Could Louis Philippe have had the will, or could he have had the power, to command the troops of the line to fire upon the National Guard ? What would have been the morrow of such a day ? "

Turn the matter as you will, this question always recurs— How happened it that the National Guard, which in 1832 fought bravely for Louis Philippe, was not to be depended on in 1848 ? To say that it was " misled by perfidious counsels " is no answer to the question. The true one will be found in the causes of disaffection which we have enumerated in our introductory chapter. Louis Philippe had brought things to such a pass, that neither resistance nor concession could avail him. Even had he gained a temporary victory over the Pa- risians, his fall would have been no less certain, and immensely more terrible.

CHAPTER VI.

RESTORATION OF ORDER.

THE day after the battle, though it passed off without any infraction of the peace, was one of strange tumultuous excitement. The streets were crowded during the whole of Friday with promenaders of both sexes, and wore the appearance of a festival. The people had not yet dismissed from their minds all apprehension of an attempt to rally on the part of those who favoured the claims of the Duchess of Orleans and her son, and they maintained a jealous attitude towards the soldiers of the line, who were still in arms. On the other hand, they displayed the most frank and generous forgiveness towards their vanquished foes. Disarmed Municipal Guards and soldiers of the regiment that had fired on the people were seen walking about the streets, and no one insulted or molested them. "At this moment," says an eye-witness, "there are certainly no symptoms of rancour, and although I have walked through a great part of the city, nowhere did I hear a cry against the late Ministers. I saw a plaster cast of Louis Philippe's bust ground to powder on the Boulevards, and workmen effacing the word 'royal' wherever it appeared, as well as the royal cypher and arms over the doors of the tradesmen to the royal family. On one sign-board, where it appeared that the proprietor was not only *breveté* by the royal family, but a provider for the *Empereur* of Russia, the Reformer conceived he had practised a joke by erasing the three first letters only, and leaving it *ereur de Russie* (Russia's error). The more practical jokes consisted of random *feux de joie* indulged in by boys ; but there are no horses to frighten, for the reason that the thoroughfares are all obstructed by barricades."

Another writer has given a description of a barricade and the mode of making it.   " Suppose the commissioners of pavements, in one of their perpetual diggings up, piled the stones of Fleet Street across the way instead of along it, inserting a shop-front or two on the top, with a few lengths of iron railing and half a dozen trees from the Temple Gardens as a finish, hat would be a barricade like scores which have been raised in Paris in the last movement. They are rude enough to the eye. but most formidable in their effect : troops can do little against them ; cavalry are quite useless ; as they are placed at all the intersections of the streets, whichever way a battalion turned it would find itself in a *cul de sac.*   And they are formed with a rapidity truly marvellous. I have examined a hundred of them with much more interest than I should feel in the Pyramids."

Among the scenes of the late conflict, none attracted more painful curiosity than the space before the hôtel of the Minister for Foreign Affairs, where the fatal volley had been fired on the night of the 23d.   Pools of blood fifty paces long stagnated horribly on the asphalte pavement.   The spot now exhibited a touching and characteristic trait of popular feeling. The railing which separates the low street called the Rue Basse du Rempart from the *trottoir* of the Boulevard was torn down in a fit of rage, at the sight of the blood of the victims ; but, by a curious reaction of tenderness, the torn railing was employed to keep people's feet from desecrating the blood, and the motive was explained by notices in chalk drawn along the *trottoir.*   On the wall of the hôtel was traced in large red letters the inscription, *A mort Guizot!*

The Boulevards, says one of our authorities, present a terrible proof of that recklessness of destruction common to all kinds of battle.   " The trees which were the ornament of these splendid streets, under which the Parisian was wont in the summer to sip his coffee while selecting his theatre for the evening, are all cut down; the stumps stood for some days exhibiting a horrid amputated look, as of ruthless surgery. They were all severed about three feet from the ground, and formed a line of posts neither useful nor ornamental. These trees will be sorely missed next July; but the next best thing to leaving them as they were is getting rid of them altogether, and this has been the occupation of a large body of labourers."

All the detached forts round Paris surrendered this day without resistance. A large body of the National Guards, and of the crowd, had marched against the fort of Vincennes, but their presence there was unnecessary. In fact, the soldiers of the line had tacitly joined the revolt. Such scenes as this occurred:—A body of the people proceeded, with obviously hostile views, to the barrack in the Rue Pépinière, in which were the 52d Regiment of the Line. They found in front of it a battalion of the 1st Legion of National Guards; one among whom asked, "What do you seek?" "The arms of the 52d." "Why?" "Because we wish to apply them to the defence of the country." "But are they not in the hands of the 52d, who have faternised with the people, and who are ready, willing, and capable of fighting for France?" This produced a pause. The National Guard then proposed that a leader of the people should accompany him to the Colonel of the 52d; which being agreed to, an interview took place, which ended in the Colonel's presenting himself at the balcony and thus addressing the people:—" Citizens! You ask for the arms of the 52d, in order that they may be given to patriots. The 52d are patriots to a man. The 52d was among the first of the regiments which in 1830 joined the people. The 52d was the first which in 1848 fraternised with the people. The 52d is no more. That which was the 52d of the Line is now the 1st Regiment of the Republic." The enthusiasm which this brief address produced on the people is indescribable. The arms were left with the regiment; and those who came five minutes previously to fight and slaughter retired delighted, and in the best possible disposition.

A sad accident happened this day. The toll-house of the Pont Louis Philippe having been set on fire about one o'clock, the flames caught the joints where the chains of the bridge are connected with the wood-work ; they gave way, and the platform was precipitated into the Seine. The shock was tremendous, and several passengers who were crossing the bridge at the fatal moment were submerged and perished.

By Friday evening order was to a great extent restored : one proof was the reopening of the Bank of France. This happy result was chiefly due to the admirable conduct of the National Guard, and to the intrepidity, energy, and good sense of the Provisional Government. To M. Lamartine especially belongs the immortal renown of having that day saved his country from anarchy the most fearful and bloody.

Among the earliest resolutions adopted by the Provisional Government were the abolition of capital punishment for political offences, and the readoption of the tricolour, which had for a while been supplanted by the ill-omened red flag. Both these measures were proposed by Lamartine, and owed their success to his extraordinary eloquence and courage. Five times on Friday he addressed the people, still fierce with excitement, assembled under the windows of the Hôtel de Ville. The "Presse" has reported one of these addresses :—

" It is thus that you are led from calumny to calumny against the men who have devoted themselves, head, heart, and breast, to give you a real Republic—the Republic of all rights, all interests, and all the legitimate rights of the people. Yesterday you asked us to usurp, in the name of the people of Paris, the rights of 35,000,000 of men—to vote them an absolute Republic, instead of a Republic invested with the strength of their consent ; that is to say, to make of that Republic, imposed and not consented, the will of a part of the people, instead of the will of the whole nation. To-day you demand from us the red flag instead of the tricolour one.

GUIZOT.

LAMARTINE.

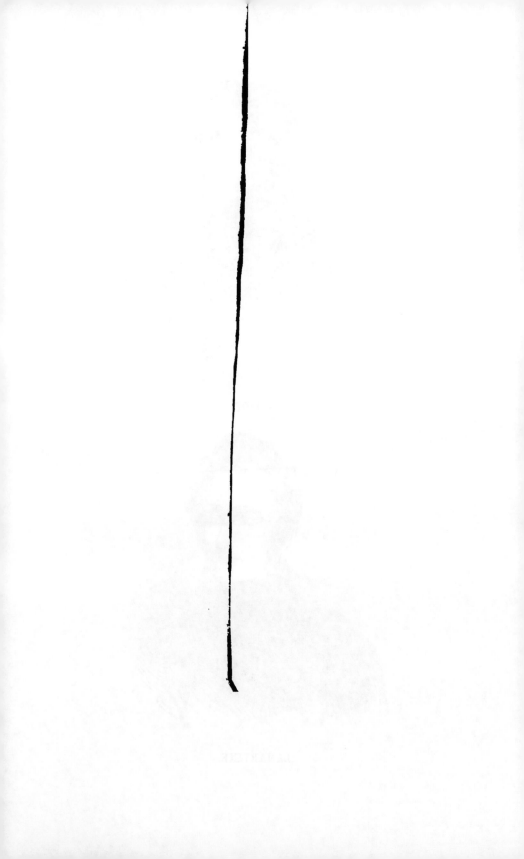

Citizens! for my part, I will never adopt the red flag; and I will explain in a word why I will oppose it with all the strength of my patriotism. It is, citizens, because the tricolour flag has made the tour of the world, under the Republic and the Empire, with our liberties and our glories, and that the red flag has only made the tour of the Champ de Mars, trailed through torrents of the blood of the people.

The effect of this oratory was all powerful. At this part of the speech of M. de Lamartine, in that astonishing sitting of sixty hours, in the midst of an irritated crowd, every one was suddenly affected by his words: hands were clapped and tears shed, and they finished by embracing him, shaking his hands, and bearing him in triumph. In a moment after, fresh masses of people arrived, armed with sabres and bayonets. They knocked at the doors; they filled the *salles.* The cry was, that all was lost; that the people were about to fire on or stifle the Members of the Provisional Government. M. de Lamartine was called for. He was supplicated to go once more, for the last time, to address the people. He was raised on a step of the staircase; the crowd remained for half-an-hour without consenting to listen to him, vociferating, brandishing arms of all kinds over his head. M. de Lamartine folded his arms, recommenced his address, and finished by softening, appeasing, and caressing the intelligent and sensible people, and determining them either to withdraw, or to become themselves the safeguard of the Provisional Government.

On Saturday, the restoration of order was completed. The public departments resumed their duties, and among them the department of Finance. It was only on the previous Monday that the notice to pay the city taxes had been issued. The whole of the coming year's taxes derived from per-centage on rents of apartments and shopkeepers' licenses would thus fall into the hands of the new Government—an enormous fund with which to begin. The million a month to the Civil List had already been confiscated, or, as the ordonnance has it, "restored to the people"—a handsome addition to the fund

applicable to the relief of distress. The streets were partially
cleared of the obstructions caused by the barricades, under
the scientific direction of the students of the Ecole Polytech-
nique, in such a way as not to compromise the security against
a surprise afforded by these popular fortifications.   This
enabled the country people to bring in provisions, of which
there was an abundant supply ; and it allowed the vast
number of coachmen and cabmen to resume their occupation.
The law courts resumed their sittings ; the shops were opened ;
every thing was done to calm apprehension.

On this day, the indefatigable Lamartine declared the
Republic : he presented himself, with the other members of
the Government, on the steps of the Hôtel de Ville, and thus
addressed the multitude : —

" Citizens ! The Provisional Government of the Republic
has called upon the people to witness its gratitude for the
magnificent national co-operation which has just accepted
these new institutions.   (Prolonged acclamations from the
crowd and National Guard.)

" The Provisional Government of the Republic has only
joyful intelligence to announce to the people here assembled.
Royalty is abolished.   The Republic is proclaimed.   The
people will exercise their political rights.   National workshops are open for those who are without work.   (Immense
acclamations.)

" The army is being reorganised. The National Guard
indissolubly unites itself with the people, so as to promptly
restore order with the same hand that had only the preceding
moment conquered our liberty.   (Renewed acclamations.)

" Finally, gentlemen, the Provisional Government was
anxious to be itself the bearer to you of the last decree it has
resolved on and signed in this memorable sitting—that is,
the abolition of the penalty of death for political matters.
(Unanimous bravos.)   This is the noblest decree, gentlemen,
that has ever issued from the mouths of a people the day after
their victory.   (Yes, yes !)   It is the character of the French

nation which escapes in one spontaneous cry from the soul of its Government. (Yes, yes! Bravo!) We have brought it with us, and I will now read it to you. There is not a more becoming homage to a people than the spectacle of its own magnanimity."

Here the orator read the following noble proclamation :—

"The Provisional Government, convinced that greatness of soul is the highest degree of policy, and that each revolution effected by the French people owes to the world the consecration of an additional philosophical truth; considering that there is no more sublime principle than the inviolability of human life; considering that in the memorable days in which we live the Provisional Government has remarked with pride that not a single cry for vengeance or for death has dropped from the mouths of the people; declares—That in its opinion the punishment of death for political offences is abolished, and that it will present that wish to the definitive ratification of the National Assembly. The Provisional Government has so firm a conviction of the truth that it proclaims, in the name of the French people, that if the guilty men who have just caused the blood of France to be spilt, were in the hands of the people, it would, in their opinion, be a more exemplary chastisement to degrade them than to put them to death."

The Provisional Government were duly rewarded for this great act of clemency, by the confidence which it immediately inspired in the justness and moderation of their views. It was indeed " the noblest act that ever issued from the mouths of a people the day after their victory;" and it did undoubtedly express the genuine, spontaneous sentiments of the victorious Parisians, and of Frenchmen generally. It is well known that M. Guizot remained in a friend's house in Paris for six days after the 24th of February, and that the Provisional Government were fully aware of his place of concealment, and that it was not till he was safe across the frontiers that they took formal steps for prosecuting him and his colleagues. Now the populace, who so often intruded into the Hôtel de Ville with clamorous importunities of all sorts, never once thought of urging the Government to vindictive measures against the fallen Ministers. On the night of the 24th, when the people were still flushed with the victory they had gained,

an individual posted up at the corner of the Rue Richelieu a
written paper, containing the name and address of the persons
with whom MM. Guizot, Duchatel, and Hébert, had taken re-
fuge. That indication was followed by an appeal to vengeance.
Already the crowd was gathering round the spot full of emotion, when a patrol of workmen advanced, with a corporal of
the National Guard at its head. The latter approached, read
the placard, and cried out, " My friends, they who make such
dastardly denunciations have not fought in our ranks!" and he
tore down the paper amidst the applause of all.

We are inclined to think with a writer in the " Westminster Review," that the abolition of the punishment of death for
political offences probably contributed, more than any other act
of the Provisional Government, to make the entire nation to
accept the new men, as the indispensable necessity of the
time, with an unanimity to which there is hardly a parallel in
history. On the part of the army, Marshal Bugeaud; on the
part of the clergy, the Archbishop of Paris; gave in their adhesion to the new Republic. On the part of the middle
classes, whether in Paris or in the provinces, and of the whole
press, without a solitary exception, there does not appear to
have been the hesitation of a moment. All seem to have felt
by instinct, that whether or not the people were prepared for
Republican institutions, the time was come when a trial of
them must be made ; for after the fall of a Government which
but a few days before had enjoyed the reputation of being one
of the strongest in Europe, and then suddenly vanished like a
mist, there could be no further hope of security for person or
property under the protection of royalty. This feeling was
put to the test by a feeble attempt on the part of the few remaining friends of the elder branch of the Bourbons, which
ended in the following ridiculous failure :—

" Ten young men attempted on Saturday evening," says the
" Courier Français," " to get up a Legitimatist manifestation
in the Faubourg St. Germain. The people, seeing them all
dressed in black, with white cockades in their hats, cried out,

'*Tiens! Tiens!* A funeral! They are undertakers' men!' The young men, finding the people in such good humour, immediately set to work. 'Friends,' exclaimed they, 'remember Henry IV. and proclaim his descendant. Long live Henry V.!' The people, in the same good humour, immediately cried out, 'Ah, how is he, the dear prince? He ain't dead? Glad to hear it! Make our compliments to him, if you please, gentlemen. How happy he will be! Henry IV. is dead! *Vive la République!*' Thus did the people turn Legitimacy to the right-about. If we relate this fact, it is merely to add that, in despair for the cause, they immediately went to inscribe themselves at their respective mayoralties, as nearly all the young men of the Faubourg St. Germain had already done. Thus Legitimacy has turned into Republicanism—the wisest thing it could do. 'Henry IV. is dead! Long live the Republic!'"

Sunday was a high festival. The barricades had all been removed; the streets were thronged, the city was as tranquil as on that day week; and nothing was wanting but better weather. The rain poured in torrents in the morning, and the wind blew a hurricane, but it cleared up in the afternoon. At two o'clock the Provisional Government reviewed the vast body of National Guards, horse and foot, before the Column of July. We quote an eye-witness:—

"It was the celebrated astronomer Arago who, from the steps of the Column of July, proclaimed the Republic, amidst the wildest enthusiasm. Arago is not an orator, but he possesses a fine person, luminous eye, and manly manner, with a voice to proclaim the Republic to the stars. The aged Dupont de l'Eure next thanked the populace for their respect for order and grand moral support of the Revolution. 'Listen,' shouted Arago: 'it is eighty years of a pure life that speaks to you,'— a far better expression than the forty ages from the Pyramids contemplating the French army; although that piece of Ossianic mysticism suited its purpose as well as did our astronomer's more touching appeal to the feelings awakened

by old age and a pure life.   Crémieux's loud but hard voice
was heard next addressing a somewhat commonplace apo-
strophe to the spirits of the victims of July, who had at length
received satisfaction; and then the procession attempted an
almost impossible performance—that of defiling round the
column through a compact mass of people, unable, if ever so
willing, to move one way or the other.

"For hours after, General Courtais devoted himself to
the preservation of order : with his white head uncovered,
and mild countenance, he harangued every group he met
along the Boulevards to the Foreign Office, recommending
order and tranquillity; and so well did he succeed that the
populace forbore to exact illuminations."

Notwithstanding this forbearance, the capital was illuminated in finer style than on the two preceding evenings.
Venetian lamps were abundantly used, and so disposed as to
make the tricolour transparent.   The Boulevards were excessively gay.   People at all the windows, and under the lamps,
were devouring the journals, which, however, did not contain
any news that had not been already known.   To attract cus-
tomers, the "death of Louis Philippe" was cried, and it was a
sad cry amidst so much gaiety. Hawkers were calling on every
body to purchase little tricoloured cockades, the national colour, the colour *qui a fait le tour du monde*, to distinguish it
from the red, which the Communists had adopted.   There
were not many of that hue to seen.

We have already dwelt upon the fact so honourable to the
population of Paris, that never was the capital freer from out-
rages against private persons and property than during the
wild turmoil of the Revolution, and up to the moment we
write this, when France has given to the world the impressive
spectacle of a nation self-governed, during five weeks, without
any military coercion and by the sole moral authority of the people.   It must not, however, be supposed that crimes were not
occasionally committed.   There are desperate malefactors in
Paris, and these men thought they saw in the confusion of the

revolutionary week safe opportunities for rapine; but their crimes were punished and suppressed by the terrible, but necessary, visitations of Lynch law. This happened several times on the 24th, 25th, and 26th.

Three men were shot in the Champs Elysées on Friday. Next day, in the Rue Richelieu, two young thieves were shot: their bodies were left for view on the spot, with a paper attached, marked in large letters with the word "*Voleur.*" A man who attempted (and with partial success) to set fire to the Palais Royal was shot near the Préfecture. Another who endeavoured to set fire to the buildings in the Parc Monceau, and a third who committed a barbarous assassination and robbery, met with a similar fate. A band of eight robbers was brought out for execution in the same unceremonious manner to the Place de la Madeleine; but the largeness of the number made the amateur executioners hesitate. Presently, however, the robbers were carried to the *mairie* of the first arrondissement, which is hard by. The Mayor, being satisfied that justice was about to be done, gave his sanction to the execution, and it was forthwith effected in the court.

On Saturday afternoon, the barricades having been opened in the principal streets, and communications made more easy, the plan of carrying culprits to the Préfecture of Police became more common; but the executions were almost equally summary.

Beyond the walls of the capital there was much wanton destruction of property. The ex-King's beautiful château at Neuilly was burnt down on Saturday; but most of its valuable contents were carefully removed, and sent to the public treasury, before the work of conflagration began. Many of the marauders suffered a fearful retribution for their criminal excesses. A large body of them rushed into the cellars, where they found wine of all descriptions, and a cask of rum, which they broke open. Some instants after they were all drunk, and then a terrific battle took place between them, their principal weapons being bottles. At length they fell to the ground, overcome by intoxication or by wounds. Meanwhile the men who got into the apartments ravaged and pillaged them completely, after which they set them on fire, and the whole building was soon in flames. A short time after the men in the cellars were burned to death or suffocated. On Sunday, from a hundred to a hundred and twenty dead bodies were dug out.

Among the most interesting items saved from the destruction of Neuilly are two volumes of the manuscript memoirs of the ex-King of the French. They terminate at the period when the Commissioners of the Consulate proclaimed the Republic in presence of the armies of the enemy. Other private papers of the ex-King have also fallen into the hands of the new Government; among them is mentioned an autograph list headed, *Hommes à moi*—" Men I am sure of."

The splendid mansion of Baron Rothschild, at Surennes, was burnt on Sunday, under the impression that it was the King's property. The Baron is deservedly very popular in France, and after the incendiaries discovered their mistake, a deputation from them, with drollery enough, waited on the unlucky proprietor to apologise for what they had done. The same day a large gang of incendiaries proceeded to Maisons Laffitte, near Paris, with the intention of burning the bridge. The National Guard immediately took arms ; but not being strong enough to oppose the banditti, they sent for assistance to St. Germain-en-Laye. A large detachment of National Guards of that town, accompanied by a squadron of dragoons, who each carried behind him an armed citizen, immediately proceeded to Maisons, where they arrived in time to prevent the destruction of the bridge. They then attacked the incendiaries, killed eight of them, and made a considerable number prisoners.

The worst destruction was that committed on the Northern Railway, the damage done to which amounted to not less than 400,000*l.* An English resident in Paris describes some traces of this sad. devastation. They began to be visible at

Beaumont. "Some detachments of three regiments of the Line were drawn up here, under the most terrific rain I ever saw—it poured down in sheets of water. The railway authorities, quite taken by surprise, could offer little or no resistance to the mob, which ravaged all the way down to this point. It was composed of the lowest ruffians of the city: and the havoc they have caused is deplored by the bulk of the people. At Isle Adam and at Anvers nothing is left of the stations but ashes and charred beams. At Pontoise the destruction appears still more extensive; a whole train of carriages that stood in front of the platform is there still, in the shape of skeletons; the iron-work of the wheels and bodies alone remaining. From this point to St. Denis, every house, hut, waggon, carriage, and shed on the line, has been burned or torn down. The stone bridges that cross the line within the city itself have had their parapets levelled; and immense masses of stone heaped together block up one line of railway completely. Fortunately, the magnificent station at Paris has escaped. The mob destroyed nothing that was not connected with the railway; the cottages and cabarets along the line have not been touched. A waggon of coke standing within sight of the Paris station was still burning when the train passed."

The damage was quickly repaired, sufficiently to render the line practicable to a certain extent; but the effect of the mischief was not confined to the heavy loss of capital we have mentioned; three-fourths of the traffic on the line were annihilated, as appears from the following returns. On the Paris and Rouen section the receipts for the week ending the 4th of March amounted only to 59,595f. 75c., and for the week ending the 11th March to 71,522f. 50c. On the Havre line, the receipts for the week ending the 4th of March amounted to 29,986f. 15c., and for the week ending the 11th March to 34,504f. 40c. The Orleans line was not damaged by the mob, and its receipts continued to be very large. For the week ending the 14th of March they amounted to 191,694f., the corresponding week of 1847 having produced 177,013f., and for the week ending the 21st March they amounted to 197,096f. 73c., while the amount for the corresponding week of 1847 was 195,635f. 47c.

The motives by which the rioters were prompted to the work of destruction were partly jealousy of the English workmen employed on the line, and partly that blind hatred of machinery which unfortunately prevails among the working classes in all countries. The latter motive led to the destruction of some printing presses in the capital, but that evil was soon effectually checked. Unfortunately, it was not in the power of the Government, or of the more enlightened portion of the public, to stop the proscription of foreign workmen. The English hands employed in the factories and on the railways were everywhere hunted out of the country; and no time was allowed them to obtain the arrears of wages due to them, or to dispose of their household effects. The barbarous fiat was as barbarously executed, and the destitute victims were ejected like malefactors from a land they were enriching by their toil and skill. These stupid persecutions were most incongruous incidents in the opening reign of Liberty, Equality, and Fraternity, but it is absurd to regard them as the natural result of Republicanism. The same ignorance of economical principles which produced these disgraceful scenes in France is repeatedly exemplified in monarchical England in the arbitrary proceedings of trade-unions, and in the fights between English and Irish labourers for exclusive possession of the field of employment. The genius of the French people is pre-eminently logical; unfortunately, the majority of them are at present possessed with the spurious theory of trade which here finds favour only with the most unreasoning portions of the community, certain dukes included; and in expelling foreign workmen, they but acted in strict accordance with the Tory doctrine of protection to native industry. It is to be hoped that the severe punishment which their fault carries with it will induce repentance, and that repentance will bring wisdom.

Whilst shoals of English workmen were drifting coast-wards before the storm of tyrannous rivalry, fear was chasing their wealthier countrymen from the capital. No fewer than five thousand passports were applied for at the British Embassy on the 22d and 23d of February, and such was the sudden demand for gold, that it rose to a premium of 15 per cent. Fortunate were those who were early in their flight: they lost, indeed, a sublime spectacle, which they had not nerve enough to look upon; but a quick run put the sea between them and the objects of their fears. But those who delayed until the railways were broken up were put to sore straits, and their terrors were aggravated by the extravagant rumours that sprang up on all sides in the provinces. An old and highly distinguished officer left Paris on the 24th of February, with his two daughters, but the train in which they travelled had only cleared four miles of the long route to the coast when it was brought to a dead stand. Neither carriage nor horses were to be had, and the young ladies were obliged to return to Paris on foot, whilst their father, who was crippled with the gout, was forced to accept the services of a stout peasant, who carried the old warrior pick-a-back all the way to his hôtel.

The close of the revolutionary week witnessed the return of order, as we have already stated; the gradual restoration of confidence—too soon, alas! to be again impaired—was the work of the succeeding week. The streets still presented a very bustling appearance, but one of a most satisfactory character, being chiefly occasioned by the active steps taken to repair the mischief done in the three days. The Provisional Government freely took all unemployed workmen into their pay, and as an additional means of securing the tranquillity of the capital, there was created a Garde Nationale Mobile of twenty-four battalions, to be clothed by the State, and paid at the rate of thirty sous daily per man. Twenty thousand of the most indigent and daring youth of Paris were quickly enrolled and marched off towards the frontiers. However objectionable these measures might be in the abstract, the strictest political

L

economist can hardly deny their expediency under the special circumstances.   Hunger is the most dangerous counsellor that ever infested a revolutionised city.   Another wise act of *largesse* on the part of the Government was the redemption, at the cost of the State, of all articles pledged subsequently to the 4th of February for sums not exceeding ten francs.   The number of articles thus released amounted to one hundred thousand, at an average cost of seven francs each.

.   Saturday, March 4th, was devoted to the obsequies of the victims who had fallen on the side of the people.   Their remains were wrapped in tricoloured winding-sheets, and laid on fifteen open biers, each containing five or six bodies.   Several corpses had been placed in the vaults beneath the Column of July on the preceding night, and those claimed by their families or friends had of course been given up for private interment.   The public funeral, therefore, afforded no opportunity for ascertaining the exact number of the slain, nor are we aware that this has been determined in any authentic manner.   At first it was supposed that between five and six hundred had been killed on both sides; a later estimate makes the number less than two hundred; whereas a correspondent of one of the London daily papers states, that he was assured by a sergeant of the 14th Regiment of the Line (a detachment of which fired the fatal volley at the Foreign Office) that the killed in that regiment alone were more than two hundred. The computation of the wounded is marked with the same uncertainty..   In the first week of March it was officially reported, that the number of wounded then lying in the hospitals was four hundred and twenty-eight, of whom seventy-eight belonged to the troops of the line or the Municipal Guard.   In the last week of March it was announced, again officially, that the total number of the wounded of February who had been received into the hospitals was seven hundred and three, of whom one hundred and fifty had died.   Taking all the circumstances into consideration, it seems not improbable that the authorities wisely forbore to publish the real amount of the carnage, at a moment when the popular passions might have been dangerously exasperated by such a disclosure.

But we must not omit to mention another cause of error, but of an opposite kind, affecting these statistics of mortality. Among the novelties produced by the Revolution was a new class of cunning speculators, called *parens de faux morts*. It appears that in the first burst of enthusiasm the different committees, appointed to register the names of the victims killed in the divers encounters with the military, had not time to examine and verify each individual case submitted to them, and so it came to pass that not a few of those who died a natural death during the three days were buried at the public expense, and their wives and children adopted by the country. Thus, amidst all the heroic unselfishness of the great week, poor commonplace human nature asserted its old prerogative. The picture would have been too ideal in its tone, but that a little farcical roguery gave it a touch of real flesh and blood.

The burial solemnity consisted of a procession from the Hôtel de Ville to the Madeleine; a performance of funeral rites at that church; a procession to the Place de la Bastile; and an interment of the dead in the vaults beneath the Column of July. The procession reached the Church of the Madeleine about noon. The church was hung with black drapery, tricoloured flags, and wreaths of *immortelles;* and inscribed over its entrance was,—*Aux Citoyens morts pour la Liberté*. A service was performed within. The route from the church to the Column of July, in the Place de la Bastile, was festooned continuously for the whole distance (nearly three miles) by tricoloured and black draperies. These were supported by posts, on which were hung shields of black cloth, inscribed with the words,—*Respect aux manes des victimes des* 22, 23, *et* 24 *Février*. Flags waved from the windows of every house on the route.

The people assembled to view the spectacle by myriads, and as portions of the mass waved to and fro, the movement

was like that of currents on the ocean. The day was beautiful,
and a brilliant sun shining on the sharp clear outlines of the
white Grecian church, on the lofty old-fashioned houses around
it, so picturesque in their complete contrast with it, and
glancing from the forest of bayonets bristling among hundreds
of tricoloured flags, above the surface of the motley and closely
packed crowd, of which no end was to be seen as far as the eye
could reach, formed a spectacle that no city save Paris could
furnish, and Paris only on such an occasion. There was something awful in that mass of human life : it was easy to imagine
how armies fail in collision with such myriads ; yet it was but
a fraction of the host the city poured forth from every street
into the main channel, in which flowed the business of the
day.

The procession from the church was led by National Guards;
then Masters of Ceremonies followed ; then the Orphéonistes—
pupils in classes on Wilhem's system, with the Société Musi-
cale. These frequently sang, with an effect even sublime.
Presently followed the clergy of the Madeleine, and the
funeral cars containing the dead. As these passed, the "Marseillaise" was sung ; one verse by the female voices alone,
and then the chorus by men. As the hymn arose the crowd
uncovered, and remained so till the cars, which were open so
as to shew the coffins under the palls, had passed. Other
bodies followed, and then came the liberated *victimes poli-
tiques*—among them, in carriages, the once Beau Barbès, now
bent and worn by eight years' incarceration, and Hubert, both
of them too weak for the fatigue of walking. More National
Guards succeeded, then the representatives of the various trades
and callings, the families of the victims, members of the municipalities, judges, freemasons, the pupils of the military schools,
and the university, &c. To these succeeded such of the wounded
as could bear the fatigue of the day ; they were all young men.
The cause for which they had fought was symbolised by the car
of Liberty, a colossal and gorgeously adorned vehicle, drawn by
eight cream-coloured horses. This harmless exhibition was

the only part of the pageant that bore any resemblance to the spuriously classical pomps of the first revolution. It is said that a bat never ceased to hover round the summit of the car during the whole procession, until it arrived at the Bastile, where the creature disappeared, leaving the superstitious in a most amusing state of wonder and alarm at so dire an omen.

The Provisional Government and the National Guard closed the long line of march, which reached the Column of July at five o'clock. In front of the column were erected two very lofty square altars, hung with black cloth set with silver stars, and with the " sacred fire" burning on their tops. The bodies of the dead were consigned to the vaults, and the vast concourse dispersed, without a single untoward occurrence throughout the day.

Here rightly terminates the French Iliad of 1848. The design of Jove was accomplished; Nemesis had done her work; and now began another *epopœia*, the business of which was the constitution of a new state on the ground laid bare by the total demolition of the old system. The Trojan epic ends with Hector's funeral rites; and if ever some Gallic Homer takes for his theme the fall of the King of the Barricades, he will close the solemn tale with the burial of the patriotic victims. But the humble chronicler is bound by other rules than those acknowledged by the poet; he must record events in their crude reality, and sometimes prolong his narrative beyond its fit ideal close, though he fall plump into inevitable bathos.

Not until after the second capture of the Tuileries, on the 7th of March, can the nation be said to have consummated its victory. The history of this burlesque affair is a follows. It seems to be the established rule in Paris, that in revolutionary times a man may be whatever he will; he has only to say, ' I appoint myself to this or that office,' and his pretensions will be acknowledged at least for a while. Some two hundred of the first occupants of the palace were pleased to constitute themselves custodians of the national property. The authorities, who would have spared them this trouble, occupied the guard-houses of the château with the National Guard, but the hint was lost on the volunteers, who always doubled each post by stationing on it a sentry of their own.   They found their quarters so much to their liking, that it is not surprising they took so much pains to guard them.   When they had exhausted the provisions in the château, they sent out every evening a detachment of foragers, who returned with bread, cheese, onions, and fruit.   The cellars supplied them with wine; and such as it was, the patriots condescended to get drunk upon it, though it gave them a very poor opinion of Louis Philippe's taste.   The charms of female society were not wanting to the Republican court; the *citoyens* were soon joined by their *citoyennes*, and there was no end of balls, concerts, and other impromptu entertainments.   The name of M. de Polignac, a son of the last Minister of Charles X., is mentioned among those of the musical amateurs who lent the aid of his talents on these occasions.   At last the noise of the revelry began to attract attention out of doors.   The Provisional Government requested the self-elected guardians to march out of the premises; but they stood upon their vested rights, and refused to resign except upon compensation.   Some of them asked 80,000 francs for the surrender of their holding; others demanded a pension of 800 francs each.   Meanwhile the people outside were growing angry; crowds of workmen assembled round the château, loudly expressing their disapproval of the conduct of the intruders.   The fellows, they said, who refused to give up the château never took it; that, in fact, it had not been taken at all, and therefore there was no honour in being found in it. At last the Préfect of Police, Caussidière, sent a final summons to the garrison to surrender.   Their answer was, that they had fifty rounds of ammunition per man, and would first set fire to the château, if attacked, and then fight their way out.   By this time several police agents had entered the palace in disguise, and recognised among its inmates a large proportion of notorious malefactors.

The authorities having made preparations to act with vigour, the intruders lost courage, and about fifty of them made their escape during the night of the 6th March, carrying with them a great deal of valuable plunder. The rest capitulated in the morning, and were marched off to the Hôtel de Ville, where they were disarmed and searched: all had dollars in abundance; some of them were found wearing three shirts and two pairs of pantaloons; and Louis Philippe landed in England without a change of either! A person in the crowd, recognising one of the fellows, asked him what they had proposed to themselves by remaining in the Tuileries,— "We intended," he replied, "to reign there for seventeen years, and afterwards to abdicate."

The amount of jewels and other valuables stolen from the château must have been very considerable, but a great portion of the spoil was afterwards recovered by the police. One of the thieves having entered a wine-shop and become intoxicated, was induced to place in the hands of another man diamonds of the value of 100,000 francs for a five-franc piece and a few litres of wine. Nearly the whole of the diamonds were found in the possession of the man who had thus obtained them. Others, valued at 300,000 francs, were recovered in Brussels from a Belgian workman, who had been among the occupants of the palace.

These are trivial facts, but they rise into an importance not intrinsically belonging to them, when we contrast them with the honest conduct of the great bulk of the population of Paris. The good fellows in blouses were not, indeed, always proof against temptation; some acts of petty larceny they did commit; a few of these were detected by their comrades and punished with death on the spot; of the rest many, if not all, were followed by voluntary confession and restitution. Several touching incidents of this kind are recorded; for instance, a working man went to the commissary of his quarter and stated, that, after fighting for the people during the Three

Days, he was amongst the first to enter the Tuileries, where a double breast-pin and chain, mounted with two large pearls, fell under his hand. He had a wife and family in a state of destitution; he yielded to temptation, purloined the pin, and pawned it for five francs, which saved four persons from starvation. Afterwards having got back to work and pay, he was able to restore the five francs with the pawn-ticket, both of which he placed in the hands of the commissary. The pin, when redeemed, was found to have belonged to the Duc de Nemours, and each pearl was worth 20*l.*

An English writer supplies us with a lively description of the Tuileries, as it appeared just after the retirement of the two hundred usurpers. A little havoc and ruin are, in his opinion, things that add greatly to the interest of places; a palace without king or throne, and still warm with the watch-fires of the populace who have had it in possession, is quite another thing from the palace of the guide-books, with every picture and couch in its proper place :—

"The apartments first taken possession of by the people comprise about half the grand front, from the Pavillon de Flore to the Salle des Maréchaux, which is exactly in the centre; they are in the left portion of the façade as you look from the Place du Carrousel. In the Pavillon de Flore, the great gallery and apartments which lead to the throne-room and the Hall of Marshals have been turned into a hospital for the wounded, and rows of beds, with pale, pain-stricken faces lying on the pillows, stand under the gorgeous paintings and gilded cornices; grey-coated convalescents pace languidly up and down before the large mirrors, or gather round the blazing wood-fires, looking as if they had had sufficient experience of regal splendour for the rest of their lives. The apartments of the Prince de Joinville are above the *salles* where the hospital has been improvised, and are at present occupied by M. Imbert, the temporary *chef* of the *invalides* of February, who but a few days ago was an exile, quietly fabricating pottery at

Brussels. As something of the mind of a man always displays itself in what Carlyle calls his ' environments,' I examined the rooms of his Royal Highness with some curiosity. The sitting-room is beautifully furnished, all the fittings are scarlet and gold; several *citoyens* had just risen from a plenteous breakfast, spread on a large round table, drawn to a comfortable proximity to the fire, and while M. Imbert was giving all kinds of directions and orders, cigars were lighted, and everybody made himself quite at home. It is delightful to see the facility with which men adapt themselves to circumstances, especially when they are an improvement on antecedents. The profession of the Prince could be traced in the numerous maps on the walls, in the lines of passage between port and port marked on them, an elephant's tooth reclining under a sideboard, marine paintings and sketches of sea-coast scenery, and a large model of a ship's stern placed over a mirror. A whole suite of rooms opens from this apartment; the two first are filled with a confused heap of furniture, a mingled mass of wreck and salvage, broken or saved from breaking. Screens are charitably drawn across to conceal the sad spectacle; beyond them is the library, exquisitely arranged, and untouched; not a book has been disturbed. Then follow sleeping-rooms, one of which is magnificent in its appointment; the others domestic, with sufficient elegance.

" A series of staircases lead down to the first of the state apartments, the *cabinet de conseil;* here, too, an extensive breakfast had been achieved, and the whole aspect of things was decidedly convivial with the slight air of disorder; an immense pile of wood on the Turkey carpet would not perhaps have been permitted if a sitting of the Ministry had been expected. The walls are hung with paintings by modern French artists; one had been torn from the frame, but I could not learn the subject. There were no other marks of violence. Passing through the grand gallery, filled with hospital beds as above stated, you enter the throne-room; here the havoc has

been ruthless enough: the throne has disappeared, the crim-
son velvet canopy over it still remains, being out of reach;
the rich tapestry is all torn down, so are the rich window-
curtains—they were converted into flags by the populace. The
surface of bare wall exposed by the removal of the hangings is
covered with inscriptions in charcoal,—*A bas les Tyrans! Vive
le Peuple! Vive la République!* with the names of some of the
invaders. ' *Conquise trois fois* ' is very conspicuously written:
the female figure which represents the French Republic, with
sword and drapeau, is vigorously drawn to the left of the chimneypiece—hastily, but with the touch of an artist. Every
royal emblem is destroyed with the completeness of hatred,
but some care must have been taken to avoid injuring, even
by accident, in such a scene of confusion, the fragile and precious objects in the room. Two costly vases, exquisitely
painted, have never been moved; the mirrors are perfect; but
more extraordinary is the escape of an enormous *pendule* in
gold, under a glass case, all perfect as on the day it was placed
there, its pulse beating as quietly as if nothing had happened.
A card table, pushed up to one of the windows, is covered with
the droppings of wax-tapers; all the chandeliers were filled in
preparation for a ball, and the mob lit up every one of them
for a daylight illumination.

"The apartment which divides the throne-room from the
then Salle des Maréchaux has not escaped quite so well; a
musket-ball has pierced the centre of an enormous mirror,
which is starred and cracked in all directions. The Salle des
Maréchaux itself is in an extraordinary state; all the furniture
from the gallery and rooms occupied by the wounded is heaped
up in it; tables, chairs, trophies, gold cornices, are all piled
together; a piano of exquisite tone is thrust among the mass;
many of the notes are mute, the royal chords probably snapped
by too vigorous an interpretation of the ' Marseillaise.' The
marble busts of the Marshals look down on the devastation
calm and cold, havoc being a contingency incident to the pro-

fession. None of the busts have been injured, but the portraits of Soult and Bugeaud are torn from the frames and carried away; that of Sebastiani is slashed with sabre cuts, which have also been bestowed freely on the portrait of Grouchy; under the empty frame which held the full-length of Soult is chalked '*Traître à la Patrie!*' A short inscription in a door panel states that 'Thieves are punished with death;' and those rude letters were an actual death-warrant to more than one poor wretch, tempted by the license of the hour. They were shot on the instant if discovered. The gallery which runs round the hall contains busts of Generals of an olden time; Custine is there, and Dumouriez, 'the shifty man,' covered with dust and neglected. The floor of this gallery is thickly strewn with fragments of broken mirrors. The view from the little recess that forms the entrance of the gallery is splendid; the window is in the very centre of the grand front of the palace and looks on the gardens, with the Obélisque and the Arc de Triomphe beyond them.

" In the court-yard an animated scene is going on. Labourers are clearing away the wrecks the storm has strewn over some of the apartments, which they bring out in baskets and shoot down ready for removal. Papers, old letters, torn prints, shoes, dolls, periodicals, bits of tapestry, but especially fragments of looking-glass, are all mixed together. The soldiers were fishing up all kinds of singularities with excessive enjoyment. A bit of mirror large enough to shave in was a great prize, for the plates were of the best quality. The appearance of the remains of an old white hat was received with shouts of laughter; it was maintained to be the identical *chapeau* of Louis Philippe when he played the *roi citoyen;* the companion umbrella did not turn up. A heavy storm of hail was the only thing that drove the military *chiffonniers* from their amusement. I scraped the heap with as much zeal as the rest; it is not every day one can tread on the dust of a dynasty."

The damage done to the building itself was not so great as might have been expected. The cost of the repairs has been estimated at not more than 30,000 francs. In the first flush of the revolutionary fervour, it was proposed that the Tuileries should be converted into an asylum for the invalided workmen; but this idea has been abandoned. The *invalides civiles* are to have their asylum at Meudon, and the chief palace of France will continue to be as heretofore the residence of the Government.

CHAPTER VII.

THE VOICE OF THE WALL.—THE POLICE OF PARIS.

THE February Revolution is, in one respect, rather curiously and unfavourably distinguished from all other political commotions in France. It seems to have excited in the population an exuberant developement of every instinct and every faculty except that of wit. This time the Parisians appear to have taken every thing *au grand sérieux*, and even when indulging in the most ludicrous freaks they have been each and all *triste comme un Anglais*. We miss the sprightly *chansons*, to the tune of which the French used to dance merrily through the most arduous evolutions of political strategy; the quaint conceits, the sly criticisms of their own absurdities, that used to vindicate the repute of the nation for quick perception and sound mother-wit. We have great reliance on the good sense of the bulk of the nation, and cannot believe that it will be long deluded by the Utopian schemes of some of its present leaders; but we shall not be convinced that the French are quite restored to sanity until they are again a laughing people. We have heard of but one solitary *bon mot* to which the events of February have given birth. " What do you think of Lamartine?" said some one to Hyde de Neuville. " *Il a bien l'air d'un incendiare qui s'est fait pompier*," was the reply—" Why he's like an incendiary turned fireman." If there was little justice in this, at least there was some wit.

During the six weeks after the fall of the monarchy there

came forth a series of caricatures, in which Louis Philippe
figures in a variety of absurd rather than amusing postures.
Altogether unlike the series which the Revolution of 1830
gave rise to, the French caricatures, on this occasion, are
poor dull jokes, indifferently told and badly drawn.   In one
we see the ex-Monarch in his blouse — in another, Queen
Victoria's astonishment at seeing him in his blouse — a third
represents him as a beggar soliciting alms — a fourth, making
his escape on foot — a fifth, hurrying into his brougham — and a
sixth, in a barber's shop having his whiskers shaved off. The
best of all represents him kneeling before a chair on which his
hat and umbrella are placed, and this inscription beneath,—
" *C'est ma faute! c'est ma faute! c'est ma très-grande faute!* "
The expression, however, is very poor — very unlike what
Gillray, or George Cruikshank, or the two Doyles, or the
French themselves in less stirring times, would succeed in
giving.

But if revolutionised Paris makes little display of wit, *en
revanche*, it abounds with dissertation, oral and written, on all
sorts of topics, moral, social, and political. The hundred
clubs that meet nightly in Paris, do not suffice as con-
duits to carry off the prodigious flood of popular eloquence.
At all hours of the day orators are to be found at every street
corner, holding forth to the passing crowd. Nor are the
patriots less busy with their pens than with their tongues.
However other trades may have languished since the Three
Days of February, the bill-printers and bill-stickers have had
no reason to complain of dull times. Not an available hand-
breadth of wall, pillar, or hoarding, but is made the vehicle
for addresses, petitions, essays, and schemes of all sorts.
Every wall has a voice, and every pillar a tongue, so that in
Republican Paris the old phrase, " between you and me and
the post," may be taken to express an intelligent conference
between three parties on equal terms. The Government,
finding their own proclamations swamped in this promiscuous
crowd, have ordained that all private addresses shall be on

coloured paper, white being reserved to distinguish official announcements.   Besides the ordinary broadsheets of the Government, the Minister of the Interior has, for his own special and most mischievous purposes, established a regular placard newspaper, called the *" Bulletin du Gouvernement Provisoire."*

As for the private placards, their matter is as diversified as are their hues.   One man, who dresses his opinions in the jaundiced tint of jealousy, declares in great type that "Morality demands the re-establishment of Divorce."   A Monsieur Lavigne, on behalf of the tailors who "make to measure," strongly denounces the ruinous competition of the "confection" houses, *i. e.* the slopsellers and establishments equivalent to our "Moses and Son."   One philosopher invites rich people not to feel alarmed, but to ride about in their carriages, give balls, keep plenty of servants, and spend their money as usual for the good of trade — advice which seems hardly likely to have much effect on dejected capitalists, mourning over their depreciated shares, and considering where to hide the small remainder of their ready cash.   The secretaries of various popular clubs paste up solemn declarations of principles, usually in a rather high-sounding, inflated strain, in which the changes are rung on fraternity, humanity, &c., *usque ad nauseam*.   It is not indeed without regret that one finds these noble phrases, and the lofty aspirations they express, which used to awaken an echo in one's heart, gradually sinking into the category of cant; and beginning to excite that sort of distaste which one comes to feel for beautiful music ground daily under one's window on a limping barrel organ.

A curious peruser of this open library of peripatetic philosophy has singled out one little written placard, which, says he, "rather touched me.   It was fixed on the doorpost of a mean house, and by the trembling characters seemed to be the production of a very old man.   It expressed the hope that the French, being so brave and generous, would not

allow the aged worn-out men of seventy years, who had but a
little while to live, to remain so destitute and so unhappy.
Some readers in the crowd had evidently shared in my feelings; for there appeared written in charcoal at the foot,
'*Approuvé;*' and under that in pencil, '*Et moi aussi;*' and
under that, in another hand, '*Oui.*' Many of the *affiches*
have similar pencilled commentaries—one I remember laughing at for its *naïve* Republicanism. It was on the *affiche* of a
club which announced its subscription at three francs per
month; which the commentator in a firm hand, with a blunt-
tipped pencil, declared 'Aristocratic;' adding, 'Working-
men ought to be admitted everywhere gratis by all true revo-
lutionaries.' It were well if graver facts, and more authori-
tative counsels, did not at every turn suggest with equal force
the inexorable question—'*Who is to pay the piper?*'

"This very question, however, is grappled with and resolved by a financial genius, evidently a master-mind, who
has brought out a great golden-yellow *affiche*, intituled,
'FRANCE RICH IN EIGHT DAYS!' The document sets forth
that there are six or seven millions of citizens in France,
having each silver plate to the value, on an average, of 300
francs—amounting, in all, to over two milliards. Let every
patriot carry his spoons to the Treasury, and exchange them
for Government stock at par; the spoons, of course, to be
coined forthwith into five-franc pieces. Observe the depth of
this combination, the subtle *engrenage* of its several elements.
Government gets the silver cheap, paying for it in depreciated securities at par. But the seller is none the worse off
for that: on the contrary, he will make a handsome profit
too; because, when the Government has two milliards in
hand, the funds will immediately go up above par. But a
practical difficulty remains,—How are the citizens to eat their
bouilli and *julienne* without the accustomed implements?
After thus literally 'forking-out' to the Treasury, how is
the business of forking-*in* to be managed? I confess, as I
read the placard, thoughtfully rapping my teeth with my.

cane, I saw nothing to fall back on, in face of this difficulty, except a cheerful resignation to three-pronged steel : still, meaner minds might have put their trust in pewter. But Here comes the crowning stroke of our financial strategist : the transaction is to be one of universal benefit; the Government and the patriot are both to pocket a handsome profit on the transaction; the Treasury is to overflow, and yet the dinner table shall not sparkle a whit less brightly. Cannot you set this egg on its end? A single word unriddles the enigma; but this word it is reserved for genius to discover. You read on hastily—

" ' Elkington ! . . .

" ' Forks plated by galvanism cannot be distinguished from the real!'

" What more need be added? 'Citizens,' cries the placard, 'a little energy—a little patriotism—and the country is saved !'

" But alas !" adds D. P., seized with a sudden despondency in his concluding line, " patriotism and energy— *c'est là toute la question!*"

There was indeed abundant food for mirth in these " voices of the wall;" but there was in them matter intelligible only to the wise, and which such men would have deemed worthy of the most serious study. Could all the libraries on earth afford such aid toward that most precious of all kinds of knowledge, the knowledge of men, as the walls of a great city covered thickly with the utterances of the individual thoughts and feelings of half a million of human beings? One more example we will quote, as it fairly justifies our emphatic assertion that the working classes of Paris are an honest and honourable race. On Saturday, April 2, there was a large gathering on the Place de la Concorde, to take into consideration an appeal from a certain " Citoyen Durclé," which had been posted on all the walls of Paris, under the title of an *Appel d'un Riche aux Riches*, and containing a proposal for a voluntary proportional tax upon property, " for this time only," and under the peculiar circumstances of the present financial difficulty. It is not worth while enumerating all the items of the table of proportion proposed, beginning at 200f. upon every capital of 100,000f., and ending at 10,000f. upon every fortune amounting to a million—the sacrifice, as the Citoyen Durclé remarked, was not immense for all friends of the Republic; but the curious part of the appeal was, that a demonstration of three hundred thousand of the lower classes was called for (to assemble on the Place de la Concorde), in order to go up to the Provisional Government and request it to *urge* this appeal upon the consideration of all the rich of France. The calling upon a monster demonstration to back a *don volontaire* by its moral *force* was evidently somewhat of an anomaly; and, says our authority, who certainly cannot be charged with an undue leaning to the popular side, " I am glad to say that I found much good sense among the working classes upon the subject. Whether the people were too much engaged in their own particular minor demonstrations to attend to any other, more patriotic, perhaps, but less showy, or whether they did not take the appeal to heart, certain it is that the project of a monster meeting utterly failed. Citoyen Durclé, a fair little active man of about thirty-five, did not manage to congregate more than a few hundreds. The sentiments of the people upon the matter were very varied, it was true; some declaimed that the rich *must* make this *voluntary* gift to the country—*must*, because if they did not, it would be a sign they desired a civil war—that their refusal would be an *appel aux armes*—that those who did not must be *forced* by such demonstrations, &c.; but there was one sturdy, little, dirty, unshaven artisan among the crowd, who dominated the assembly by his energetic language, and carried away the majority; he declared that the people were too just to give an appeal to the generosity of the rich the air of a *menace*, and that they were too proud to give it the air of begging. He completely knocked Citoyen Durclé's demonstration project on the head. The name of this orator of the people, in the name of their good feeling and their good sense, would have been worth recording."

Alarmed by the formidable rivalry of the wall, the conductors of the newspaper press urgently insisted upon a repeal of the stamp-duty, and gave the Provisional Government no rest until their demand was complied with. The newspaper stamp was wholly abolished. The first effect of this was, of course, a reduction of price, in which "La Presse" led the way. Its price to the annual subscriber in Paris is reduced from 40f. to 24f. per annum, the postage being added for the subscribers in the provinces and foreign places. This makes the price of the paper *daily* 6 centimes and 6-10ths, or little more than six-tenths of a penny for one of the most ably conducted journals of the French capital. Before the recent revolution the circulation of " La Presse" was 36,000 ; its present circulation is reported to be nearly 80,000.

It is an interesting and significant fact that M. Emile de Girardin, than whom no man in France has a keener eye to his own personal interest, and who is one of the most formidable opponents of the wild theories of M. Louis Blanc and of the extreme Communists, has adopted the example of commercial communism set by the Northern Railway. That company, early in March, announced its purpose of making all individuals of every rank and class in its employment, from the president of the company and the engineer-in-chief to the humblest station-man, stoker, and plate-layer, virtual partners in the enterprise and participators in its profits. Many private establishments have adopted the same course. The following announcement appeared at the head of the leading column of " La Presse : "—

" COUNCIL OF PROPRIETORS OF 'LA PRESSE.' — MEETING OF MARCH 5.—M. de Beville, president ; M. Laboy, secretary ; M. Coutzen, auditor. The proprietors of the ' Presse,' called together by M. Emile Girardin (one of them), agree unanimously to the principles hereafter stated, already adopted by the company of the Northern Railway Company :—Association of labour and capital — division of profits. Henceforward, in every industrial enterprise, all the salaries of labourers, workmen, foremen, clerks, engineers, directors, and managers, shall be made a common fund with the capitalists, with reference to the labour of one and the capital of the others. The profits remaining, after the payment of labour and dividends on capital, and for providing a sinking fund to pay off the capital, shall be divided between all, according to the amount of salary or dividend of each. In consequence they decide, that the division of the proceeds of the 'Presse' shall be made as follows :—1. Payment of salaries. 2. Interest of capital at five per cent, according to the average profits of the 'Presse,' from the 1st August, 1839, the day of its purchase, comprising therein the sinking fund. 3. Division of the profits in the proportion of capital in money to capital in labour represented by the amount of salaries. This word 'salaries' must have some more noble import. The proprietors of the 'Presse,' therefore, extend it, without distinction, to editors, clerks, compositors, correctors, printers, distributors, and folders. The accounts of the participation shall commence from January 1, 1848. A commission composed of three members has been charged with the drawing up the legal agreement. The reduction of the price of subscription from 44f. (average) for Paris to 24f. per year (difference 20f.), from 52f. (average) for the departments to 36f. per year (difference 16f.), is approved, for all the subscriptions made after this day. All the proprietors of the 'Presse' giving their consent severally.''

We are now writing in the seventh week of the French Republic's existence, and up to this time the peace and security of the capital has been admirably preserved under a fearful combination of the most trying circumstances. There are fewer marauders, and less uneasiness is to be felt in a midnight excursion through the streets of Paris than under the old system. The self-elected Préfect of Police, Caussidière, does his duty wonderfully well, and is universally confessed to be the only man in France who could so soon have re-established order and security. He is a veteran of the Old Guard, has for years been one of the stanchest Republicans in the country, and has suffered much both in person and fortune for the cause. Immediately on his seizing the, vacant place of Préfect, he set about organising the system of night police upon a totally new system, and which succeeded beyond expectation. He formed a band of four hundred individuals of his own choosing; taking some from the most active members of the old police; others from among the workmen on the wharves of Paris, a very daring and powerful race of men;

and many from the very prisons of the capital — selecting them for strength and activity — and, by liberal pay, making it worth their while to remain faithful to his service.

No greater proof can be given of the wisdom of suiting the work to the workman, than in the success of the system of Caussidière. This lawless band, which might have become, in such a time of trouble, the terror of the whole city, has been, ever since the Revolution, its protection and safeguard. The troop is lodged night and day at the Préfecture, and is ever ready, arms in hand, to obey the orders of its chief. Caussidière has been heard to boast that his band of Montagnards, as he calls them, have not suffered a single robbery to go unde-tected since he has been installed in office, and asks if such had ever been the case during a month's administration of his predecessor. The National Guard, from all parts of Paris, upon the first appearance of danger, send immediately for the Montagnards, who succeed with admirable promptitude in dis-persing an obnoxious crowd; from their personal acquaintance with the principal leaders in these turbulent movements, they can immediately dispel the effect by arresting the cause. The Jacobin Club, in the Faubourg du Roule, had given some little uneasiness to the people in the neighbourhood of its sittings, by the immense crowd which it attracted, and by the violence of the opinions emanating from its members. Caussidière was applied to, the National Guard of the quarter having been found inadequate to cope with the infuriated orators. He in-stantly despatched thither about a dozen of his sturdy Mon-tagnards, in the dress of Auvergnats—the hewers of wood and drawers of water to the good *bourgeois* of Paris: for it had not been deemed prudent to alarm the timid, or excite the unruly, by suffering them to appear in their well-known uniform. At the very first symptom of uproarious behaviour, the Auvergnats arose and called out, *A bas l'Orateur—à bas le Président!* which cry, of course, excited the honest indignation of the worshipful assembly, just then voting the sacrifice of the pro-perty of all aristocrats; to be accompanied by that of their

heads also, in case of resistance. A frightful tumult began;
the Auvergnats, unarmed, by the sole assistance of their fists,
and the terror of their war-cry, *Au Montagnard!* succeeded in
clearing the room in the space of seven minutes, the president
being the first to decamp in all haste; and the very next day
the walls of the faubourg were placarded with the announcement of the dissolution of the club, and of its fusion into that
of *le Reveil du Peuple* of the Rue de Laborde.

One of the most remarkable of this band of Montagnards
is Ledru, known among his associates as Jean de Nivelle, who
in 1845 escaped from La Force, where he was confined for
coining, by hollowing out, with no other instrument than a
shoemaker's awl and a common clasp-knife, a subterranean
passage running across two streets to the Fountain in the Rue
du Parc—the boldest prison enterprise since the days of Baron
Trenck. He is the very life and soul of every undertaking;
and by his extraordinary courage and agility never fails to return victorious from his expeditions against the best-organised
plan for disturbing the public peace. The regiment rejoices
also in the possession of another individual not less remarkable—a man of letters, author of several successful theatrical
pieces, besides two or three novels. This man began life as
an actor of the Funambules, where he frequently played with
great success in pieces of his own composition, and where he
would no doubt have risen one day to eminence, had not a
little miserable incident occurred in 1838, which, quite insignificant in itself, proved, nevertheless, of the utmost consequence to him, for it changed the freedom of his joyous *vie de
Bohème* into the disgrace and dishonour of the pillory—the
slavery of the prison-house. A lady belonging to the company
of the Funambules—one of those clever women whose knowledge of arithmetic and rigid economy are both so admirable
that they can manage to procure the most brilliant clothes
and jewels, the most splendid furniture and appointments,
sometimes, indeed, to keep a handsome carriage, with the poor
stipend afforded by their second-rate talent at this low theatre

—missed from her dressing-room a splendid diamond bracelet which her wonderful prudence and economy had, no doubt, enabled her to purchase.   In consequence of the hue and cry made by the fair lady, a diligent inquiry was made, and every person about the theatre was compelled to submit to a search. Now it fell out, we know not how, but the missing valuable was found upon the person of our hero—in his very pocket! He says in his memoirs that it was a conspiracy; that the lady in question contrived to slide the bracelet into his glove, which he had laid upon her dressing-table for a moment, and that when called in a hurry to enter the stage, he had taken it up and thrust it into his pocket unawares!   However, the judges seem not to have been of this opinion, for he was condemned without mercy to two years' imprisonment at Poissy. At the end of this time, being disgusted with theatricals, he endeavoured to find employment with the press.   In this he succeeded, and wrote for several of the leading journals.   He then published his impressions of prison life, a novel or two, and a volume of memoirs.   He might have acquired both competence and fame, but the dissipated habits he had acquired in prison, the loss of his own self-respect, the consciousness of degradation, had unfitted him for labour of any kind, or for any regular course of life, and he was soon once more hopeless and destitute.   He had been several times an inmate of the Depôt de Mendicité at St. Denis, and his recital of the sufferings he endured when confined there are touching in the extreme.   Four years ago, having wearied all his friends, and having tried every kind of office, he was too glad to accept the place of chief scavenger of Paris!   It was a subject of deep reflection to behold this man of talent at the head of his brigade of men and women, sweeping away in measured cadence the accumulated mud and filth of the dirtiest streets in the world; it was indeed an awful lesson to those who feel inclined to dissipate God's goodly gifts, or to misuse the time and talent bestowed for wise and great and holy purposes.   He was one of the first to whom Caussidière applied to fill the office of clerk to his battalion of Montagnards, and he appears to give satisfaction in the employment so well suited to his romantic disposition and restless roving habits.

The uniform of the corps is remarkable, being tricoloured, and, although of the coarsest and cheapest materials, perfectly graceful, and well calculated to shew to advantage the brawny muscular forms of these wild brigands. It consists of a common dark-blue blouse, confined at the waist by a scarlet sash; a red woollen cap; and white trousers. They are armed to the teeth, and with their dark beards and swarthy weather-beaten countenances, present a most formidable appearance. Jules Gerard, the lion-killer of Africa, sometimes accompanies them, but quite *en amateur*, and merely for the sake of enjoying the excitement of pursuit and capture, to the gratification of which passion he seems to have devoted every faculty. He was first beheld at the storming of the Tuileries and at the sacking of the Palais Royal. His cry of *Mort aux roleurs!* was adopted on the instant, and from that moment he has never ceased to wage war against all thieves and plunderers. He is dressed in the rich costume of the African Zoaves, to which regiment he originally belonged, and walks in his own allotted place at every public ceremony. He carries a long cord twisted round his arm, at one end of which is suspended an iron hook, the other end being formed into a running noose; at the first cry of alarm, Gerard rushes into the crowd, and with unerring aim flings the iron hook towards the thief, hooking him at once by the garments; then drawing him thus nearer to himself, he flings the running noose over his head, and secures him effectually. It is impossible to describe the terror which the very name of Gerard produces in a crowd. In vain the wretched culprit, when detected, essays by dodging into the thickest of the *mêlée* to escape—the steady aim and cool determination of his enemy are invincible—and with a cry of distress he sees the fatal noose drawn over him, and knows that from thence there is no escape.

The vigilance of Caussidière is beyond all praise, and,

like the great Haroun al Raschid, he disdains not to seek
every opportunity of judging personally of the manner in
which his orders are obeyed.   He wages war to the death
with every species of vice, which never fails to rear its head
in the midst of popular commotion ; and the gaming-houses
were never so watched and persecuted as at the moment we
write this.   He has, moreover, announced his intention of
putting down all those haunts so favoured by M. de Rambuteau,
and so approved of by the " system " of Louis Philippe, as
tending to amuse and enervate the youthful population of
Paris, thus diverting their attention from public affairs.   All
those nurses of vice and infamy — the juvenile theatres — are
likewise to be discontinued ; and he has announced, with
great nobleness of sentiment, that under his administration,
" although it may be impossible to destroy corruption altogether in so large a capital as Paris, yet it shall henceforth
be made necessary for the citizens to go forth in quest of
seduction, and not have it brought, as hitherto, to their very
doors."   One day Caussidière, walking through the Rue
Guéneg, was attracted by the display of some forbidden pub-
lications in the shop of a bookseller.   He entered and purchased one of these, and, as he laid the money down upon the
counter, inquired of the worthy shopkeeper how many more
copies of the work remained on hand?   " Two hundred."
" You will deliver them up to my agent, who will burn
them," replied Caussidière.   " I am the Préfect of Police,
and will order a *visite domiciliaire* this evening."   The shop ·
keeper laughed in derision.   " Before then," said he, " the '
book will be safe enough, and your agent will have nought
but his trouble for his profit."   " Well, then, I shall just
stand for a moment opposite your door, and having read from
this book some few sentences to those who choose to listen,
leave you to enter into your own justification with the crowd."
The threat was too terrible ; the bookseller was glad enough
to promise every thing ; and, before he quitted the shop, the
Préfect had the satisfaction of consigning to the flames with

his own hand every copy of the offending publication which existed on the premises.

The papers found by Caussidière in the Préfecture of Police laid bare many acts of infamous perfidy committed by professing Republicans. The affair of Lucien de la Hodde, one of the curled darlings of the world of fashion, excited an extraordinary sensation. One version of the tale is as follows :—

It appears that this young hero, who was one of the most renowned exquisites and gallants of the salons of Paris—who was acknowledged to be a first-rate artist, a tolerable poet, and supposed to be a gentleman of fortune, was one of the first to apply to the Provisional Government for some kind of employment suited to his talents. His friend Caussidière, who had already elected himself Minister of Police, got him named to some office of trust in the Hôtel de Ville, which he fulfilled to the satisfaction of all around him until Thursday, March 23, when, as he was about to leave his office, he was accosted by a fellow in blouse and sabots, who hailed him as an old friend and comrade, congratulating him upon his fashionable appearance and the apparently flourishing circumstances in which he was found. Although the gay Lucien was observed to change countenance at the sudden recognition of his self-styled friend, yet, of course, he stoutly denied any former acquaintance with him, and by stepping into his cabriolet, which, with its dark grey horse, was waiting at the door of the Hôtel de Ville to convey him home, he soon left the obtrusive friend far behind, and arrived at the Café Hardy, where he was engaged to dine with a party of fashionable acquaintance, rather flurried, of course, with the adventure, but fully determined to forget it as soon as possible in the enjoyment of good wine and good company. He was fulfilling this laudable intention to his heart's content when waited upon by a messenger from Caussidière, bearing a request to see him directly at the Préfecture de Police. De la Hodde was rather disturbed at the summons, for he was preparing to

honour Grisi's benefit at the Italian Opera; however, the
message was too peremptory to admit of refusal, so he once
more jumped into the dark brown cabriolet picked out with
orange, which had for so long a time been the delight and
pride of the Champ Elysées; and again did the high-trotting
iron-grey bear him at a towering pace through the streets of
Paris. Arrived at his destination, he was immediately ushered
into the presence of his friend Caussidière, whom he found
surrounded by his numberless myrmidons, and flanked, as
usual, by the redoubtable brace of horse-pistols which have
never left his side since his first nomination to office. None
of this would have created the slightest alarm in the mind of
young De la Hodde, for he was accustomed to the tone and
bearing of his friend Caussidière, and knew that after all he
was a *bon enfant*, whose bark was worse than his bite, and he
advanced fearlessly with outstretched hand and a gay greeting
upon his lips. Presently, however, he started back, and
would have fled had not the door been bolted behind him immediately on his entrance; for behind the chair of Caussidière
he had beheld his other friend of the Hôtel de Ville, and
spread out upon the table certain papers and documents which
he but knew too well, and which had been taken from the
archives of the police! In an instant De la Hodde felt that
he was lost, and fell upon his knees to beg for mercy; while
Caussidière spurned him with his foot as he exclaimed
—" Go, thou base, vile miscreant! in the first moment of
wrath I had designed to have destroyed thee with my own
hand; but my anger is cooled into contempt, and I resign
thee into the hands of those who will deal towards thee with
more justice and with more severity than I should have done
by depriving thee of life." De la Hodde was immediately
hurried away to the Conciergerie, where, during the night,
his trial was heard and his judgment pronounced. He was
condemned to be shot in the courtyard of the prison. Like
Marshal Ney and the Duc d'Enghien, execution was to follow
immediately upon the sentence. The criminal was brought

forward with pinioned arms and bandaged eyes, and placed against the wall ; the word was given, fourteen muskets fired on the instant, and the unhappy man fell forward on his face, while a burst of laughter echoed from the executioners, who ran to pick him up. The execution was but a farce, meant to intimidate the miserable wretch, and make him feel the horrors of judgment and of death, without the curse of blood upon the conscience of his judges ; but the event has filled them, nevertheless, with remorse and with alarm, for De la Hodde was taken up senseless, and put to bed in the most alarming condition. All that night he moved not, nor gave signs of life. For some time he was thought to be in reality dead, but he recovered in time sufficiently to open his eyes and to give tokens of returning consciousness ; but, although he could partake of nourishment, yet he neither moved nor spoke for many a day since that memorable Thursday night.

According to another account, the conclusion of this affair was not quite so melodramatic, though not much less sternly impressive. It states, that the guilty man was at once transferred from the Préfecture of Police to the Conciergerie. In the evening a party of ardent patriots, who had access to the prison, took him out, and carried him before an extemporane-ously-formed military tribunal, which soon found the culprit guilty of treason, and sentenced him to be shot. It was with difficulty that some of the National Guards prevented them from carrying the sentence immediately into execution ; but ultimately they allowed him to be taken back to prison, on the promise that he should be speedily brought to trial before the regular tribunals.

The man whose presence behind Caussidière's chair struck De la Hodde with such horror was his old comrade and fellow-spy Raynal. The letters in De la Hodde's handwriting, found in the archives of the police, were to the number of five hundred. They go back for some years, and the last was written as late as the afternoon of the 23d of February—that is to say, the second of the three glorious days. In this last letter he informs M. Delessert that he has at last induced the Republicans to make a stand in the streets; that the most ardent Republicans were that evening, at eight o'clock, to be at the Port St. Martin and the Port St. Denis, and if he would send a party of Municipal Guards at that hour he might seize the whole of them.　M. Delessert acted, it appears, on this information.　He sent the Municipal Guards at the hour appointed, but they arrived nine minutes before the hour fixed, and the Republicans consequently escaped from falling into the trap.

CHAPTER VIII.

THE HÔTEL DE VILLE.—THE PROVISIONAL GOVERNMENT.

"*A l'Hôtel de Ville!*" shouted some one in the Chamber
of Deputies on the 24th of February, and thousands of voices
instantly took up that oldest and most familiar rallying cry of
plebeian Paris.   From the time when the boatmen of Lutetia
first built their huts upon the mud-banks of the Seine, down
to the present hour, through all the vicissitudes of the national
existence, through all the momentary and secular mutations .
exhibited by a people proverbially noted for fickleness and love
of change, the old municipal heart of Paris has maintained its
indefeasible prerogative.   Its history is the most complete
summary of the history of France.   The Hôtel de Ville is
the Frenchman's Caaba — the monumental cynosure of his
political faith — the centre to which gravitate all the movements of the capital and the country.   Whatever power possesses the Hôtel de Ville, is for the time the dominant power
in France.

Impossible as it would be to give any adequate description
of the turbulence and confusion that prevailed in the Hôtel
de Ville on the 24th and 25th of February, what we have
already related on this subject is enough to confirm the
assertion we made in our opening page, that the Revolution
was, from first to last, the spontaneous work of the people of
Paris.   They began the revolt of their own accord, carried it
on without leaders, and consummated it in accordance with
their own unanimous desires, and not as they were impelled

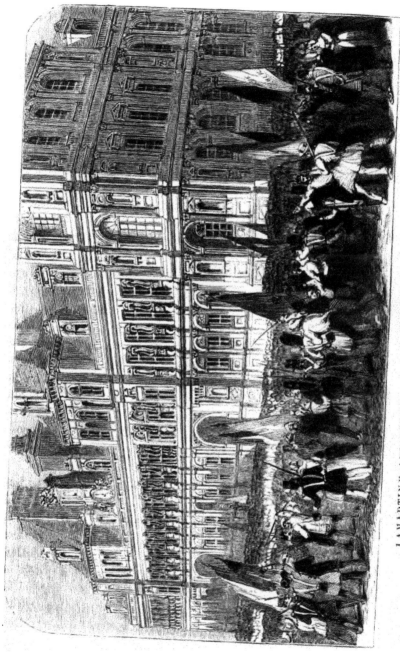

LAMARTINE ADDRESSING THE POPULACE AT THE HOTEL DE VILLE.

to do by any extraneous promptings. Remembering how they had conquered in vain in 1830, they were resolved that this time they should not be defrauded of the fruits of their victory. They would sweep away every vestige of the old system, they would hear of no compromise with royalty; and instead of acquiescing in the establishment of a Republic because it was recommended to them by the Provisional Government, they accepted the Provisional Government because it promised them a Republic. The conduct of the people at the Hôtel de Ville bespoke any thing but the docility of men awaiting the decisions of known and tried leaders. The heads of the Republican party (whose tactics, ever since the failure of the attempt made by Barbès in 1839, had been to sit still and watch for such an opportunity as that which presented itself in February) did then come forward at the right moment, and when they had satisfied the people that they were the right men, they were allowed to be and remain the Government. But before their powers were confirmed by the popular sanction, they had to stand with muskets and bayonets pointed at their throats, and undergo many a tremendous examination by choleric and suspicious judges. Their lives were never worth five minutes' purchase, until they had put it beyond doubt that the popular cause would be safer in their hands than it had been in those of Lafayette in 1830.

It was, indeed, as trying a task as ever devolved upon any set of men, to overcome the extreme distrust that filled the minds of the armed citizens. Often, as they were soothed and charmed by Lamartine's eloquence, their suspicions would still return as soon as his voice had ceased to delight their ears. The more the orator had enchanted them, the more enraged they felt at the thought that all his fine words might be nothing but cajolery. Their perplexity would have been in the highest degree comic, had it not threatened to result in a most tragic catastrophe. They insisted that the Provisional Government should, every quarter of an hour, make a report of their proceedings to the people. On one occasion

Lamartine came forward and said, — "Citizens, I come to impart to you the ideas of the Provisional Government." *"We won't have any ideas — down with ideas!"* shouted the mob. Another time Lamartine began thus, — "The first necessity of the Republic is order." *"We won't have any order — down with order!"* exclaimed the sovereign people.

Although, as we have said, the leaders of the Republican party were vigilant waiters upon opportunity, and never ceased to hope for the time when they should reduce their doctrines to practice, there seems reason to think that the Revolution took them by surprise almost as much as it did any other class of men in the country. How otherwise can we explain the fact that they had not come to any common understanding as to the individuals who were to constitute this new Government? Four different lists were simultaneously published in different parts of Paris. The names announced at the Chamber of Deputies were those of Dupont (de l'Eure), Arago, Lamartine, Garnier Pagès, Marie, and Crémieux. The writers of the "Réforme" newspaper put forth another list, composed of the names of Arago, Flocon, Louis-Blanc, Recurt, Lamartine, Ledru-Rollin, Albert, and Marrast. A third list was concocted at the office of the "National," and a fourth at the Hôtel de Ville itself, before the arrival of the members designated elsewhere.

When the candidates thus named had met together, their first business was mutually to discuss their several claims; but how they were able to do this, and afterwards to draw up the many proclamations they issued, amidst the stunning noise and the pressure of a delirious multitude that scarcely left them space enough to breathe, is one of the inexplicable marvels of the wondrous week. On the 26th, they began to be somewhat more at ease, having succeeded in clearing the building of all but some thousand persons, the greater part of whom persisted in offering their services as a guard of honour. The Government made a virtue of necessity, and accepted the patriotic offer with the best possible grace.

Thenceforth they were secure from the promiscuous irruption of the multitude, and some degree of order began to prevail in the interior of the Hôtel de Ville ; but still they were not secure from the violence that lurked in their own council-room, and sometimes broke out in the most stormy demonstrations. Preserved repeatedly, almost by as many miracles, from death by the weapons of the frantic multitude, Lamartine's invaluable life was again put in most imminent peril by the same hand that had fired the fatal shot at the Hôtel des Affaires Etrangères. The high consideration in which Lagrange was held by the Republican party may be inferred from the fact, that to him Lieutenant Aubert Roche, of the 5th Legion of the National Guard, formally transmitted Louis Philippe's act of abdication, which had been put into his hands by an officer of the château. The Provisional Government, though in dread of the well-known incendiary principles of Lagrange, felt compelled to nominate him to some post of eminence, and for two days he figured as Governor of the Hôtel de Ville. At the end of that time he was replaced by another, and no more was heard of Lagrange, who, as creator and father of the Revolution of 1848, had of course attracted considerable attention at first.

It appears that on the Monday following the flight of Louis Philippe, a grand council was held of all the revolutionary leaders, assembled to dictate terms à huis clos to the Provisional Government. The wise and calm demeanour of Lamartine seems to have irritated in no small degree the boiling, passionate nature of Lagrange, whose excitement was so fierce and terrible that several members of the Assembly prepared to withdraw in alarm. Lamartine alone blenched not, and the sang froid and self-possession displayed in his replies only served to increase the savage anger of his opponent all the more. At length, exasperated beyond control, the infuriated Republican, drawing a pistol from his pocket, rushed towards Lamartine, and exclaiming, " Thou art no true patriot!" pointed the weapon at the head of the Minister.

N

" What hinders me from taking thy life now—at once—upon
the instant?" shrieked he, with redoubled fury as the calm
glance of Lamartine met his eye. " Your own conscience,"
coolly replied the Minister, " and the utter uselessness of such
an outrage; for should I fall, there will still remain my colleagues, who all, to a man, have resolved to die rather than
submit to violence, or to return to the senseless anarchy of
'93!"   The words had the effect of calming for an instant the
fury of Lagrange—he dropped the weapon which he held, and
turning pale as death, while his eye quailed before the steady
gaze of Lamartine, he muttered between his teeth, " Thou art
not a true Republican, nor yet a true patriot; but I verily believe thou art an honest man!" and then sank again upon his
seat at the council-board, trembling in every limb, and apparently exhausted with the effort of passion to which he had
given way.   It was then that his neighbour, La Caussidière,
managed to seize the pistol which he had placed beside him,
and by this presence of mind saved the Assembly from a dread-
ful catastrophe; for in the space of a few moments Lagrange
arose, and with the most frightful yells and howlings began to
rend the clothes from his back and to tear the flesh from his
bosom, until the blood spurted forth, all the while uttering the
most fearful imprecations and blasphemies.   In an instant the
whole Assembly was in an uproar—the terror of the scene was
greater than words can describe.   It was evident that the
fierce excitement of the last few days had turned the brain of
Lagrange and produced a fit of raging madness.   He was secured with difficulty, and borne to a *maison de santé* at Montmartre, where, for aught we know, he now remains, still a
raving maniac.   The Assembly all gathered round Lamartine
with congratulations, but the effect of the scene was such that
many were forced to retire, and the meeting broke up.   Much
commiseration was felt for Lagrange, who, it could not be
doubted, was a warm and disinterested, though misguided,
Republican, and who had made himself conspicuous in the
insurrection at Lyons, not only for his energy and daring, but

by some signal acts of magnanimous clemency. In person he is a model of manly beauty, and he possessed great power over the lower class.

After the removal of this maniac, the Provisional Government might have had reasonable leisure to apply themselves to their most arduous and multifarious tasks, but for the false direction which they themselves had unhappily given to the course of social reform. The working men of Paris from the first announced their determination that the Revolution of February should result in some improvement of their condition, and not merely in the creation of a multitude of places for the middle and upper classes, as in the case of the Revolution of July. The Provisional Government acquiesced in this principle, and issued the following decree :—

"Considering that the Revolution made by the people ought to be made *for* them ; — that it is time to put an end to the long and iniquitous sufferings of workmen ; — that the labour question is one of supreme importance ; — that there is no other more high, or more worthy of the consideration of a Republican Government ; — that it belongs to France to study ardently, and to resolve a problem submitted at present to all the industrial nations of Europe : — The Provisional Government of the Republic decrees a permanent commission, which shall be named *Commission de Gouvernement pour les Travailleurs*, which is about to be nominated, with the express and special mission of occupying itself with their lot. To shew how much importance the Provisional Government of the Republic attaches to the solution of this great problem, it nominates President of the Commission of Government for Workmen one of its members, M. Louis Blanc, and for Vice-President another of its members, M. Albert, workman. Workmen will be invited to form part of the Committee. The seat of the Committee will be at the Palace of the Luxembourg."

So far all was fair and reasonable on both sides. The condition of the working classes called imperatively for amendment. How to place the relations between the employer and the employed on a wholesome footing is, of all social problems in our times, at once the most urgent and the most difficult. In France, all the laws and regulations made on this subject during the last reign were dictated by fear and hatred of the working classes, and therefore there was so much the more obvious need of a mixed commission to inquire into the whole system, apply present remedies to the most crying abuses, and by sage and cautious induction prepare the basis of a sound code of trade legislation.   Unfortunately the Labour Parliament, assembled at the Luxembourg, began its work at the wrong end, making sentence precede inquiry.   It was, in fact, only a cumbrous contrivance for disguising the absolute dictatorship of Louis Blanc and Albert "*ouvrier*." Before the Republic was a week old, we have decrees signed by those two functionaries (March 1 and 2), fixing the duration of a day's labour at ten hours, *the wages to remain as before*, and abolishing *marchandage*, or the customary division of large contracts among a number of sub-contractors, without which no great work can be executed, except at a greatly enhanced cost.

The Provisional Government having thus sanctioned the popular delusion that the amount of wages may be fixed by direct legislative enactment, their reception-hall was forthwith invaded by deputation after deputation from the members of every calling in the capital, all demanding a maximum of pay for a minimum of work.   Never was a Government so beset: they had need to have among them a Moreau de St. Méry, who in the first Revolution was recorded to have given, in one brief hour, three thousand orders.   The cabmen, omnibus-drivers, and conductors, struck for increase of wages, and had their demands ratified by the Government.   The example was immediately followed by all the other working classes. "Half regiments of men in blouses," says a spectator, "defile before you, two-and-two, mount the steps of the Hôtel de Ville, and disappear—gone to see the Ministry face to face, to speak with it, hear it speak, assure it of their adhesion to the Republic, remind it that it is there 'to organise labour,' and so withdraw, shouting, '*Vive la République!*' Not a dozen men in Paris, united by any professional bond, but come in this way to give in their adhesion. On Thursday, again, came a deputation from the School of Medicine, to adhere, and ask respectfully that henceforth they may be allowed to elect their own dean! Then came the players of the Théâtre Française, to adhere, and beg that Monsieur So-and-so, their manager and 'tyrant,' should, in these days of liberty and universal election, be deposed! Everybody comes 'adhering,' and many stay to ask for places. Some minister or other has to receive everybody, and give everybody a polite answer. Fancy what hard work to be a member of this Provisional Government of France!"

To no part of the proceedings of the Provisional Government can we turn with feelings of such lively admiration as to the official manifestoes of its foreign policy, issued by the generous and pure-souled Minister, to whom, happily for France and for Europe, has been consigned the task of representing his country in her relations with the surrounding states. The first specific intimation of the international views that were to govern the conduct of the new Republic was given to the world on the 5th of March, in the shape of a " Circular from the Minister for Foreign Affairs to the Diplomatic Agents of the French Republic." It is as follows:—

" Monsieur,—You are acquainted with the events of Paris, the victory of the people, their heroism, their moderation, how soon appeased, order re-established by the concurrence of all citizens, as if in this interregnum of visible powers the general reason alone directed the government of France.

" The French Revolution has thus entered its final period. France is a Republic. The French Republic has no need of being recognised in order to exist. It stands by natural right and national right; it is the will of a great people, who ask no title but from itself. However, the French Republic, desiring to enter into the family of instituted Governments as a regular power, and not as a disturbing phenomenon of European order, it is fitting that you promptly make known to the Government to which you are accredited the principles and the tendencies which are forthwith to direct the foreign policy of the French Government.

" The proclamation of the French Republic is not an act of aggression against any form of government in the world. Forms of government have with all people their diversities as legitimate as diversities of character, of geographical situation, and of intellectual developement, moral and material. Nations have, like individuals, different ages. The principles

which rule have different phases. Monarchical, aristocratical, constitutional, Republican Governments, are the expression of those different
degrees of maturity of the genius of nations. They demand more liberty
as fast as they feel themselves capable of supporting more; they demand
more equality and democracy in proportion as they are inspired by more
justice and love for the people. It is a question of time. A people lose
themselves in anticipating the hour of this maturity, as they dishonour
themselves when they allow its escape. Monarchy and the Republic are
not, in the eyes of true statesmen, absolute principles engaged in a death
struggle—they are things which stand in contrast, and which can live face
to face on a mutual understanding and with mutual respect.

" War is not then the principle of the French Republic, as by a fatal
and glorious necessity it had become in 1792. Between 1792 and 1848 there
is half a century. To return after half a century to the principle of 1792,
or to the principle of conquest of the empire, would be not to advance but
to retrograde with time. The Revolution of yesterday is a step in advance,
not in arrear. The world and ourselves alike wish to march to fraternity
and to peace.

" If the situation of the French Republic in 1792 accounted for the
war, the differences which exist between this epoch of our history and the
present explain peace. The differences endeavour to comprehend, and to
be made comprehended about you.

" In 1792 the nation was not one. Two people existed on the same
soil. A terrible struggle was going on between the classes dispossessed of
their privileges and the classes that had just gained equality and liberty.
The dispossessed classes with captive royalty, and with the jealous foreigner, wished to deny to France her Revolution, and to reimpose monarchy, aristocracy, and theocracy upon her by invasion. There are no
longer at this day distinct and unequal classes: liberty has enfranchised
all : equality, before the law, has levelled all : fraternity, whose application
we proclaim, and whose benefits the National Assembly will organise,
shall all unite. There is not a single citizen in France, of no matter what
opinion, who does not rally to the principle of country above all, and who
does not by this same union render her inexpugnable to the attempts and
disquietudes of invasion.

" In 1792, it was not the entire people who entered into possession of
its then Government—it was the middle class alone who desired to exercise
and enjoy liberty. The triumph of the middle class was then selfish, as is
the triumph of every oligarchy. It desired to keep for itself alone the
rights conquered by all. It became necessary for its purpose to operate a
strong diversion to the advent of the people in precipitating them upon the
field of battle, in order to prevent their entering upon their own proper
government. This diversion was war. War was the thought of the

Monarchists and of the Girondins : it was not the thought of the more advanced democrats, who desired, as we do, the sincere, complete, and regular reign of the people themselves, comprehending under this name all classes, without exclusion and without preference, of which the nation is composed.

" In 1792, the people were only the instrument of revolution and not the object. To-day the Revolution is made by them and for them—the people and themselves the Revolution. In entering into it they bring new necessities of labour, of industry, of instruction, of agriculture, of commerce, of morality, of comfort, of property, of cheap living, of navigation—in fine, of civilisation—which are all necessities of peace ! The people and peace are synonymous terms.

" In 1792, the ideas of France and of Europe were not prepared to comprehend and to accept the great harmony of nations amongst themselves for the benefit of the human race. The thought of the age which has ended was confined to the heads of a few philosophers. Philosophy is at this day popular. Fifty years of liberty of thought, of speech, and writing, have produced their result—books, journals, the tribunes, have operated as apostleship of European intelligence. Reason beaming everywhere beyond the frontier of nations has created amongst minds this grand intellectual nationality, which will be the finishing work of the French Revolution, and the constitution of international fraternity upon the globe.

" In fine, in 1792 liberty was a novelty, equality was a scandal, the Republic was a problem. The title of the people, hardly discovered by Fénélon, Montesquieu, Rousseau, was so forgotten, buried, profaned by old feudal, dynastic, and sacerdotal traditions, that the most legitimate intervention of the people in their own affairs looked a monstrosity in the eyes of statesmen of the old school. Democracy caused thrones and the foundation of society to tremble alike. At this day, both thrones and people are alike accustomed to the word, the forms, the regular agitations of liberty, exercised in different proportions, in nearly all states, even the monarchical. They will habituate themselves to the Republic, which is its perfect form among mature nations. They will recognise that there is a conservative liberty ; they will recognise that there may be in a republic not only a better order, but that there may be more real order in this government of all, for all, than in the government of some for some.

" But, apart from these disinterested considerations, the sole interest of consolidation and of duration of the Republic will inspire the statesmen of France with thoughts of peace. It is not the country alone that incurs the greatest dangers in war—it is liberty. War is always a dictatorship. Soldiers forget the institutions for the men. Thrones tempt the ambitious.

Glory dazzles patriotism. The prestige of a victorious name veils the design against the national sovereignty. The Republic desires glory undoubtedly, but for its own sake, and not for the sake of Cæsars and Napoleons.

"Do not deceive yourselves for all that; these ideas that the Provisional Government commission you to represent to the powers as a gauge of European security are not intended to ask pardon for the Republic for her boldness in coming to life; less again to humbly demand the place of a great right and of a great people in Europe. They have a more noble object—to cause sovereigns and people to reflect—not to allow themselves to fall into involuntary mistakes upon the character of our Revolution—to give its true light and just physiognomy to the event; to give, in fine, guarantees to humanity before giving them to our rights and to our honour if they be slighted or menaced.

"The French Republic will not then provoke war against any one. She need not say that she will accept it, if the conditions of war be laid down to the French people. The feeling of the men who govern France at this moment is this; happy France, if war be declared against her, and if she be thus constrained to increase in power and glory despite of moderation! terrible responsibility to France, if the Republic herself declares war, without being provoked to it. In the first case her martial genius, her impatient desire of action, her power accumulated during so many years of peace, would render her invincible at home; redoubtable, perhaps, beyond her frontiers. In the second case she would turn against her the recollection of her conquests, which disaffect nationalities, and she would compromise her first and most universal alliance; the mind of nations and the genius of civilisation.

"According to these principles, Monsieur, which are the coolly-adopted principles of France—principles which she can present without fear, as without defiance, to her friends and to her enemies—you would do well to ponder over the following declarations :—

"The treaties of 1815 exist no longer as a right in the eyes of the French Republic; however, the territorial limits of these treaties are a fact which she admits as bases and starting-points in her relations with other nations.

"But if the treaties of 1815 only exist as facts to be modified by common consent, and if the Republic declares aloud that she has for right and for mission to arrive regularly and pacifically at these modifications, the good sense, the moderation, the conscience, the prudence of the Republic exist, and are for Europe a better and more honourable guarantee than the letters of these treaties, so often violated or modified.

"Endeavour, Monsieur, to cause to be comprehended and admitted candidly this emancipation of the Republic from the treaties of 1815, and to shew that this frankness is by no means irreconcileable with the repose of Europe.

"Thus we say it openly; if the hour for the reconstruction of some oppressed nationalities in Europe or elsewhere appear to us to be announced in the decrees of Providence—if Switzerland, our faithful ally, was constrained or menaced in the movement of growth that she is effecting within herself to lend an additional force to the aggregate of Democratic Governments—if the independent states of Italy were invaded—if limits or obstacles were imposed upon their internal transformations—if, by force of arms, their right should be disputed of forming alliances among themselves for the consolidation of an Italian country, the French Republic would believe herself authorised to arm for the protection of these legitimate movements of the growth and nationality of those people.

" The Republic, you see, has at her first step bounded over the era of proscriptions and dictatorships. She is decided never to veil liberty at home; she is equally decided never to veil her democratic principles abroad; she will never permit the hand of any one to intrude between the pacific beam of her freedom and the vision of nations; she proclaims herself the intellectual and cordial ally of all rights, of all progress, of all the legitimate developements of the institutions of nations who desire to live on the same principles as her own; she will make no underhand or incendiary propagandism among her neighbours; she knows that there are no durable liberties but those that spring from themselves upon their proper soil: but she will exercise by the light of her ideas, by the spectacle of order and of peace, that she hopes to give to the world the sober and honest proselytism—the proselytism of esteem and of sympathy. It is not war—it is nature. It is not the agitation of Europe—it is the life. It is not to inflame the world—it is to shine from her place upon the horizon of nations—to advance and to guide them at once.

" We desire for humanity's sake that peace may be preserved. We even hope it. A sole question of war had been laid down a year ago between France and England.

" This question of war, it was not Republican France that laid it down, it was the dynasty. The dynasty carries with it this danger of war, that she had raised for Europe, by an ambition altogether personal of family alliances in Spain. Thus this domestic policy of the fallen dynasty, which weighed for seventeen years upon our national dignity, weighed at the same time, by its pretensions to another crown at Madrid, upon our liberal alliances and upon peace. The Republic has no ambition. The Republic has no nepotism. It does not inherit family pretensions. Let Spain rule herself; let Spain be independent and free. France counts more for the solidity of this natural alliance, upon conformity of principles, than upon the succession of the House of Bourbon.

" Such, Monsieur, is the spirit of the councils of the Republic.   Such
will invariably be the character of the frank, strong, and liberal policy that
you will have to represent.

" The Republic, at the moment of its birth, and in the midst of
the heat of a contest not provoked by the people, have pronounced three
words which have revealed its soul, and which will call down upon its
cradle the benediction of God and of men—Liberty, Equality, Fraternity.
She immediately gave, by the abolition of the penalty of death for political
offences, the true commentary of these three words at home : give to them
also their true commentary abroad.   The sense of these three words,
applied to our foreign relations, is this—enfranchisement of France from
the chains which have weighed upon her principles and her dignity—restoration of the rank which she sought to occupy on a level with the great
European powers—in fine, declaration of alliance and friendship with all
people.

" If France has the consciousness of her part of the liberal and civil-
ising mission in the age, there is not one of those words signifying *war*.   If
Europe be prudent and just, each of these words signifies *peace*.

" Receive, Monsieur, the assurance of most distinguished consideration.

" LAMARTINE,
" Member of the Provisional Government, and
Minister for Foreign Affairs."

The effect of this eloquent, temperate, and dignified state
paper was generally to produce a feeling of confidence in the
stability of peace on the Continent.   Some supersubtle critics
were pleased, however, to consider the document as am-
biguous in tone ; and Austria, especially, took umbrage at
the paragraph expressive of sympathy with " oppressed nationalities."   The red-tape school of politicians were shocked
by the violation of diplomatic propriety displayed in the
announcement that " the treaties of 1815 exist no longer as
a right in the eyes of the French Republic," only the territorial limits fixed by those treaties " are a fact which she
admits as bases and starting-points in her relations with other
nations."   Now France had a perfect right to regard the
Treaty of Vienna as null and void, and in submitting to be
bound provisionally by its territorial arrangements she gave
proof of very commendable moderation.   The principle laid
down by Lamartine had been pointedly expressed more than

a year previously by Lord Palmerston, in his speech on the extinction of the independence of Cracow, when he made the memorable declaration, that " If the Treaty of Vienna is void on the banks of the Vistula, it must be equally void on the banks of the Rhine or the Po." But it was not left for France to give effect to that equitable verdict; that has been accomplished by the force of events in which she has had no participation, except in the way of example. As to the perfect good faith with which Lamartine pledged himself, in the name of France, to abstain from every act of aggression, every undue interference with the internal affairs of other states, all doubts on this subject were completely extinguished by his replies to the various deputations of foreigners who sought the aid of the French Republic in their projected attempts to revolutionise their own respective countries.

When the deputation of the Poles waited on the Government on March 26, M. Godebski, one of the members of the deputation, expressed himself in the following terms:—

" Poland, citizens, casts off her blood-stained shroud, and her exiled sons come to offer through you their thanks to France for the hospitality they have received from her in their days of misfortune. We doubt not, citizens, that, at this supreme moment, you will know how to reconcile the imperious exigencies of the national sentiment with the difficulties of your position. After so many cruel deceptions, the hour is now come when Poland may decide her own fate by her own hand. It is to concur in this work that we are about to march, and we believe that we have a right to hope that you will aid us to perform our duty as soldiers. We rely upon you, citizens, because we consider you as the true representatives of the French people, who are our brothers. *Vive la République Française! Vive la République Polonaise !*"

M. de Lamartine replied:—

" Citizens of Poland !—The French Republic receives as a happy omen the homage of your adhesion and of your acknowledgment of its hospitality. I have no need to express to you its sentiments towards the sons of Poland. The voice of France has annually declared them to you, even when the monarchy endeavoured to suppress it. The voice and gesture of the Republic are still more sympathetic, and it repeats its fraternal sentiments towards you. You will find them in every instance compatible with the justice, moderation, and peace which she has proclaimed to all the world. Yes, since your last disasters, since the day when the sword effaced from the map of nations the last vestige of the existence of Poland, she has not only been the reproach, but a living cause of remorse in the heart of Europe. France owes you not only her best wishes and her tears, she owes you a moral and eventual support, in return, brave Poles, for that blood which you have shed for her on all the fields of battle in Europe. Be assured that France will repay you all that she owes to you. Only, you must leave to her that which she alone can appoint—the hour, the moment, the mode for giving to you, without aggression, without effusion of blood, the place which is due to you in the list of nations. I will make known to you, if you know them not already, the principles which the Provisional Government has adopted invariably for its foreign policy. France is undoubtedly Republican. She proclaims this to the world. But the Republic is not at war, either openly or secretly, with any of the existing nations or governments, as long as those nations and governments refrain from making war upon it. It will not, therefore, voluntarily commit, or suffer to be committed, any act of aggression or violence upon the Germanic nations. They are at this moment labouring to modify by themselves their own internal system of confederation. It would be insensate or treacherous to the freedom of the world to disturb and derange their labours by demonstrations of war, and thus turn into hostility and hatred that pure disposition to promote liberty which makes them incline, with all the best feelings of their hearts, towards us and towards you. And at what a moment have you come to us to require us to commit this contravention against all good policy and liberty? Is the treaty of Pilnitz being brought into action against us? Is there a coalition of absolute sovereigns assembled in arms upon our frontiers or upon yours? No! Every courier brings us victorious acclamations of people, which strengthen our cause precisely for the reason that we have declared its principle to be respect for the rights, the wills, forms of government, and the territories of all nations and people! Are the results of the external policy of the Provisional Government so bad that it must be forced to change it, and march to the frontiers of its neighbours, bayonet in hand, instead of presenting it as the harbinger of liberty and peace? No! The firm and pacific policy of the Republic succeeds too well for us to wish to alter it until the hour comes when we may be forced to change it to other powers. Look at Belgium — Switzerland— Italy—all Southern Germany! Turn your eyes towards Vienna and Berlin! What more is necessary? Even the possessors of your own land open to you a path to your country, and call upon you to come and re-establish it in peace! Be not unjust either towards God, towards the Republic, or towards yourselves! The sympathising States of Germany, the King of Prussia, are opening the doors of their

citadels to your martyrs ; the gates of Poland are open ; Cracow is enfranchised ; the Grand Duchy of Posen has again become Polish. These are
the arms which we have given you in one month! Do not demand any
more from us. The Provisional Government will not allow its policy to
be changed in favour of any foreign people, however much we may in our
hearts sympathise with it. We love Poland, but we love France better
than all the rest of the earth. At this moment we have in our hands her
future destiny, and perhaps that of Europe. This is a responsibility which
we will relinquish to none but our own nation. Trust, therefore, in her—
trust in what has passed in the last thirty days, which have gained more
ground for the democracy of France than thirty pitched battles. Do not,
therefore, either by arms or by agitation, disturb the great work which
Providence is accomplishing, with no other weapons than ideas, for the
regeneration and fraternity of all mankind ! ''

M. Godebski expressed the warmest gratitude for these
sentiments, but added,—

'' Now that the flag of Poland is waving over the tombs of the ancient
sovereigns of her republic, the impatience of the Polish emigrants must be
easily conceived. This impatience is a duty which does not permit us to
remain inactive, and view our brethren from afar, again rising, again entering into new battles, again, perhaps, making themselves martyrs, while
we remain in all the enjoyment of your hospitality. We hold ourselves
bound in duty to endeavour to procure the means of accomplishing our
holy mission. It is for you in your wisdom to consider the manner in
which you can comply with our wishes.''

M. de Lamartine replied :—

'' You have spoken admirably as a Pole. Our duty is to speak to you
as Frenchmen. As Poles you are justly eager to fly to the land of your
fathers, answering the appeal to her noble children from a part of Poland
restored to liberty. To this feeling we can only give our applause, and
furnish such pacific means as may assist you in returning to your country,
and enjoy at Posen the commencement of its independence. We, as
Frenchmen, have not only to consider Poland, but the universal policy of
Europe. The vast importance of these interests prevents the Provisional
Government of the Republic from abdicating in favour of any partial
nationality, any portion of a nation, however sacred may be the cause it
maintains, the responsibility and freedom of its resolutions. The Republic
cannot, will not, act in contradiction to its words. What has it said in its
manifesto to the powers of Europe? Referring to you it said, When it
shall appear to us that the hour is struck for the resurrection of a nationality unjustly effaced from the map, we fly to its succour. But we right-

fully reserved to France to recognise the hour, the justice of the cause, and the most fitting mode of intervention. Hitherto we have chosen and resolved upon pacific means. If you do not find that these pacific means have availed us, you deceive yourselves. In thirty-one days the natural results of this system of peace and fraternity have been more valuable to the cause of France and liberty, and of Poland herself, than ten battles with torrents of blood. Vienna, Berlin, Italy, Milan, Genoa, Southern Germany, Munich, all these constitutions,—all these unprovoked, spontaneous explosions from the souls of the people—your own frontiers, in fine, opened to your steps through the acclamations of Germany, are the advances made by the Republic, thanks to its system of respect for the liberty of the soil and the blood of men. We will not retrograde by adopting any other system. Do not, therefore, attempt to divert us in any way from it, even by the influence of that paternal sentiment which brings you to us this day ; leave us to the free exercise of our minds, being assured that we can never entertain an idea of separating two people whose blood has so often been mingled together on the field of battle. Our solicitude for your future well-being shall be as great as our hospitality, as wide as our frontiers. Our anxiety shall follow you into your country. Carry with you that hope of regeneration which has had its commencement for you in Prussia, even where your flag is now floating at Berlin. France requires no other compensation for the asylum she has afforded you than amelioration in your national destinies, and the remembrance of the French name, which you will carry with you. Never forget that it is to the Republic you owe the first step you are about to take towards your own country.''

A Pole came forward and said,—'' We will take our departure, and go without arms.''   Another Pole took M. Lamartine by the hand, and begged his pardon for some strong expressions which had escaped from him on the preceding day in the warmth of his patriotic feeling. M. Lamartine cordially returned the pressure, and said,—'' Let not a word more be said of this. Patriotism always carries with it its own justification. I shall never recollect the expressions in question, and France will never recollect anything but her love for Poland.'' The deputation withdrew amidst cries of *Vive la République !*

A very numerous deputation of the Italian Association went on the 27th of March to the Hôtel de Ville. M. Mazzini, the president, read an address expressing their sympathy

for the Provisional Government, and announcing that the
Association had been definitively constituted. The object of
the Association was the political unity of the Peninsula, the
complete emancipation from the sea to the Alps of that land,
the foundation of a compact and strong nationality, which
might, for the welfare of the world, take rank in the confederation of nations, and bring to the common task the inspiration and sincere devotedness, the thought and action, of
twenty-four millions of free men, brethren, and associated in
one single national belief, "God and the people"— in one
single international belief, "God and humanity." Italy, he
said, from the earliest up to the latest times, had declared
such to be her belief, and that her national tradition was
Unity and Liberty.   M. Lamartine replied as follows :—

"Citizens of the National Association for the Regeneration of Italy,
citizens, I believe, of all parts of Italy (Yes ! yes ! of all Italy !)—It is to
me one of the happiest days of this young Republic,—it is to me one of the
most glorious functions which the Provisional Government could confer
on me, to receive the adhesion which you are kind enough to offer, at this
moment, to its principles and acts.   And I also, I venture to say, am a
son of adoption of your dear Italy. (Loud acclamations, and cries of
Vive Lamartine !)   I venture to say, and I repeat it with glory and
with love, that I am an adopted child of that great country. (Renewed
acclamations.) Your sun warmed my youth, and almost my infancy.
Your genius has coloured my poor imagination,— your liberty, your independence,—the day that I see arise, at length, has been for me, your
friend, as for you, the most beautiful dream of my ripe life. (Bravo,
bravo ! Long live France and Italy regenerated !) You must feel by
these words how much I am delighted at the honour of being called by
Providence to see realised here by the contract of these two great nationalities, which have no longer to combat each other, which have only to
love and strengthen one another, to defend one another, that dream of
patriotic hearts, which I do not doubt will become in a few months the
most unexpected of all realities. (Bravo !) The Republic, as you will
readily believe, has not displaced Italy in my heart; I called her not long
ago at the tribune, not the Queen of Nations, but the Queen of Human
Races. She has only to resume her place, and the universe will recognise that intellectual royalty of Italian genius which she consecrated in
other centuries. The Provisional Government does not feel surprised at
this proceeding of the Italians, who are united in such great numbers

around this palace of the people. Your cause is ours, and you have admirably enumerated your titles to that cause ; but those titles need not be
recalled to human kind—they are written in ineffaceable characters by
your magnificent ruins, by your imperishable monuments on your soil ;
they are also eternally written in your hearts, and that is why no tyranny
can efface them, if they should revive in the future. (Bravo, bravo !)
Amongst those titles you just now cited, perhaps the most glorious, the
most imperishable of all—the name of those great men, which, in all ages,
rendered the soil of Italy illustrious ; so long as those titles of nations
have not been, so to speak, countersigned by immortal names, they have
not the seal of time, they are not graven so deep, so strikingly, in history.
Amongst the glorious names which you have mentioned there is one alone
which I reproach you with having called to mind, in consequence of the.
signification which is commonly attached to the name of Machiavel. (Cries
of Yes, yes, he is out of place.)   Efface henceforth that name from
your titles of glory, and substitute for it the pure name of Washington ;
that is the one which should now be proclaimed ; that is the name of
modern liberty.   It is no longer the name of a politician or of a conqueror
that is required, it is that of a man the most disinterested, the most devoted to the people. That is the man required by liberty. (Cries of,
Yes, yes ! Bravo, bravo !)   The want of the age is an European
Washington ; that of the people, peace and liberty. (Loud acclamations.)
I shall not enter with you into any of the details of the different political
questions which your national meeting will discuss in the plenitude of its
free will, and freed from any international influence. We have proclaimed
the dogma of respect for nationalities, governments, and people ; we shall
never contradict this dogma, which is as respectful for the people and the
governors as for ourselves.   The independence of nations in the choice of
the international *régime*, which is best suited to them, is the standard of
the French Republic. We wish it to wave on both sides of the Alps and
the Pyrenees, and on both banks of the Rhine. Neither fear, nor complaisance, nor even a feeling of predilection, shall make us swerve from
this principle. It is that of the dignity of the people, and of the security
of the governing powers in their relations with us.   But I reproach
myself with having detained you so long. (Cries of No, no !) You
must excuse me, for I see a brother in every son of the Italian family.
(Applause.)   These are, doubtless, adieux which I offer to you in the
name of France. You hear your brethren of Naples, of Turin, of
Rome, of Florence, of Genoa, call on you. You doubtless go to join
them, and to strengthen them by your co-operation in that pacific
and, I hope, already accomplished work, of forming new constitutions suited to the wants and interests of the different governments and
states of Italy. (Cries of Yes, we are all going there !) Since France

and Italy only make a single name in our common sentiments for her liberal regeneration, go, and tell Italy that she also has children on this side of the Alps. (Hear, hear.) Go, and tell her that if she is attacked in her soil or her sentiments, in her limits or her liberties, that if your arms are not sufficient to defend her, it is no longer wishes merely, it is the sword of France that we shall offer to preserve her from all encroachment! (Great applause.) And do not, citizens of free Italy, be disquieted or humiliated by that word. Time has enlightened France, given her in reason, wisdom, and moderation, what formerly she had in impatient longing after victory, and in thirst of conquest. We want no more conquests but with you and for you. We want only the peaceful conquest of the human mind. We have no longer any ambition, except for ideas. We are sufficiently reasonable and sufficiently generous at present to correct ourselves even of a vain love of glory. Our love for Italy is disinterested, and we have no other ambition but to see her as imperishable and as great as the soil which she has rendered eternal by her name."

Loud cries of *Vive Lamartine! Vive le Gouvernement Provisoire! Vive la République!* followed this address. M. Mazzini replied in terms of acknowledgment, declaring his joy that Italy was at last breaking her chains, and expressing a hope that she would be able to suffice for herself. After some words in reply from M. de Lamartine, the deputation withdrew.

The answer given by Lamartine to the envoys from the Irish Confederation was even more impressive (more explicit it could hardly be) than his replies to the Poles and the Italians. After some graceful expressions of sympathy with the Irish people, he addressed himself as follows to the Irishmen's request for support in their intended rebellion :—

" We are at peace, and we are desirous of remaining on good terms of equality, not with this or that part of Great Britain, but with Great Britain entire. We believe this peace to be useful and honourable, not only to Great Britain and the French Republic, but to the human race. We will not commit an act—we will not utter a word—we will not breathe an insinuation at variance with the principles of the reciprocal inviolability of nations which we have proclaimed, and of which the continent of Europe is already gathering the fruits. The fallen monarchy had treaties and diplomatists. Our diplomatists are nations—our treaties are sympathies! We should be insane were we openly to exchange such a diplomacy for

o

unmeaning and partial alliances with even the most legitimate parties in the countries which surround us.   We are not competent either to judge them or to prefer some of them to others; by announcing our partizan-ship of the one side, we should declare ourselves the enemies of the other. We do not wish to be the enemies of any of your fellow-countrymen. We wish, on the contrary, by a faithful observance of the Republican pledges, to remove all the prejudices which may mutually exist between our neighbours and ourselves.

" This course, however painful it may be, is imposed on us by the law of nations as well as by our historical remembrances.

" Do you know what it was which most served to irritate France and estrange her from England during the first republic ?   It was the civil war in a portion of our territory, supported, subsidised, and assisted by Mr. Pitt.   It was the encouragement and the arms given to Frenchmen, as heroical as yourselves, but Frenchmen fighting against their fellow-citizens.   This was not honourable warfare.   It was a Royalist propa-gandism waged with French blood against the Republic.   This policy is not yet, in spite of all our efforts, entirely effaced from the memory of the nation.   Well, this cause of dissension between Great Britain and us we will never renew by taking any similar course.   We accept with gratitude expressions of friendship from the different nationalities included in the British empire.   We ardently wish that justice may found and strengthen the friendship of races ; that equality may become more and more its basis : but while proclaiming with you, with her (England), and with all, the holy dogma of fraternity, we will perform only acts of brotherhood in conformity with our principles, and our feeling towards the Irish nation."

Similar in tenour with the foregoing declarations were Lamartine's replies to the Belgians, the Germans, and the Savoyards.   In no instance did he stoop to the arts of the vulgar demagogue, or selfishly catch at a spurious popularity by flattering the worst prejudices and propensities of his countrymen.   Truly has it been said of him that " his words, as a public man, have been as reserved as disinterested, and as noble as private and chivalric honour would dictate."   And his acts were strictly consistent with his words.   He lent no furtive support to those to whom he refused open aid ; on the contrary, he gave timely notice to every neighbouring state whenever a movement was directed from France against its frontiers.   Had he done less, he would have been false to the

LEDRU ROLLIN.

LOUIS BLANC.

principle of strict neutrality which he professed. Some of his colleagues were less scrupulous. A band of marauders, who made an unsuccessful incursion into Belgium, were furnished with arms and ammunition from the Government stores at Lille. The responsibility of this and other similar acts of perfidy rests alone with Ledru Rollin, the Minister of the Interior. To this man and his confederate, Ferdinand Flocon, with Louis Blanc, and Albert " the workman" (who is not a journeyman but a capitalist), are chiefly ascribable all those disasters in the early history of the Republic, which were not the inevitable result of circumstances beyond the control of human prudence. The principle of the first two was terrorism (the modified terrorism of an age averse to bloodshed), and, in the name of liberty, they demanded of all France implicit obedience to their own despotic will! In the name of liberty, they seized upon the very engine which had been constructed and used for the enslavement of France, and which could serve no other purpose; they augmented the machinery of centralisation, and worked it as unsparingly, as wickedly, and with as bad effect, as ever their Doctrinaire predecessors had done. Blanc and Albert pursued their impracticable schemes with more subtlety, with less personal obtrusiveness, and a [less glaring display of fraud and violence, but the political tendency of their theories was nearly the same. They, too, aimed at extinguishing the free action of each man's individual nature : in their Utopia there was to be no such thing as personal freedom, but all men were to be passive members of a vast corporation, moved only by the will of one abstract being, the State.

Louis Blanc, as the ablest and most enterprising of the minority, was the most dangerous of the four, until he was self-disarmed by the total failure of his experiment, made with the whole power of the state at his command. The personal characteristics of this acute and eloquent apostle of unreason are as singular as his doctrines. His figure is that of a boy of twelve, while his limbs and face are undeveloped and childish, and his voice possesses that falsetto squeak which usually marks the age of transition from boyhood to adolescence.   These peculiarities place him at an immense disadvantage as a public speaker, and yet such is his eloquence, his lucidity, and fine conception, that his harangues are generally listened to with pleasure.   On one occasion, when he went out with the other members of the Provisional Government to talk familiarly with the crowd assembled round the Hôtel de Ville, an ardent admirer caught him up in his brawny arms, and held him aloft, that his little figure might be visible above the heads of the throng.   It is probable that Louis Blanc was more mortified than pleased by such an evidence of his popularity.   His whole life has been one constant struggle between the pride of conscious talent and the humiliation caused by the defects of his person.

Louis Blanc, born in Madrid in 1813, is come of the best blood of Corsica—his mother being own sister to Count Pozzo di Borgo, the celebrated diplomatist.   He was remarkable at college for his great natural talents and perseverance in study; and from its having become a thing understood in the family that he was to pursue the same career for which his uncle had obtained so much power and influence, his attention had been early directed to the study of history and the art of government.   Few men in Europe possess a greater book-knowledge of foreign policy than Louis Blanc, and had he chosen to follow the profession of diplomacy he would doubtless have risen to eminence and distinction.   He had already experienced much suffering at college from the mockery of his fellow-students, to whom his dwarfish figure and childish appearance were of course a fruitful theme of epigram and insult.   It is not in the nature of his countrymen to make any display of passion or hatred, and so the young student bore the ridicule in silence, kept aloof from his comrades, and lived the life of a hermit, amply consoled for present suffering by the reflection of the future fame which his unceasing application to study would enable him to acquire in the diplomatic world, in which it was agreed that he was to make his *début* as Secretary to his cousin, Count Charles Pozzo di Borgo, who was then applying for the Brussels legation.

It was thus, invested with the style and title of *Secrétaire d'Ambassade*, that Louis Blanc first appeared upon the stage of public life, by attending one of the far-famed diplomatic *soirées* of the Duchess de Dino, whose influence in the great world of Paris was at that time undivided and undisputed. The report both of the talents and pretensions of the young *diplomate* had, of course, reached the *coterie* over which presided the Duchess, and excited therein various sentiments—some of interest, others of envy; and his appearance was looked for with some little degree of curiosity. He was presented by the veteran Pozzo himself, and on the announcement of that well-known name, all eyes were turned to the door, and wandered from the tall and portly person of the old Ambassador to the diminutive figure beside him, in so much amazement that a murmur escaped from the usually well-bred crowd —whether of surprise or mockery, it would have been impossible to decide. Louis Blanc bore the impertinent scrutiny of which he had become the object with ill-disguised impatience, and by the time he had reached the head of the room, where reclined in languid state the fair hostess, his temper had waxed rather warm. "Permit me to introduce to your notice my nephew," said the old Count, bowing with courtier-like dignity to the Duchess, who—perhaps still under the impression of some incomparably witty saying which had just reached her ear, concerning the poor little diplomatist,— raised herself, with a languid air, from the sofa, and, gazing vacantly over the shoulder of the Count, exclaimed, in a tone of sweet bewilderment, "*Where* is he?—I should like to see him!"

This direct criticism upon the almost invisible proportions of her visitor, caused a titter to run through the assembly;

and many and many a compliment, no doubt, did it procure
for the lovely lips which had uttered it so boldly.   But the
Corsican blood of Louis Blanc, to this very hour, has forbidden forgiveness of the cruel insult.   From that moment
did he eschew all idea of a career to be pursued amid the
heartlessness of a court, and of success to be obtained only by
the sacrifice of his personal dignity.   He declared to his
uncle that very night, that he had resigned all pretensions to
the appointment which he had been at so much pains to
obtain for him ; and when the old man, although readily guess-
ing at the cause of his disgust, ventured to remonstrate and
to propose other posts of importance to his notice, Louis
answered bitterly, that feeling that he had no right to intrude
himself amongst the more favoured, he had resolved upon
turning his attention to the service óf those to whom such
service might be of value.   The result of this unfortunate
soirée may be traced in every line of his book, " The History of Ten Years."   Louis Philippe has often been heard to
declare that those volumes had acted as a battering-ram to
the bulwarks of royalty in France ; if so, the Duchess de
Dino and her bevy of *attachés* have much to answer for.

The humble employment of a clerk in a notary's office
was the first resource that offered itself to the poor, insulted
man of genius.   He afterwards found more congenial occupation as tutor in a private family, and then we find him making
his way to the highest eminence among the journalists of
Paris, and winning renown and influence by his " History of
Ten Years," his " Organisation of Labour," and other works,
which have had an immense circulation.   Meanwhile he led
a solitary life, nurturing the mighty ambition that swelled
within his pigmy frame, and urging himself to the pursuit of
a visionary philanthropy by the morbid stimulus he derived
from pondering over the sufferings and indignities he had
himself endured.   At last the secluded theorist was hailed by
the acclamations of the forum as the lawgiver from whose

lips industrial France awaited her new code of laws, and on the 20th of March he announced the following as the Government plan for organising labour :—

" The Government would take into their own hands such ateliers as the proprietors chose to dispose of, for an indemnity payable out of the future resources of the State. The workmen in these ateliers would receive *equal wages*. The Government would rely on the *point of honour* instead of competition to ensure hard work. Idleness, under these regulations, would soon become as disgraceful among workmen, as cowardice among soldiers. The profits, after reserving the sum requisite to pay the interest of the capital, the wages of the men, and the repairs of the machinery, will be divided into four parts:

" One fourth for the amortissement of the capital.

" One fourth as a fund for the old, the wounded, and the sick.

" One fourth to be divided among the workmen.

" One fourth as a reserve fund.

" These Government institutions would exist as models, in competition with the private ateliers, which would not be suppressed or interfered with. The Government would rely on the superior advantages of their system to procure its universal adoption."

The majority of the workmen themselves were among the first to declare their strong disapprobation of this perverse scheme, which, after all, was but a fragment of a larger system — a first step towards a great measure for extinguishing both the rights and the existence of private property, and totally subverting the immutable principles of human nature. The whole system is thus summed up by its author himself, in the concluding chapter of his "Organisation du Travail:"—

" The Government would be regarded as the supreme regulator of production, and invested, for the accomplishment of its task, with powers of the largest kind.

" This task would lie in making use of the arm of competition itself, to effect the abolition of competition.

" The Government would raise a loan, to be employed in the creation of *social workshops* in all the most important branches of the national industry.

" As such a creation could be effected only at a considerable cost, the number of original workshops would be rigidly limited; but, in virtue of their very organisation, these would be endowed with an enormously expansive force.

" The Government being considered the only founder of the social workshops, the statutes regulating these would be framed by it. This code, deliberated on and voted by the representatives of the nation, should have the form and force of law.

" All workmen provided with guarantees of their moral character should be invited to work in the *social workshops*, in competition for the capital first of all collected for the purchase of the implements of labour.

" Although the lying and anti-social education given to the present generation makes it difficult to seek any motive of emulation and encouragement other than an increased recompense, the wages should be equal —an altogether new education being destined to effect, in this respect, a change of ideas and customs.

" For the first year after the establishment of the social workshops, the Government would regulate the appointment and tenure of the office-bearers (*hierarchie des fonctions* — hierarchy of functions). After the first year, this would no longer be the case. The workers, having had time to appreciate each other's merits, and being all equally interested, as will be shewn immediately, in the success of the association, the appointment of office-bearers would be determined by election.

" Every year an estimate would be made of the net profits, which should be divided into three parts : one of these would be distributed equally among the members of the association; the other would be employed, first, in the maintenance of the aged, sick, and infirm—second, in alleviation of the crisis weighing on other branches of industry, since all of these owe each other aid and succour; the third, finally, would be devoted to the purchase of implements of labour for persons desirous of being admitted into the association, so that this might extend itself indefinitely.

" Into each of these associations, formed for such branches of industry as are practised on a great scale, might be admitted persons belonging to those professions which their very nature forces to scatter themselves over different localities ; so that, in this way, each social workshop might be composed of different professions, all grouped round one great branch of industry—all different parts of one and the same whole—obeying the same laws, and participating in the same advantages.

" Each member of the social workshop would be entitled to dispose of his wages according to his own choice ; but the evident economy and incontestible excellence of living in common would not be long in educing from the association of labour the voluntary association of wants and enjoyments.

" The capitalist would be a member of the association, and would receive interest for the capital furnished by him, which interest would be guaranteed him in the budget; but it would be only as a labourer, like the rest, that he would have a right to share in the profits.

" The social workshop once established in conformity with these principles, it is easy to understand its results. In every chief branch of industry (that of machine-making, for instance, or that of silk, or cotton, or printing) there would be a social workshop competing with private industry. Would the contest be a long one? No; because the social workshop would possess over the private workshop the advantage result-ing from the economy of living together, and from a mode of organisation in which all the workers, without exception, are interested in producing swiftly and well. Would the contest be a destructive one? No; because the Government would always be able to check its effects, by preventing the products of its workshops from sinking to too low a price. At present, whenever a very wealthy individual enters the lists with others who are less so, this unequal contest cannot fail to be disastrous, seeing that a private individual looks only to his own personal interests: if he can sell twice as cheaply as his competitors, to ruin them and remain master of the field, he does it. But when, in the room of this private individual, you substitute the state, the question assumes quite a different aspect.

" Will the state, such as we wish it to be, have any interest in over-throwing industry, in convulsing the general existence? Will it not be, from its nature and its position, the born protector, even of those with whom, in order to metamorphose society, it will be entering into a holy competition? Between the industrial war, therefore, which at present the great capitalist wages against the small, and that which the state, in our system, is to wage against the individual, there is no possible comparison. The former necessarily consecrates fraud, violence, and all the woes en-gendered by injustice; the latter would be conducted without ferocity, without convulsions, and solely in such a way as to attain its aim—the successive and peaceful absorption, namely, of the private by the social workshops. Thus, instead of being (what at present every great capitalist is) a master and tyrant of the market, the Government would be its regu-lator; it would make use of competition as a weapon, not violently to overturn private industry—a result it would be pre-eminently interested in avoiding—but to bring it, insensibly, to terms. Soon, in reality, in every sphere of industry where a social workshop had been established, we should see capitalists and labourers hastening towards this workshop, from the advantages it would hold out to its members. At the end of a certain time—without usurpation, without injustice, without irreparable disasters, and to the gain of the principle of association—we should see presented to us that phenomenon which at present operates so deplorably, and by a despotic power, to the gain of individual egotism. At present a very wealthy producer can, by aiming one great blow at his rivals, leave them

dead upon the field, and monopolise a whole branch of industry.   In our
system the state would, little by little, make itself the master of industry ;
and, instead of monopoly, we should have obtained, as the result of our
success, that victory over competition — association.   Let us suppose our
aim attained in any one branch of industry — let us suppose the machine-
makers, for example, brought to enter the service of the state, that is to
say, to submit themselves to the principles of the general scheme,—as one
and the same branch of industry is not always practised on the same spot,
and as it has different seats, there would be room to establish between all
the workshops belonging to the same branch of industry the system of
association within each particular workshop ; for it would be absurd to
allow the existence of competition among corporations, after having annihilated it among individuals.   There would then be, in each sphere of
labour which the Government had succeeded in conquering, a central
workshop towards which all the others would radiate, as a kind of supple-
mentary workshop," &c. &c.

" If I were allowed," says that able economist, Michel
Chevalier, " to compress this exposition into three lines,' I
would say, that M. Louis Blanc's organisation of labour consists of the following innovations :—1st, The suppression of
competition ; 2d, After a period of transition, perfect equality
for all, without taking into account the skill and activity of
each ; 3d, The abolition of all profits of capital, beyond legal
interest ; 4th, The election, by the rank and file, of the commanding and subaltern officers of the industrial works.

" Speaking from my conscience, I believe that this
abridgment of the system will suffice to enable any one to
pronounce a verdict on it, who has the least knowledge of
what labour in a workshop is, or who knows the composition
of the human heart, and what are the ordinary motives which
guide men in their daily business.

" With this organisation of labour, production would
sensibly slacken.   There would be much fewer products to
distribute, consequently, much more of misery.   The cause
may be easily guessed ; nobody would be directly interested
in making an effort, or be impelled to it by the rivalry of his
neighbour.   M. Louis Blanc believes that the social workshops, thus constituted, would be gifted with an *immense*

expansive force, and that none of the actually existing industrial establishments could maintain a *long contest* with his. I appeal to any one who has had the management of a workshop—I declare myself converted beforehand to the doctrine of M. Louis Blanc, and I pledge myself to become the apostle of his organisation of labour if, among all the inhabitants of Paris who are familiar with industrial occupations, he find three who are of opinion that an establishment thus organised could sustain the competition of others, and go on for three months, without becoming bankrupt.

" A perfect equality of wages, whatever the work done may be, would be the height of injustice. M. Louis Blanc has adopted it because he thinks that the feeling of duty is, in industrial employment, a motive sufficiently strong to stimulate to do much, and to do it well. Here is his fundamental error—an error which does him honour, since he adopted it from his own mind—a mind wholly devoted to the public weal, but an error which surprises us on the part of a man who has so deeply studied history and ethics. Industry, like all the other institutions of society, presupposes, assuredly, the sentiment of duty; but it also presupposes, more rigidly, the sentiment of personal interest. Religion and the laws of polity recommend duty to men, and glorify self-sacrifice. Society would fall into decay, if self-sacrifice and self-denial were not to receive the homage of men.

" Erect your statues to Cincinnatus, offer your palms to martyrs; but do not hope that in the ordinary business of life, in questions of the larder, mankind in the mass will impose on itself the imitation of virtues which have been manifested, on solemn occasions, by the select few,—here in presence of the interests of a fatherland—there before God, beneath the sway of an exalted religious faith. In his daily transactions man follows the bent of his interest. The human heart is made *so*. So much the worse for the human heart, M. Louis Blanc will say. No; it is so much the worse for—your scheme.

" But M. Louis Blanc will retort, You are mistaking my

system ;—*all the employed, without exception, are interested in
producing swiftly and well.*   Yes, certainly, the mass of the
employed, in its indivisible unity, is interested in the abundance of the production—in there being much produced, and
that of good quality ; but no one is individually interested in
being laborious and zealous, for the individual is not allowed
to claim the result accruing from his personal efforts : he
only receives, by way of return, the thousandth or ten-thou-
sandth part of it.   It is just as if he received not a fraction
of it.   This system annihilates the personality of man, and
drowns it in a confused Pantheism.   It does for each of us
what the criminal law does to the convicted felon,—gives
each a number, thus making all of them alike.   Industry lies
within the domain assigned to the feeling of individualism.
The main-spring of production is individual interest excited by
personal rewards, and exhibited in competition, just as capital
forms its wheel-work ; and on that account, in suppressing
individual interest, you disorganise industry, just as you to all
effect destroy a watch when you take away its main-spring.

  " True equality, that proclaimed by our fathers in 1789,
amid the applause of the whole world, has nothing in common with the phantom which you are presenting to the gaze
of the fascinated multitude which is crowding after you.   All
Frenchmen are equal ; that means that the French nation is
one, that public distinctions belong to talent and to services,
without regard to birth.   It signifies that the state owes every
interest an equal support,—that it is bound to protect this
man's fields, that man's dividends, and the labour of another,
who has neither fields nor stock.   The meaning of this fruitful and generous equality is, that through the instruction it
extends, the state ought to prepare every man to be useful to
society and to himself,—and that a vast and liberal system of
national education ought anxiously, in hamlet as in city, beneath thatch and rags as beneath the roof of opulence, to
seek out those superior natures of which society so stands in
need, with the view of developing them and making them

worthy to become the depositaries of the destinies of the country. But to subject to the same material existence all men without exception, from the highest dignitaries of the state to the humblest workman, is one of those chimeras pardonable only in the young collegian whose unsophisticated imagination dreams of the black broth of Sparta, — when out of the college refectory, however, and when his own hunger has been appeased. What! the President of the Republic is to reside, not in the noble palace of the successors of Washington, but in a ticketed chamber, precisely the same as that of the lowest citizen ; he is to eat at the general mess the common rations, and unbend himself from his grave anxieties in the public green, at the same sports as the mob ! When he wishes to meditate on the affairs of his country, he will have around him for inspiration, just like the workman, the household utensils and the squall of children ! Such an equality would be the degradation of all that is noble and pure upon the earth,—would be a shameful promiscuousness !

" This system, for the rest, like many of the ideas now uppermost, is merely a passionate reaction against the in equalities which preceded it. It would be organising the despotism of the ordinary over the superior natures — of egotists, fools, idlers, over the active, the intelligent, and the devoted. To employ an expression consecrated by one of the decrees of the Provisional Government, it would be the *exploitation* of good workmen by bad. It was not for such a result that we made the Revolutions of 1789 and of 1830 ; nor will it be the finale of that of 1848.

" That competition makes commodities cheap is a truth which runs the streets. Well ; what is cheapness of commodities, if not the physical enfranchisement of the poor man ? Competition is the stimulus of industry ; it is through competition that those improvements, so advantageous to the majority, are discovered and propagated. Suppress competition, and torpor succeeds to that ardent activity which characterises modern industry. Competition is the industrial phasis of

liberty,—of that holy liberty with which our fathers were impassioned in 1789 ; which they conquered and made ours by
so many heroic labours, at the cost of so many sacrifices.
Systematically to condemn competition is, therefore, to reject
the immortal principles of 1789 —is to wish that France, beating its breast, should ask pardon of human kind for having
led it into error, and should then set forth to retrace her
steps, with shame upon her brow.   ^

   " But, says M. Louis Blanc, competition is the curse of
society.   According to him, competition is fatal, not only to
the employed, but to the employer ; for M. Louis Blanc is
good enough, in his book, to shew a great deal of anxiety for
the employers of labour.   It is true, indeed, competition has
its abuses.   The arena of competition is sown with ruins.
How many well-founded hopes have been destroyed there !
how often have the prospects of families been there annihilated !   I do not conceal the fact ; I deplore it.   But has not
the career of liberty, too, been covered with wreck and rub-
bish ?   Acts of infamy have sullied its sacred soil ; it has
been drenched with gore. · On it the monstrous *guillotine*
was for a moment inaugurated, sanctified ; for we were told
of the ' holy *guillotine*.'   On it Atheism sat enthroned for
days, and monsters worthy of the execration of mankind
strutted triumphant.   Must we therefore declare Liberty ac-
cursed ?   Why, then, make the principle of competition
responsible for the falsities or the misdeeds which have been,
or are being, accomplished in her name ?

   " All things, the very best of things, and the very noblest
of principles, are liable to abuse.   Yes ; but not the less is it
an abuse of one's own imagination to fancy that it is possible
to arrive at a social organisation in which there shall be practised neither violence nor fraud.   On this earth of ours there
will always be good and bad men.   The great matter is, that
the good should not be systematically sacrificed to the bad ;
that, on the contrary, good shall get the upper hand over evil.
Now, all things considered, this state of things does actually

exist, and exists with considerable emphasis, so long as industry ranges herself beneath the flag of freedom or of competition ; for I cannot repeat it too often, these two are one.
Competition is only the industrial phasis of freedom.   Competition is a goad, incessantly impelling society towards a
state of things in which the quantity of commodities produced will be at last large enough to give to each the share
which the claims of his human nature demand for him.   It
is from the application of this goad that all industrial improvements arise, and the general and absolute character of
every industrial improvement is to multiply the quantity of
products resulting in any one branch of industry.   Sharp,
indeed, is this goad ; and the wounds it gives are sometimes
cruel enough.   It must be considered to what degree it
might be possible to make these sores less painful, without
blunting the good, or suspending its activity night and day,
as a powerful stimulant; but to throw it away altogether, as
proposed by M. Louis Blanc, *that* would simply be decreeing
perpetual wretchedness for the majority of mankind.   *That*
would bring the forward march of industry to a dead halt.

   " Nations or individuals,—none should flatter themselves
that on this earth they will ever have a tent fixed in which
they may take sweet slumbers at their ease, with a ceaseless
accompaniment of smiling dreams.   We are placed here below to struggle, to be tried; and progress is the fruit of
struggle and of trial.   Not only for the advancement, but
for the very existence of society, it is necessary that the social
system be in accordance with the fundamental postulates of
human nature.   The system of M. Louis Blanc ignores these.
Whether he himself respects justice or not, his system violates it.   In a word, in his system, evil triumphs over good,
and extinguishes it.   Beneath the sway of freedom and competition, the result is just the contrary.   It remains only to
be seen if it be not possible still further to diminish the extent of evil by which we see freedom and competition accompanied in our day.

" I have at last, then, arrived at a region in which I may
be on a good understanding with the Socialists in general,
and, perhaps (a thought which gives me great satisfaction),
with M. Louis Blanc himself.   I have insisted on the necessity of preserving competition, for the sake of the future
happiness of the working classes themselves ; but, because a
principle is good, or even excellent, that is no reason why we
should follow it out indefinitely to its furthest consequences
without looking about one.   The men who are at the head of
affairs in a society have to lead to victory several principles,
all equally deserving our respect.   These appear to exclude
each other ; but there is room for each.   Heaven be thanked !
these principles, in appearance mutually exclusive, may be
checked one by another, as, in a piece of mechanism, forces
more or less opposed finally resolve themselves into a single
force,—the harmonious result of all that are acting.   Just as
it is needful to ally with political freedom that principle of
order, without which it would be making, ever and anon,
dangerous starts ; so also may we hope to guard against the
most striking inconveniences of competition, by the intelligent
application of a principle justly lauded in an enthusiastic tone
by all the Socialist schools,—the principle of ASSOCIATION.

" Thus M. Blanc has good reason to recommend to the
working classes, as a means whereby they may enhance the
fruits of their labour, the plan of living together ; this social
organisation, when applied to consumption, is very remarkably productive of economy, and consequently enables the
happiness and pleasures of each member to be increased, the
original fund of resources remaining the same.   By means of
association, the income which was want for the individual
living alone becomes an existence of tolerable comfort.   Nor
is that the only good result which may be expected from the
principle of association.   Even in production, association is
possible ; it is still more desirable in production than in consumption."

CHAPTER IX.

FINANCE.

IT is lamentable to think at what an enormous cost of wealth and human suffering France purchased her knowledge of the futility of Louis Blanc's scheme for the organisation of labour. "La Presse" gives the following calculation of the loss incurred by the depreciation of only two kinds of property, namely, government and railway securities :—

"The depreciation of securities at the Bourse since the 23d February to 12th April, amounts on the funds, the Bank of France, and railways, to the enormous sum of 3,749,060,811f., and there may be added to this more than 1,000,000,000f. for other securities, such as canals, bonds, mines, gas, assurances, &c., the greater part of which have not been quoted for six weeks past.

		Francs.
The 3 per cents, amounting to 68,114,833f., represented on 23d February, at the then price of 74f. 70c., a capital of		1,670,021,959
The 4 per cents, amounting to 26,507,375f., at 99f., a capital of....		656,057,531
The 4½ per cents, amounting to 1,026,000f., at 104, a capital of....		23,725,866
The 5 per cents, amounting to 146,752,528f., at 116·10, a capital of....		3,407,573,700
		5,757,379,056
On 12th April the 3 per cents had fallen to 42·50, representing a capital of ..	964,960,842	
The 4 per cents, to 46, a capital of.....	301,834,962	
The 4½ per cents, to 50, a capital of	11,406,600	
The 5 per cents, to 61, a capital of......	1,190,380,841	
		2,468,533,245
Being a loss of		3,288,795,811

This loss was much greater eight days earlier, since at that time the 3 per cents had fallen to 32, and 5 per cents to 50.

P

	Francs.
The 67,000 Bank Shares were, on 23d Feb., at 3·180 francs, being a total of	223,060,600
On 12th April, at 1·120 francs	76,380,000
Being a loss of	146,680,600

The railways, on 23d Feb., six lines were quoted above par, viz. :—

	Francs.
Orleans, at 1·180 for 80,000 shares, being a capital of....	94,400,000
Rouen, at 858·75 for 72,000 shares, being..............	61,130,000
St. Germain, at 660 for 180,000 shares, being	11,880,000
Marseilles, at 53·250 for 40,000.......................	21,300,000
Vierzon, at 501·25 for 66,000........................	23,182,500
North, at 536·25 for 400,000	114,000,000
	325,892,500

The capital on April 12, was reduced as follows :—

Orleans at 440......................	35,200,000	
Rouen at 305	21,960,000	
St. Germain at 350	6,300,000	
Marseilles at 190	7,600,000	110,640,000
Vierzon at 220	8,580,000	
North at 327·50	31,000,000	
Being a loss of		215,252,500

The other lines were already below par, but the depreciation has, since the 23d, been enormous, and the loss on April 12, as follows :—

							Francs.
Versailles (r. d.)	295	fell to	95	Loss	..		4,400,000
Versailles (r. g.)	195	,,	95	,,	..		2,000,000
Bâle	157 50	,,	77 50	,,	..		6,700,000
Boulogne	360	,,	150	,,	..		15,750,000
Lyons	385	,,	305	,,	..		32,000,000
Bordeaux	475	,,	385	,,	..		11,700,000
Nantes	380	,,	335	,,	..		3,600,000
Strasburg	411 25	,,	340	,,	..		15,312,500
Montereau	237 50	,,	125	,,	..		4,500,000
Dieppe	257 50	,,	125	,,	..		4,770,000
Havre	417 50	,,	170	,,	..		9,900,000
				Loss........			110,632,000

RECAPITULATION.

				Francs.
Funds......loss on				3,285,793,811
Bank Shares ,, ...				146,680,000
Railways ,,	six lines	205,952,500	⎞	316,585,000
,, ,,	eleven lines........	110,632,500	⎠	
	General total			3,749,060,811

GARNIER PAGES.

ARMAND MARRAST.

Before the 23d February eleven lines were below par, having lost 143,347,500f., according to the prices at the Bourse, which brings the total loss on railways to 459,932,500f.

A part of this enormous loss must, of course, be set down simply to the account of the Revolution ; another part is chargeable to the bad political economy of those who expelled the foreign workmen from France ; another to the embarrassments bequeathed to the Republic by the profligate expenditure of the late Government ; Ledru Rollin, his ukases, and his insolent and tyrannous Commissioners, are answerable for a large portion : but after making these and all other due deductions, there will remain a huge balance to be debited against the chief disorganiser of French industry, Louis Blanc.

On the 9th of March, Garnier Pagès (who had shortly before succeeded to the office vacated by M. Goudchaux, being himself succeeded in the mayoralty of Paris by Armand Marrast) made his financial report. On the 1st of January, 1848, the national debt of France, deducting the government stock belonging to the sinking fund, amounted to 207,185,789l. The whole of this burden it was necessary for the Republic to accept, and as the best possible pledge that it would accept it, and of its anxiety to uphold public credit, the Provisional Government commenced paying in advance on the 6th of March, out of the balance they found in the Treasury, the dividends due on the 22d. This measure, although reassuring, did not prevent, as it was hoped it would, the great depreciation of government and railway stock.

The failure of banking-houses holding large securities in railway bonds, was one of the first symptoms of commercial alarm.   But the subject of greatest uneasiness was the deficit of 1847, for which a loan of fourteen millions sterling had been contracted by the fallen Government in November, on which 3,280,000l. only had been paid.   The balance of 10,720,000l. remained to be paid by instalments of 400,000l. per month, and as the loss to the subscribers would be ruinous, the contract price having been 75f. 25c. in the 3 per cents, it became a problem whether even the house of Rothschild, through whom the contract had been taken, would not break down under its responsibility.

To check the run upon the Savings' Banks, the interest allowed the depositors was raised to 5 per cent, but this did not have the effect of quieting their fears. The run continued; and it became necessary to declare the inability of the Government to meet it with any means at their disposal. The property of the depositors, amounting to 14,200,000*l.* was chiefly invested in the funds. To convert this into cash by sales of stock after a fall of 35 per cent, or to obtain the cash by any other mode, was obviously impossible. The Government at once announced the fact. It arranged to pay each depositor 4*l.* in cash, to meet the case of the very poor withdrawing it from actual need, and to pay the surplus in exchequer bills at four and six months' date, and 5 per cent stock at par. This measure, instead of relieving the pressure, aggravated it into panic. The depositors finding that a transfer warrant, given them as 100f., would only sell for 75f. (although they were not obliged to sell it in an unfavourable market), considered themselves robbed. The anxiety to obtain gold or silver to hoard, in the event of worse contingencies, increased on every hand; a run commenced upon all the banks throughout the country, including the Bank of France, which finally (March 15) was obliged to suspend specie payments. The Government then adopted the only course which remained; it issued a decree, authorising the substitution of notes for coin, and declaring the notes of the Bank of France a legal tender. By a subsequent decree, the notes of the banks of Lyons, Marseilles, and seven other provincial towns, were made a legal tender, but for limited amounts, in no case exceeding 1,000,000*l.*

The day after the decree was issued for suspending cash payments, a thousand-franc note was sold for 825 francs. Vast quantities of silver plate were carried to the Mint, and exchanged, by weight, for five-franc pieces. The amount coined in this manner within the month ending March 24, was about 15,000,000 francs. But very little of this appears to have found its way into circulation; the greater part of it was, probably, reserved for future emergencies, being considered as property converted into the most available form. The Government cannot be charged with want of zeal in their efforts to retrieve the financial and commercial affairs of the country, but the mischief done was not to be remedied by any sudden process. So great was the distress of the Treasury, that the Government were compelled to decree an addition of 45 per cent to the direct taxes; but such was the impoverished state of the country, that they found it necessary soon afterwards to declare that those who were unable to pay the extraordinary contribution of 45 centimes, should be exonerated therefrom in an equitable proportion. Week after week the returns of the Bank of France shewed a continuous deterioration in its condition. Within the week ending April 21, the stock of bullion had diminished by 2,000,000 francs; that of the branch banks in similar amount. The overdue bills in the hands of the Bank had been increased by 5,000,000; the sum to the credit of the Treasury had been diminished by 7,000,000; the amount current by 2,000,000; the bank-notes in circulation had increased by 4,000,000. The state of the Treasury was desperate, and it seemed likely that M. Garnier Pagès would soon have to apply to the Bank for another loan of its paper. It was also very probable that the Bank would be forced to suspend its cash payments altogether, and that paper money would shortly be the circulating medium, even for the smallest transactions.

The propounders of the notable scheme for equalising the distribution of wealth, forgot that the really essential thing was, in the very first place, to increase the sum of the national fortunes. They found France a poor country, and they made her incalculably poorer. They partly destroyed and partly

frightened out of the country the capital, for want of which
the hands of her labouring classes were condemned to inactivity.   Chevalier calculates, that if the whole annual produce of France was equally divided among her children, it
would give each Frenchman 78 centimes to expend per day
in clothing, meat, lodging, instruction, and enjoyment, and it
is out of that sum that any saving for a future day must be
made.   " At the price at which all the necessaries of life are,
can any thing like comfort be procured for 78 centimes per
day? Evidently not.   Even on the supposition that an equal
division of the products could be made, France is not in a
state to give to each of her inhabitants what is necessary for
their comfort; the part which the poor would have would only
keep them poor—the poor would only increase in number.
There are, however, 15,000,000 of Frenchmen spread over
the country, and in certain quarters of large cities, whose
labour does not procure them even this average sum.   The
production of France must, therefore, be materially increased,
in order to cure her of the leprosy of misery which affects so
many parts of this great and illustrious nation.   A practical
conclusion may be therefore drawn.   It is more particularly
the increase of production that should excite our solicitude.
It is not that I contest the importance of a good and equitable
division of the produce; but henceforth it is impossible that
the division should not be good.   The most numerous class
has in its favour the irresistible force of the rising tide; every
increase of production will necessarily turn to the profit of the
working classes.   What government, what pretenders to privilege, can now mistake that God wills it, and that the fate
of whoever opposes such a tendency must be to be carried by
the current to confusion and to ruin?"

Lamartine appears to be aware how needful it is to give
a much greater developement to the ample productive ca-
pacities of France; but, unhappily, neither he nor his colleagues have yet applied themselves to the solution of that

most urgent problem. A glimpse of his views on this subject is afforded us in a report given by an English gentleman of an interesting conversation he had with the poet statesman.

"M. de Lamartine is a tall spare man, with features somewhat worn and eager; the nose aquiline and prominent; the lips rather thin, slightly compressed, and nervous. His eye, as it rests on you, has that peculiar expression which I have observed in men whose vision is perpetually gazing beyond the actual, the individual,—fixed on futurity,—ranging in the ideal and the universal. Had we been talking in the open air, I should have thought that he divided his attention between me and some star in the horizon. His utterance is rapid—his language fluent—his ideas ready—his imagery copious and striking. He is fond of walking up and down the room with his interlocutor; varying his pace with the varying current of his ideas. He speaks, I think, more than he listens; presenting, in this respect, the same contrast to our English statesmen that the French *initiative* plan of government bears to our cautious and merely *regulative* system. He apologised for not speaking English, and asked me, as an impartial observer, what I thought of their situation.

" I said that the financial difficulties struck me as the knot of the question.

" ' Yes, yes!' he replied, ' we have financial difficulties; but we shall get through them perfectly well.'

" ' In time, no doubt,' I rejoined; ' but in six months? in——'

" ' In a very short period,' he interposed quickly.

" ' Can you increase your production of food sufficiently to fulfil your promises—your guarantees to the workmen?' I inquired.

" ' We shall increase it very largely and very rapidly,' he replied; ' we have great facilities for doing so, and we shall take full advantage of them.'

" ' To an English apprehension,' I observed, ' it seems dangerous for a government to descend into the arena of commerce, and initiate enterprises — such as banks, work-shops, and so forth. We think that this tends to defeat private calculation, and to damp the ardour of individual enterprise. In short, to us, centralisation——'

" ' Centralisation,' he cried, ' is the sign of a high and intense social life. In the animal kingdom, the lowest forms of life are the most diffuse ; as you ascend through the scale of organisms you meet life in more and more centralised forms. It is the same with societies.'

" I think this is the substance of what he said ; but he spoke very rapidly for several minutes, and, I own, my attention was diverted by the secret care of hunting up a suitable image in support of my rejoinder.

" ' I accept your illustration,' said I, ' and I take the human body, governed by the brain, as the most perfect example of centralisation. Now, when bile is wanted, does the brain undertake to secrete it? Certainly not. It leaves that to the special organ appointed for the purpose. It stimulates the liver, if necessary, by sending it some vital impulse — and in this manner, no doubt, it *indirectly* promotes the secretion ; but the brain itself never furnishes bile. The more the brain is centralised in an animal, the more centralised and independent of interference is each organ of the body. Now, in the social body, take the banking system, and consider that the analogue of the liver — the organ, so to speak, for the *secretion of credit*. We say that the Govern-ment, which is the brain, should never turn liver, and take to banking on its own account. It may stimulate, if neces-sary, the elaboration of credit through its natural organs ; but it should not assume the special functions of producing it. That is my objection to government competition, and to discounts advanced by the state. I should have preferred to operate through the bankers.'

" ' But we applied to the bankers,' he returned, ' and found them inadequate to the crisis. We had no choice but to act ourselves. Besides, you overlook the essential difference

between our character, our system, our antecedents, and
yours. If you place yourself in an exclusively English point
of view, you will never understand France, her peculiar
questions, her distinctive merits and defects, and her social
requirements. We do not appeal to exactly the same motives;
we do not respond to precisely the same desires; we cannot
govern by absolutely identical means. Our material civilisation is less advanced than yours; our commerce less certain and mechanical in its operation; our negotiants less
experienced and less enterprising. On the other hand, our
intellectual and moral developement has in some respect the
advantage of yours. Our working population is animated by
certain sympathies and instincts, on which experience shews
that we can rely; sympathies and instincts less regular perhaps
in their individual manifestation, but not less real nor less
normal, in their collective influence, than the economical
principles on which your system is almost exclusively based.
These are the qualities which give France her pre-eminence
as an initiative people, and which respond with sensitive
vibration to every well-timed appeal. Neglect them, and
France suffers *ennui;* trample on them—and the result is
explosion. They are accompanied, in the mass of our people,
with great patience, good sense, and *droiture;* and their indi-
cations, conjointly with economical principles, will enable us
to work out the new destinies of France.'

" Here the conversation was interrupted by the arrival of
a messenger, whose news called M. Lamartine away; and I
soon after took my leave. The above sketch renders, pretty
accurately, the impression left on my mind by this conversation; I do not pretend to have retraced it phrase by phrase."

The Provisional Government left untouched one grand
administrative reform, which would have promoted alike the
wealth and the civil liberties of the nation. " Our system of
administration," says Chevalier, "among other defects, presents
that of being infinitely meddlesome (*réglementaire* — regula-

tion). With great pretensions to liberty, ours, of all European nations, is the one most interfered with by its Government, and consequently, I do not hesitate to say, the least free, in all its undertakings. In France, a compact despotism is extant, which works by official circulars. The despotism of the old *régime* has been overthrown; that of Napoleon sank as soon as military glory ceased to be there to support it. But the despotism of a bureaucracy flourishes more vigorously than ever, and the last thirty years have enabled it to strike root deeply. We are obliged to give account to it of every scheme, to seek permission from it for every act. It receives our applications with an air of nonchalance, turns and returns them, and bandies them about, during official hours, from one of its subalterns to another. It wears our patience, rusts our enterprise, thwarts our most justifiable wishes. Some years ago, there was published the series of formalities necessary to be observed by the owner of a field bordering on a river to place a skiff in the latter. Not less than forty or fifty despatches are needful, and, if you followed the ordinary routine, it would last as long as the siege of Troy. This monstrous abuse of centralisation and the spirit of interference does great damage to the public weal; it is, besides, distasteful to liberty. But this is not the view which ought to influence me now. The effects of the bureaucratic despotism may be summed up thus—that it robs us all of an hour or half-hour daily, out of eight or nine hours devoted to actual labour. The result, therefore, is precisely the same as if society were deprived of the eighth or ninth, or, at the very least, of the sixteenth of its capital,—of that which gives us wealth, comfort, or subsistence. I leave to each the task of deducing the conclusion to be arrived at."

Although it is certain that the price of labour cannot be fixed by legislative enactment, it is no less clear that good or bad legislation may greatly augment or diminish the actual value—that is to say, the purchasing power—of the workman's wages. The enactment tending to enhance the price of food should be tolerated under any pretext. The Provisional Government tardily and partially acknowledged this principle by repealing the salt duty, and the toll on meat levied at the gates of Paris.

CHAPTER X.

PRELIMINARIES TO THE ELECTIONS.

THE following decree prescribed the manner of electing the Constituent Assembly which was to shape the new Republican constitution. The time of holding the elections, which was at first appointed for the 9th of April, was afterwards fixed for the 23d and 24th :—

" The Provisional Government of the Republic, wishing to hand over as soon as possible into the hands of a definitive Government the powers which it exercises for the interest and by command of the people, decrees,—

" Art. 1. The electoral cantonal assemblies are convoked for the 9th April next, to elect the representatives of the people at the National Assembly which is to decree the constitution.

" Art. 2. The election will be based on the number of the population.

" Art. 3. The total number of representatives will be nine hundred, including Algeria and the French colonies.

" Art. 4. They shall be divided among the departments, agreeably to the subjoined list.

" Art. 5. The suffrage shall be direct and universal.

" Art. 6. Every Frenchman twenty-one years of age is an elector, if he has resided in the commune for six months, and not judicially deprived or suspended from the exercise of his civil rights.

" Art. 7. All Frenchmen who have attained the age of twenty-five years, and not deprived or suspended of their civil rights, are eligible to be elected.

" Art. 8. The ballot shall be secret.

" Art. 9. All electors shall vote at the principal town of their canton by ballot. Each bulletin shall contain as many names as there shall be representatives to be elected in the department. No one can be elected representative who has not received two thousand votes.

" Art. 10. Each representative shall receive an indemnity of twenty-five francs per day during the session.

" Art. 11. An order from the Provisional Government will regulate the details of the execution of the present decree.

" Art. 12. The National Constituent shall open on the 20th April.

" Art. 13. The present decree shall be immediately sent into the departments, and published and posted up in all the communes of the Republic.

" Done at Paris, by the Government in Council, this 5th March, 1848."

Soon after the publication of the decree for the elections appeared two official circulars on the same subject, both of which provoked much well-grounded displeasure. M. Carnot, the Minister of Public Instruction, addressed the masters of the primary schools, calling on them to take an active part in guiding and determining the choice of the electors, and desiring them to inculcate the strange doctrine that to be an efficient member of the National Assembly it was not necessary to possess either fortune *or education*. This was, probably, but a verbal mistake; M. Carnot's meaning being, apparently, that superior scholarship was not requisite in a member of the Assembly. This, at least, may be inferred from his subsequent explanation, in which he referred to the peasant legislators, who are certainly not uneducated men, however little acquaintance they may have with Latin or Greek. But there is no excuse to be offered for the following arrogant ukase of M. Ledru Rollin, addressed to his commissioners in the provinces : —

" The circular which has reached you, and which has been published, traced out your duties. It is, however, important that I enter with you into some details, and that I state more clearly what I expect from your patriotism, now that by your care the Republic is proclaimed. From several departments demands have been sent in to me, inquiring what your powers are. The Minister of War has been in some anxiety as to your relations with the military leaders. Several amongst you desire to be informed as to the line of conduct which you ought to follow with respect to the law functionaries; finally, the National Guard and the elections, particularly the latter, ought to be the object of your constant attention.

" 1. What are your Powers ?—They are unlimited. Agent of a revo-

lutionary authority, you are revolutionary also. The victory of the people
has imposed on you the duty of getting your work proclaimed and consolidated. For the accomplishment of that task you are invested with its
sovereignty; you take orders only from your conscience; you are to act
as circumstances may demand for the public safety. Thanks to our state
of public morals, that mission is not a very terrible one. Hitherto you have
not had to break down any serious resistance, and you have been able to
remain calm in your force; you must not, however, deceive yourself as to
the state of the country. Republican sentiments ought to be strongly
forwarded there, and for that purpose all political functions must be allotted to men sure, and of Republican principles. Everywhere the Préfects
and Sub-Préfects ought to be changed. In some localities their con-
tinuance in office is demanded; it is your duty to make the population
perceive that those persons who served a power, each act of which was a
corruption, cannot be preserved. The nomination of Sub-Commissioners
to replace those functionaries belongs to you; and you can refer to me
whenever you feel any hesitation. Choose in preference men belonging
to the chief town. You are not to take them in the arrondissement
itself, unless you know them to be perfectly free from all spirit of coterie.
Do not set young men aside, as ardour and generosity are the privilege of
that age, and the Republic has need of those fine qualities. You must
also provide for the replacement of mayors and their deputies. You will
appoint them provisionally, investing them with the ordinary power. If
the municipal councils are hostile, you will dissolve them, and, in concert
with the mayors, you will nominate a provincial municipality; but you
will not have recourse to that measure except in cases of rigorous necessity. I am of opinion that the great majority of the municipal councils
may be preserved by placing at their head new leaders.

  "2. Your Relations with the Officers in Command of the Troops.—
You are exercising the powers of the Executive authority, so that the
armed force is under your orders. You can call it out, and put it in
movement; you can even, in grave cases, suspend a commanding officer,
referring the case immediately to me. But you ought to shew the greatest caution in this part of your functions. All that on your part might
offend the just susceptibilities of the officers or soldiers would be an inex-
cusable fault. I understand that in several departments the Commissioners
have not at once established a bond between them and the military authorities; I am astonished at that, and I recommend you not to sin against
these simple rules of good policy and propriety. The army, in the late
events, shewed a lively sympathy for the Republican cause, and it must be
attached to it more and more. It is of the people, as we are, and it is
the first barrier that would be opposed to an invasion. It is about to
enter for the first time on the possession of its political rights. Therefore

honour it, and do what you can to obtain the good wishes of those who command it. Do not forget that your powers do not extend to the regulations of discipline; they may be summed up in these two words—to make use of the military force, and to gain it over by marks of esteem and cordiality.

" 3. Your Relations with the Law Functionaries.—These magistrates depend on the Executive authority, only in the circle precisely traced out by the law. You will demand from the law officers a devoted co-operation, and wherever you do not find it you will inform me; at the same time mentioning such persons as are remarkable for their probity and firmness. I shall communicate the same to the Ministry of Justice. As to the law officers, who are immovable, you will keep a close eye on them, and if any of the members should exhibit public marks of hostility, you may use the right of suspending, which your sovereign authority confers on you.

" 4. National Guard.—You will receive from me detailed instructions on the organisation of the civil force. I have endeavoured to provide against all the difficulties which you may meet with. Those which arise from local and unforeseen obstacles must be surmounted by your patriotism. In proceeding to the elections, you will conform yourself to the decrees of the Government—that is to say, that, in derogation to the law of 1831, you will cause to be named all the officers, without exception, by the National Guard, commencing by the superior ranks. You will carefully watch over the action of the sub-commissaries and of the municipalities, and will oblige them to render you an exact account of their operations.

" 5. The Elections.—The elections are your great work; they will prove the salvation of the country. It is on the composition of the Assembly that our destinies depend. It must be animated by a revolutionary spirit; if not, we shall go on to civil war and anarchy. On this subject put yourself on your guard against the intrigues of double-faced men, who, after having served royalty, call themselves servants of the people. Those will deceive you, and you must refuse them your support. Let your *mot d'ordre* be, ' New men,' and, as much as possible, from the ranks of the people. The working classes, who form the living strength of the nation, should choose from amongst them men recommended by their intelligence, their morality, and their devotedness; united to the *élite* of thinking men, they will bring force into the discussion of all great questions which will be agitated under the authority of their practical experience. They will continue the Revolution, and they will limit it within the bounds of possibility and reason. Without them it will be led away in vain Utopian ideas, when it will be stifled under the efforts of a retrograde faction. Enlighten the electors, and repeat to them incessantly that the reign of the men of the monarchy is finished.

" You comprehend how great is your task. The education of the

country is not complete : it is for you to guide it. Cause on all points of
your department the meeting of electoral committees ; examine closely the
qualifications of the candidates, and stop at those only who appear to present the strongest guarantees of Republican opinion, and the greatest
chance of success. No compromises, no complaisance. Let the day of
election be the triumph of the Revolution.

" LEDRU ROLLIN."

Great was the indignation excited by this manifesto of
unmitigated despotism. A deputation from the Republican
Club for the liberty of election waited on the Provisional
Government, on the 15th of March, to remonstrate against the
circular. Lamartine replied at considerable length, virtually
disavowing the document. He declared that " the Provisional
Government had not directed any one to speak in its name to
the nation, and especially to speak a language superior to the
law." A proclamation was soon afterwards issued in the name
of the whole Government, tending to remove the bad impression
made by Ledru Rollin's circular, and it was resolved that, for
the future, no official proclamations should be issued on the
sole authority of any individual minister.* The Minister of
the Interior did not easily submit to this correction. During
the deliberations of the Provisional Government on the night
of the 15th, he made a proposition which was disapproved of
by his colleagues and rejected. Upon this M. Ledru Rollin
threatened, that if his proposition was not agreed to he would
call in the people assembled in the court, and force the Government to accede to it. M. Garnier Pagès upon this
immediately arose, and, drawing a pistol from his pocket,
declared that if M. Ledru Rollin attempted to put his threat
into execution he would shoot him through the head. The
affair went.no further.

So much had the Minister of the Interior disgusted all
moderate men, that it is probable he would have been forced

---

* This, however, did not prevent Ledru Rollin from continuing to
issue his periodical placard, headed " Bulletin of the Republic, Ministry of
the Interior."

to retire but for a miserable blunder committed by a portion of the National Guard, the grenadier and chasseur companies. These were picked companies, selected from the general body, distinguished by certain badges, such as a bear-skin cap, yellow epaulettes, &c. By a decree of the Minister of the Interior, these companies were to be broken up and fused with the general mass. This led to an open revolt. On the 15th of March, a body of Guards, principally those of the Banlieu, Belleville, Vaugirard, and Batignolles, presented themselves at the Hôtel de Ville, and demanded the recall of the decree in question. No promise of compliance was given ; whereupon they said, "We come unarmed to-day to demand a right : you took us unfairly and by surprise. If by nine o'clock to-morrow morning that decree be not annulled, we will be here and armed." The next day (Thursday) they appeared to the number of fifty or sixty thousand at the Hôtel de Ville, *en masse*, but not *avec les sabres* as promised. The people assembled in multitudes, hissed them, and saluted the companies *d'élite* with cries of *Egalité! A bas les aristocrats!* The Government replied with unexpected spirit. They regretted that their measures "should have caused manifestations inconsistent with public order : " they would resist counsels taking the form of menace or force ; and they refused the requests of the Guards.

A great meeting of working men took place on the 17th. The numbers present appear to have been nearly 200,000 men. A deputation of about forty persons from the corporations and clubs was received by the Provisional Government within the hôtel. The demands made were—first, the removal of troops from Paris ; secondly, the postponement of the elections of the National Guard to the 5th of April ; and thirdly, the postponement of the National Assembly to the 31st of May. A long and conciliatory conversation ensued. M. de Lamartine displayed all his intrepidity, adroitness, and skill in elocution, and contrived to parry the searching and rather dangerous cross-examination of the demagogues. He

Q

fairly talked the crowd over. But he and his colleagues
thought it safest to render some substantial compliance with
their demands.

The correspondent of the "Morning Chronicle" makes
the following comments on this affair :—

" The demonstration made by the companies d'élite of the
National Guard on Thursday last, and the attempt they made
to force the Government to withdraw the decree by which
they were dissolved and thrown into the general mass of the
different legions, is admitted on all hands to have been not
only a most injudicious one, but to have been excessively injurious to the cause of moderation and order.   Unfortunately,
the object which the companies had in view was not one
which could rouse the sympathies of the public, or even those
of their colleagues of the National Guards themselves.   In
these Republican times privileges are not much tolerated by
the populace, even when these privileges entitle the possessor
to no greater distinction than that of wearing a bear-skin cap
or yellow epaulettes.   But in the present case the pretensions
of the companies d'élite were much more important and more
offensive.   They claimed the right of being an exclusive and
aristocratic body among their democratic fellows.   They
claimed the right of selecting those whom they should consider worthy of being admitted into their ranks, and of electing their own officers.   In short, they endeavoured to form
themselves into a select society in the National Guards, so
superior to the ordinary chasseurs that the latter were not
thought worthy of associating with them.   Such pretensions
were clearly incompatible with the principle of equality which
is the pride of the Republic, and the Provisional Government
could clearly not admit them.   But the manner in which they
attempted to force these inadmissible pretensions on the Government was still more objectionable.   They went to the
Hôtel de Ville without arms, to be sure, but they made no
secret of their intention to adopt forcible measures if the
peaceable demonstration should not be successful.   They even

declared that they would insist on the dismissal of M. Ledru Rollin, who signed the decree; and, unfortunately for themselves, they mixed up with their own quarrel the affair of the circular to the provisional delegates, and alleged the two affairs as sufficient grounds for the step they took This attempt on the part of the National Guards to coerce the Government, so far from having the effect they expected from it, operated exactly the other way. It gave the out-and-out Republicans an opportunity, which they did not lose, of stimulating their partisans, and frightening their adversaries by the demonstration of force which they made on Friday. Such is the effect of the injudicious step taken by the National Guards. The errors committed by M. Carnot and M. Ledru Rollin in their circulars had disgusted the public and annoyed their colleagues. M. de Lamartine went so far as to give them a public disavowal, and to issue a new and very moderate proclamation, to counteract their effect. M. Ledru Rollin had become so unpopular, even among the Republicans, that he could not have remained another week in office, when this unlucky *demarche* of the National Guards came to spoil all, and to place M. Ledru Rollin in such a position that his cause is now considered that of the revolution, and any attempt to get rid of him would be the signal for a deluge of blood. The fact is, that the step taken by the National Guards has made M. Ledru Rollin, M. Louis Blanc, and M. Flocon, the masters of the Government, instead of being, as they were a few days ago, a small minority in it."

Ledru Rollin now pursued his despotic career with unabated insolence; and so well was he seconded by his agents in the departments, that many of the latter were almost impelled to plunge into civil war. One of these agents, M. Emmanuel Arago, took upon himself to double the taxes in Lyons, and to prohibit all persons who left the town from carrying with them more than 500 francs. The Ultra-Republican Clubs in Paris indulged in the most inflammatory language, and talked vehemently of taking up arms against the

National Assembly, unless it should consist altogether of men of their own party.   Meanwhile the working classes, craving excitement, and withdrawn more and more from all useful occupations, amused themselves with planting " trees of liberty" all over Paris.   These trees were full-grown poplars, likely to prove but sapless and unsightly emblems of freedom, though their roots were plentifully bedewed with holy water by the clergy, who were forced to take part in these fooleries. At night the inhabitants were obliged to illuminate their houses, and they were kept awake by volleys fired in honour of the idle ceremony.

We have mentioned Ledru Rollin's bulletin newspaper. On the 15th of April the walls of Paris were placarded with its fifteenth number, from which the following is an extract :—

" The elections, if they do not cause social truth to triumph —if they are but the expression of the interests of a caste, extorted from the confiding loyalty of the people—the elections, which should be the safety of the Republic, will be its ruin, of that there can be no doubt.   There would then be but one means of safety for the people, who made the barricades—it would be to manifest a second time its will, and to adjourn the decision of a false national representation.

" Will France force Paris to have recourse to this extreme, this deplorable remedy ?   God forbid !   As France has confided to Paris a great mission, the French people would not render their mission incompatible with the order and calm necessary to the deliberations of a constituted body.   Paris looks on herself with reason as the representative of all the population of the national territory.   Paris is the advanced post of the army that combats for the Republican idea.   If anarchy works in the distance—if social influences pervert the judgment, or betray the will, of the masses of the people, dispersed and scattered, the people of Paris believe and declare themselves guardians of the interests of the whole nation."

" Never," observes the " Constitutionnel," on this astounding document, " never at any period did the counter-revolutionary spirit itself attack with more audacity the liberty of election.   What ! on the eve of the day when a whole people is about to exercise its rights for the first time, you place all the committees of France under the cannon of Paris. You tell them, in the name of the capital, ' Your vote or your life.' Why this the deprivation *en masse* of citizens! What is the deprivation of functionaries to this? A whole independent nation menaced with the deprivation of its sovereignty. The bulletin prays the citizens of the departments to allow themselves to be persuaded, and so save Paris the pain of vanquishing — whom? All France, if she be not wise."

A reaction took place at last. An attempt was made on Sunday, the 16th of April, to overthrow the moderate section of the Government, and substitute for it a so-called Committee of Safety. This plot was defeated without a blow by the prompt and hearty support given to the cause of order by the National Guard. Two hundred thousand men, of all ranks and conditions, rallied instantly around the Government. The most cordial unanimity pervaded the whole armed mass ; but if any portion of it was more conspicuous than another for its zeal in behalf of the Government, the poor, ill-clad soldiers of the Garde Mobile might fairly claim the palm of civic virtue. The great bulk of the working men of Paris emphatically declared their adhesion to the honest and rational portion of the Provisional Government, and distinctly separated their cause from that of the selfish demagogues and spurious philanthropists, Ledru Rollin, Louis Blanc, and Flocon. This fact teaches a great lesson. The populace, the *canaille*, who were treated as the most dangerous enemies of " the system " under the late monarchy, were now found to be among the trustiest supporters of an honest government. The event proved the good policy of admitting the workmen into the National Guard, for had they been excluded, they would now, probably, have been made tools of the Communist and selfish factions. The abortive attempt of the latter immensely strengthened the hands of Lamartine and the better portion of his colleagues, and enabled them to bring back the army to Paris with the entire approbation of the vast majority of the citizens.

The germ of the affair was a perfectly harmless and legitimate meeting of the Trades in the Champs Elysées, for the purpose of electing fourteen of their number as staff-officers of the National Guard. This meeting had been announced several days before : it was known that the workmen intended to march in procession to the Hôtel de Ville, to present their elected officers to the Government, and also to bring, in a decorated basket, a patriotic offering of money collected among themselves on the occasion.

Two parties resolved to graft on this movement manifestations calculated to fortify their own respective interests.

Blanqui's party took the initiative. He is a man of restless, plotting, underhand character, who has been all his life a conspirator, and has since February been President of the Central Republican Club, one of the most violent of the popular societies. He had placed himself in strong opposition to the moderate section of the Provisional Government; who, on their part, endeavoured to crush him by causing him to be charged with having betrayed the former secret societies, of which he was a member, to the Government of Louis Philippe ; and in support of the accusation they printed in the " Retrospective Review" a paper purporting to have been written by him, and carried off from M. Guizot's hôtel during the Revolution. Blanqui, in his defence, declared this paper a forgery, and threatened retaliatory disclosures, such as should cover several of the Ministers with everlasting infamy. The clubs were violently agitated ; but after several days of discussion and hesitation the majority declared in favour of Blanqui, who was brought back in triumph to the Central Republican Club, from the presidence of which he had been provisionally suspended. It may easily be imagined that Blanqui, thirsting for revenge, fanned the fire of his supporters' zeal. He worked them up to denounce Lamartine and the moderate members of the Government as treacherous apostates from the cause of freedom ; and to declare that they should be overthrown, and Blanqui, with his friends, set up in their stead. On Saturday night the storm of hatred and defiance reached its height; and at the meeting of the Central Republican Club it was resolved to take advantage of the next day's meeting to stir up the people against the Government, and to bring about the desired *émeute*.

Louis Blanc and Albert were also on the alert. They seized this occasion to revive their fading prestige; and they contrived that the Trades should be furnished with placards to affix on their banners, bearing this inscription:—

" Abolition of the *Exploitation* of Man by Man—Organisation of Labour by Association."

MM. Blanc and Albert are asserted to have taken this step without the knowledge of their colleagues.

On Sunday morning the Trades assembled in the Champ de Mars, and proceeded peaceably to the business of their meeting. A large body of workmen belonging to the Club des Ateliers were also assembled in the Hippodrome for a similar purpose. And the supporters of M. Blanqui began to collect, in comparatively insignificant force, in the Champs Elysées. Towards noon the Blanqui party endeavoured to mix themselves with the general body of the workmen, hoping so to fraternise with them, and shape their cry into a form hostile to the moderate section of the Government; but their overtures were rejected by the workmen.

Between one and two o'clock the Trades in vast columns began to move towards the Hôtel de Ville; bearing on their banners the Louis Blanc placards. But meanwhile, Marrast, the Mayor of Paris, and Lamartine, had taken their measures. The *générale* was beaten in all quarters of Paris, and in the banlieue early in the forenoon, and with such effect that before twelve o'clock 60,000 National Guards were concentrated on the Hôtel de Ville, and supported by some pieces of cannon. Along the Quays, the Boulevards, and the other principal streets on the north side of the river, were assembled 160,000 more, including 40,000 of the National Guards of the banlieue, and the 20,000 of the National Guards Mobiles. Moreover, they were provided with ball-cartridge, and certainly a more determined-looking body of men has rarely been seen. The attempt of "The Trades" to reach the Hôtel de Ville was, nevertheless, made; but when they had arrived near to the Pont Neuf they found a dense mass of National Guards, with a rather fighting air, who refused them permission to go farther, and there the greater portion of them remained until a body of the Mobiles had been allowed to pass to the Hôtel de Ville, whither "The Trades," finding an opening, followed in their wake. A portion of them obtained admission to the Provisional Government, stating that they had an offering of money to make for the public service. The plot was crushed without a blow being struck.

An Englishman who made an extensive promenade this day through the midst of the armed masses, says that the most frequent cries uttered were in favour of Lamartine ; the names of Louis Blanc and Ledru Rollin did not once strike his ear. This was the more remarkable, as in former manifestations theirs were almost the only names heard.

At about half-past four o'clock, when the National Guard filled the Place de Grève, M. de Lamartine and M. Crémieux were observed at one of the windows of the Hôtel de Ville. Suddenly, and by enchantment, shakos, hats, and caps, were placed on the ends of the bayonets, and waved, and cries of *Vive Lamartine! Vive le Gouvernement Provisoire!* rent the air. An instant afterwards M. Louis Blanc appeared at another window. Some persons saluted him with *vivats,* and the same manifestation was made in the ranks of the National Guard, but less spontaneously and less generally. In the evening another manifestation took place, still greater and more solemn. The *rappel* was again beaten, all the legions assembled to go to the Hôtel de Ville. They defiled on the quays, beginning at eight o'clock, and at ten they had not finished. During the whole march shouts, tremendous and continuous, were heard from 200,000 voices, *A bas les Com-*

munistes! A bas Cabet! A bas les Fainéans! Vive la République!
Vive la Gouvernement Provisoire! Vive Lamartine! Such were
the shouts which exhibited the dispositions of the people on
the events of the day. At nine o'clock the Provisional Government addressed the National Guard. All Paris was spontaneously illuminated.

It appears that M. Blanqui, during the commencement of
the manifestation, took up his station in the Champs Elysées,
surrounded by a sort of staff, or body-guard. Emissaries
were constantly proceeding from this band, to mix with the
masses in the Champ de Mars, for the purpose of ascertaining
their temper and disposition towards M. Blanqui. The intelligence brought back by these scouts was, however, so
unfavourable to the views of the agitator, that he disappeared
at an early hour, and was not seen in public during the
remainder of the day.

In the evening, says a writer in the "Weekly Chronicle,"
" I witnessed, at the theatre of the Port St. Martin, an incident which is, perhaps, worth recounting, as illustrative of
the fermentation which reigned on this day in the public
mind.

" The celebrated actor, Fréderic Lemaître, was performing
the character of Robert Macaire. Lemaître is, as you are
aware, an actor of great genius, but somewhat extravagant,
and of most excitable temperament. During his performance,
the *rappel* was heard in the street, and all the National
Guards present quitted the theatre hastily to join their
respective companies. Upon this, Lemaître dropped his
voice, and almost became inaudible. Cries of 'Speak up!'
issued from all parts of the house. Lemaître suddenly
stopped short, rushed forward to the foot-lights, and exclaimed, in a voice that seemed broken by emotion,—

" ' Messieurs ! you tell me to speak loudly ; but my voice
is stifled with my tears — with the beating of my heart !
Ah, Messieurs, our France — our unhappy country — torn
with dissensions'—(here he stopped, sobbing ; and the whole

house, which had risen in amazement, cheered him enthusiastically). 'Forgive this emotion—these tears. I was till three o'clock to-day, with my sons, on guard in the Place de la Grève—I hear the *rappel* again beaten—perhaps at this moment the conflict is engaged—the blood of my countrymen may be flowing while I speak; my own sons ——' (here he broke down again, and again the audience manifested their sympathy by loud cheers). 'Ah, Messieurs!' he resumed, 'beneath this rouge—these trappings—there is, after all, the man—the father. (Cheers and emotion.) Messieurs, at such a moment, I am here, playing the buffoon, *à contre cœur*—not for myself—but to keep this house from being closed—to save my brother actors from inactivity and distress. (Immense cheers.) Messieurs, I crave your indulgence; this task is too odious to me; I hate and scorn myself to be here jesting, and playing these miserable antics, while my country bleeds. (Sensation.) Ah, Messieurs! come to me a few months—a few weeks hence—when France is tranquil and happy—then I will play before you with a light heart—but not now—not now.' (Loud cheers, and cries, 'Let us go!'—'Drop the curtain!' and counter-cries, 'No, no!' continue the piece!') 'Messieurs,' he cried, with a voice of thunder, suddenly bounding on the stage in a sort of frenzy, 'I am a MAN—not a puppet!—Away with these fooleries!'—and as he spoke he tore off his wig, his patched coat, his tawdry Macaire waistcoat, and dashed them on the stage; then, trampling them under foot, he went on speaking with vehement gesticulations, amidst an uproar of conflicting cries, which entirely drowned his voice. In a few moments the manager came upon the stage; and, approaching him, said a few words in his ear. Lemaître then raised his hand deprecatingly to the audience; and, with a gesture of resignation, stooped, and picked up successively the wig and the motley vestments, and put them on. These being re-adjusted, he folded his arms, and, in a humble attitude, seemed awaiting the restoration of silence to resume his drolleries. I thought

I could discern a slight curl of suppressed contempt at the corner of his lip. The majority, however, were bent on having their money's worth—in quantity if not in quality; but a certain number of persons left the house. I withdrew also, and walked home, pondering on the infeodations of genius to society; on the actor weeping behind his mask; on poor Hood writing comic on his deathbed; on Seymour quitting a half-finished sketch for 'Figaro' to blow out his brains. I remembered Retzsch's outlines of the captive Pegasus, with his wings bound, bleeding beneath the cartlash,—fainting at the plough; and I thought that the intellectual workman is as deeply concerned as the artisan in the great question of the organisation of labour."

The grand fête of fraternity to celebrate the return of the troops of the line to Paris took place on Thursday the 20th of April. Paris that day presented a spectacle of which no other city in the world could offer an example. Upwards of 250,000 armed men (some accounts say, 350,000), and more than 300,000 spectators, were mixed together during seven or eight hours, one might almost say without confusion,—certainly without an instance of bad or unkind feeling. Only one accident has been reported, which was caused by a National Guard, who, in true Cockney spirit, fired a loaded gun, as he intended, into the air, and shot a man at the other side of the quay dead on the spot. The illumination in the evening was very brilliant, and had the peculiarity of being general. Paris illuminations are, ordinarily, confined to the boulevards, quays, and principal streets; but on this occasion the whole city, and even the suburbs, were lighted up.

The Parisians were now in a condition to proceed without fear of violence to the election of their representatives in the National Constituent Assembly.

George Barclay, Castle Street, Leicester Square.

ption has been reported in a number of cases after
of artillery, is true. Do they imply that a better plan of
treat ... the ... to meet the requirements of ...

was very different, and the actual working of those parts of
these discussions are erroneously occupied in the tendency in
question of principal interest. Thus on this occasion the whole
meeting must deal with the amendments.

The Parisians who now in a condition to oppose and pre-
pared the class of violence to the electors and their representatives in the
National Constituent Assembly.

London, November 1847.

A

CATALOGUE OF BOOKS,

PUBLISHED BY

CHAPMAN AND HALL, 186 STRAND.

Comprising

Books of Travel and Adventure.
Works of Fiction.
Illustrated Books and Works on the Fine Arts.
Poetry.
Biography, History, and Politics.
Works of General Interest and Utility.
Atlases and Maps.
Works in General Literature.
Cheap Editions.

INDEX.

Catalogue of Books.

BOOKS OF TRAVEL AND ADVENTURE.

THE EXPEDITION TO BORNEO OF H.M.S. DIDO,

For the Suppression of Piracy. With Extracts from the Journal of His Excellency JAMES BROOKE, Rajah of Sarāwak, Governor of Labuan, &c.

By CAPTAIN THE HON. HENRY KEPPEL, R.N.

THIRD EDITION, with an Additional Chapter, comprising Recent Intelligence, by W. K. KELLY. With Six Maps and Eleven Views in Tinted Lithography.

2 vols. 8vo, cloth, price 1l. 12s.

"This is an important book upon an important subject. Captain Keppel's characteristic sketches will amply repay perusal. One volume contains the diary of Mr. Brooke, and we know not when we have read a history of true greatness so modestly narrated; a series of events so full of interest and striking novelty. We recommend the work with real pleasure to the notice of our readers."—*The Times.*

WAYFARING SKETCHES
AMONG THE GREEKS AND TURKS,
AND ON THE SHORES OF THE DANUBE.

By A SEVEN YEARS' RESIDENT IN GREECE.

Post 8vo, cloth, price 9s.

"The Wayfaring Sketches are admirable pictures, a series of bold and vigorous drawings of a grand subject, well chosen, and graceful in their vigour. The author's style is perfectly charming—simple, playful, earnest, eloquent, and always adapted to the subject."—*Jerrold's Newspaper.*

"Pages full of grace, sweetness, and variety. The view of Greek manners and society is more complete than any given by a recent writer."—*Morning Chronicle.*

"These Sketches are by a Lady, and have the vivacity and grace of the female mind. The narrative is eloquent, entertaining, and forcible; the descriptions are of a high order of beauty; and the sentiments exhibit much originality of thought."—*Britannia.*

"This is a delightful volume in the full and literal meaning of the word, for it is written with taste, feeling, a high classic enthusiasm, and a sparkling brilliancy of st —*John Bull.*

NOTES OF A JOURNEY FROM
CORNHILL TO GRAND CAIRO.
By MICHAEL ANGELO TITMARSH.
With a Coloured Frontispiece.
SECOND EDITION, *small 8vo, price 6s.*

" We ask for no better *compagnon de voyage* than Mr. Titmarsh; he is the very man to travel with; his book the very one to write or read."—*Times.*

" There is much of entertainment in these pages. . . . . As we laugh we gather wisdom." —*Literary Gazette.*

THE IRISH SKETCH-BOOK.
By MR. M. A. TITMARSH.
With numerous Engravings on Wood, from the Author's Designs.
SECOND EDITION, 2 *vols. post 8vo, price 14s.*

" One of the most valuable books of travelling Sketches that has been published for many a day. * * * Taken as a whole, the book is capital."—*Spectator.*
" Michael Angelo Titmarsh is precisely the writer who should sketch Ireland as it is.

He has caught the very characteristics of the clime; and his narrative runs on with a never-failing interest, which leaves one no chance, having once opened the book, but to read it to its very last page—ay, and to profit by it too."—*Morning Chronicle.*

CAMP AND BARRACK-ROOM;
OR, THE BRITISH ARMY AS IT IS.
By a late Staff-Sergeant of the 13th Light Infantry.
Post 8vo, cloth, price 9s.

" We recommend the Staff-Sergeant's history, as narrating a life that few of us are familiar with, in a fair and honest manner, and

conveying with it a deal of material for after-thought."—*Morning Chronicle.*

AMERICAN NOTES,
FOR GENERAL CIRCULATION.
By CHARLES DICKENS.
FOURTH EDITION, 2 *vols. post 8vo, cloth, price 1l. 1s.*

IRELAND, SCOTLAND, & ENGLAND.
By J. G. KOHL.
In one volume, 8vo, cloth, price 11s.

" Mr. Kohl's work on Ireland is beyond all comparison *the most succinct and faithful that we have yet seen,* and exhibits the *lamentable condition of that country* in a light in which none but a foreigner, or at

least a sagacious traveller, could paint it. His testimony is doubly valuable from the weight of experience and authority which name carries with it."—*Times.*

RUSSIA.

St. Petersburgh, Moscow, Karkhoff, Riga, Odessa, the German
Provinces on the Baltic, the Steppes, the Crimea, and the Interior
of the Empire.

By J. G. KOHL.

A NEW EDITION, with a Map, and Illustrations in Tinted Lithography.
In one volume 8vo, cloth, gilt back, price 12s.

AUSTRIA.

Vienna, Prague, Hungary, Bohemia, the Danube, Galicia, Styria,
Moravia, Bukovino, and the Military Frontier.

By J. G. KOHL.

In one volume, 8vo, cloth, price 11s.

"Mr. Kohl's volumes upon Russia and Austria deserve the rank which has, by universal consent, been awarded to them. They are the very best books about the two countries which have yet appeared, containing a greater quantity of solid information, digested into the pleasantest possible form, than all the tours and journals extant."—*Fraser's Mag.*

EGYPT AND NUBIA

Popularly Described; their Scenery and National Characteristics, Incidents of Wayfaring and Sojourn, Personal and Historical Sketches, &c.

By J. A. ST. JOHN,

AUTHOR OF "EGYPT AND MOHAMMED ALI," "MANNERS AND CUSTOMS OF ANCIENT GREECE," &c.

Illustrated with One Hundred and Twenty-five Wood-Engravings.
8vo, price 9s. cloth gilt ; or in morocco, 15s.

SYRIA AND THE HOLY LAND

Popularly Described; their Scenery and their People, Incidents of
Travel, &c. From the best and most recent Authorities.

By WALTER KEATING KELLY.

Illustrated with One Hundred and Eighty Wood-Engravings.
8vo, price 8s. 6d. cloth gilt ; or in morocco, 14s.

"Never was information more amusingly conveyed—never were the results of voluminous works of travel more spiritedly condensed. The execution is truly admirable. The moral, social, physical, political, and geographical features of the East are well brought out, and the reader is at home with the Turk, the Arab, the Jew, the Druse, and the Maronite."—*Westminster Review.*

Mark Wilton, the Merchant's Clerk.

A Tale.

BY THE REV. CHARLES B. TAYLER,

AUTHOR OF "MAY YOU LIKE IT," "RECORDS OF A GOOD MAN'S LIFE," &c.

With numerous Illustrations on Wood.

In one volume, small 8vo.

The Bachelor of the Albany.

A Novel.

BY THE AUTHOR OF "THE FALCON FAMILY."

In one volume, post 8vo, cloth, price 9s.

"The 'Bachelor of the Albany' is a book with hardly a grave sentence in it. But its mirth is neither emptiness nor flippancy. It is good, honest mirth: made up of lawful enjoyment or well-directed ridicule; and the fruit of a quick and clear understanding, as well as of a cultivated and well-stored mind."—*Examiner.*

"One of the cleverest, smartest, most amusing sketches of English middle life which we have ever had the gratification of reading."—*Liverpool Journal.*

"The book scintillates with wit. The charm of its cutting vivacity never flags; it

is impossible to take it up without reading it to the last line; and it is impossible to put it down without being impressed by the literary taste, the wit, the genial feeling, and sound sense that are assembled in its pages."—*Atlas.*

"The perusal of this work has afforded us the highest gratification—our interest has never been allowed for a moment to flag—full of the quaintest conceits, and abounding with a species of dry humour which is irresistible, we have no doubt that it will add largely to the reputation of the author of 'The Falcon Family.'—*Dublin University Magazine.*

The Half-Sisters. A Novel.

By GERALDINE E. JEWSBURY,

AUTHOR OF "ZOE; THE HISTORY OF TWO LIVES."

In two volumes, post 8vo, cloth.

Tales of Woman's Trials.

BY MRS. S. C. HALL.

Embellished with Seventy Illustrations on Wood, drawn by

J. NOEL PATON,	H. C. SELOUS,	J. FRANKLIN,
E. M. WARD,	J. GILBERT,	F. W. HULME,
E. CORBOULD,	R. R. M'IAN,	F. W. TOPHAM, &c.

In a handsome large octavo volume, elegantly bound in cloth and gilt, price 1l. 1s.; or in morocco gilt, 31s. 6d.

"Mrs. Hall's talents appear to great advantage in these tales. The book is magnificently printed and bound, and crowded with fine thoughtful woodcuts. It is altogether presented with such an eye to costliness that it is well entitled to take rank among the gift-books."—*Atlas.*

Ranthorpe.

Post 8vo, cloth, price 9s.

"A tale of the life of a man of letters, conceived in a manly, healthy spirit."—*Examiner.*

"A work of great power. 'Ranthorpe' is the production of no common writer."—*John Bull.*

"The work of a writer of distinguished abilities—animated, skilful, and eloquent, with remarkable powers of narrative ; aptitude for dramatic dialogue."—*Su... Times.*

"Bespeaks great talents, admirably ciplined. The story is exceedingly inter ing."—*Jerrold's Newspaper.*

Mount Sorel ;

Or, the Heiress of the De Veres. A Novel.

BY THE AUTHOR OF THE "TWO OLD MEN'S TALES," &c.

2 vols. post 8vo, cloth, 18s.

"A tale of singular beauty."—*Examiner.*

"'Mount Sorel' is its author's best invention. * * * We have rarely read a book exciting so strong an interest, in which the mean, the criminal, and the vulgar had so small a share; and for this, as a crown charm and an excellence too rare, alas ! these days, does it give us pleasure to co mend and *re*-commend 'Mount Sorel.'' *Athenæum.*

Father Darcy. An Historical Romance

BY THE AUTHOR OF

"MOUNT SOREL," "EMILIA WYNDHAM," &c.

2 vols. post 8vo, cloth, price 18s.

"In 'Father Darcy' there is more of graphic description than in any other work from the same pen."—*Atlas.*

"This, like most of the productions of its writer, is a remarkable book. For deep and just feeling, for judgment, power, discrimi tion of character, and delicate perception moral and physical beauty, few recent pul cations can compare with 'Father Darcy.' *Examiner.*

The Whiteboy. A Story of Ireland in 1822

By MRS. S. C. HALL.

2 vols. post 8vo, cloth, 18s.

"Indisputably Mrs. Hall's best novel."—*Athenæum.*

"Full of vivid descriptions, life-like sketches of character, dashes of genuine Irish humour, with occasionally scenes exhibiti the strong passions and affections of the Iri people, drawn with exceeding energy a power."—*Atlas.*

Long Engagements.

A TALE OF THE AFFGHAN REBELLION.

Post 8vo, cloth, 9s.

"A story more exciting both to the heart and imagination than any thing we have met with for a long time."—*The Indian News.*

"*This work is a rare exception to a large ss; for it is a good, an amusing, and a* true picture of life in India."—*Morni Herald.*

"A work of great power, full of lively terest, and abounding with masterly sketch of character."—*Liverpool Courier.*

Posthumous Papers of the Pickwick Club.

By CHARLES DICKENS.

With Forty-three Illustrations by R. SEYMOUR and " PHIZ."

8vo, cloth, price 21s.; half-morocco, marbled edges, 24s. 6d.;
morocco, gilt edges, 26s. 6d.

=====

Life and Adventures of Nicholas Nickleby.

By CHARLES DICKENS.

With Forty Illustrations by " PHIZ."

8vo, cloth, price 21s.; half-morocco, marbled edges, 24s. 6d.;
morocco, gilt edges, 26s. 6d.

=====

Sketches by " Boz."

Illustrating Every-Day Life and Every-Day People.

A New Edition, with Forty Illustrations by GEO. CRUIKSHANK.

8vo, cloth, price 21s.; half-morocco, marbled edges, 24s. 6d.;
morocco, gilt edges, 26s. 6d.

=====

Life and Adventures of Martin Chuzzlewit.

By CHARLES DICKENS.

With Forty Illustrations by " PHIZ."

8vo, cloth, price 21s.; half-morocco, marbled edges, 24s. 6d.;
morocco, gilt edges, 26s. 6d.

=====

The Old Curiosity Shop.

By CHARLES DICKENS.

With Seventy-five Illustrations by G. CATTERMOLE and H. K. BROWNE.

Imperial 8vo, cloth, price 13s.

=====

Barnaby Rudge.

A Tale of the Riots of 'Eighty.

By CHARLES DICKENS.

th Seventy-eight Illustrations by G. CATTERMOLE and H. K. BROWNE.

Imperial 8vo, cloth, price 13s.

The Cheap Edition of
The Pickwick Papers.
By CHARLES DICKENS.

With a Frontispiece from a Design by C. R. LESLIE, R.A.

In one volume, crown 8vo, price 4s. 6d. stiff wrapper; 5s. cloth; or 7s. 6d. half-morocco, marbled edges.

The Edinburgh Tales.

A Series of Stories and Novelettes, illustrative of English, Irish, and Scottish Character, Domestic Manners, and Social Duties, by

MRS. JOHNSTONE.	AUTHOR OF "MOUNT SOREL."	MAURICE O'CONNELL.
MRS. GORE.	M. FRASER TYTLER.	WILLIAM HOWITT.
MISS MITFORD.	MRS. FRASER.	JOHN MILLS.
MARY HOWITT.	SIR T. D. LAUDER.	EDWARD QUILLINAN.
MRS. CROWE.	ROBERT NICOLL.	COLONEL JOHNSON.

EDITED BY MRS. JOHNSTONE.

In Three Volumes, imperial 8vo, cloth gilt, price 4s. 6d. each.

*** *These Stories, printed in the usual way of Modern Novels, would fill Twenty-Seven Volumes post 8vo.*

" Capital volumes for light reading, worth half-a-dozen common fictions."—*Spectator.*

" Mrs. Johnstone is the Edgeworth of Scotland. If we knew higher praise, we would bestow it."—*Dublin Review.*

" Amazingly cheap, but that is its least merit. The tales are delightfully told—naturally, cheerfully, with great refinement of feeling, and a skilful variety of manner."—*Examiner.*

Tales from the German.

Comprising Specimens from the most celebrated Authors.

By J. OXENFORD and C. A. FEILING.

Cloth, price 11s.

" Mr. Oxenford is one of the best German scholars we have. Mr. Feiling, with whom he has before been associated in foreign literature, is a German known for his proficiency in the studies of his native language. The combination was the most fitting conceivable for a work of this kind. Selection and translation are alike characteristic and spirited."—*Examiner.*

LIFE IN DALECARLIA.
The Parsonage of Mora.

By FREDERIKA BREMER.   Translated by WILLIAM HOWITT.

Small 8vo, ornamental boards, price 5s.

" There are, in the ' Parsonage of Mora,' as in every thing else that Miss Bremer writes, beauties of a rare kind, charming and cheerful pictures of the domestic affections and household habits of educated and happy middle life, and vivid fancy shedding lustre on all on which it glances or plays."—*Tait Magazine.*

ILLUSTRATED BOOKS AND WORKS ON THE FINE ARTS.

HEATH'S ILLUSTRATED NEW TESTAMENT.

Embellished with a Series of beautiful Engravings, and each page surrounded by an Elaborate Decorative Border, drawn by the First Artists, and Engraved in the highest style of the Art on Wood, under the superintendence of

Mr. CHARLES HEATH.

Publishing, in Monthly Parts, elegantly printed in Small Folio, price Two SHILLINGS, *or on Large Paper* THREE SHILLINGS, *each.*

Five Hundred Borders, of surpassing beauty, each generally illustrative of the Text enclosed, will ornament the Work. In addition, there will be between Two and Three Hundred Vignettes, embodying all the most prominent subjects in the New Testament. These will be mostly from Original Designs, but will also include some of the finest specimens of the Ancient and Modern Schools; thus making the Work a complete Gallery of Scriptural Subjects.

" We have no recollection of having ever met, amongst the magnificent editions of the Scriptures that have recently been issued, any work more truly superb than this. The typography and paper are beautiful, but the strength of the work is in its engravings. In this respect it has no equal. And all who appreciate the application of the highest art to the finest subjects, will place on this New Testament a very high value."—*Tait's Magazine.*

"A truly superb work; there is no falling off as it proceeds, in the execution, and, as for choice of subject for illustration, it can have no rival."—*New Monthly Magazine.*

THE PRINCIPLES AND PRACTICE OF ART;

Treating of Beauty of Form, Imitation, Composition, Light and Shade, Effect and Colour.

By J. D. HARDING,

AUTHOR OF "ELEMENTARY ART," &c.

With numerous Illustrations, drawn and engraved by the Author.

Imperial 4to, price 3l. 3s.; proofs on India paper, 4l. 4s.

" The plates in this volume are no less various than excellent, and admirably adapted to elucidate the letter-press. We know of no work from which amateurs, and even persons wholly unacquainted with every principle, could so readily gather a guiding knowledge."—*Art-Union.*

FINDEN'S BEAUTIES OF MOORE;

Comprising Forty-eight Portraits of the Principal Female Characters in his Works, from Paintings made expressly for the Work, by the following Eminent Artists:

S. HART, R.A.	H. O'NEIL.	W. FISHER.
S. NEWTON, R.A.	J. WRIGHT.	A. DERBY.
W. P. FRITH, A.R.A.	R. T. BOTT.	E. HAWKES.
A. ELMORE, A.R.A.	H. WARREN.	W. MADDOX.
FRANK STONE.	J. G. MIDDLETON.	W. ROOM.
E. M. WARD.	F. WOOD.	F. CROWLEY.
A. EGG.	J. WOOD.	A. DE VALENTINI.

Engraved in the highest Style of Art, by, or under the immediate Superintendence of, MR. EDWARD FINDEN.

With Descriptive Letter-Press.

In one thick vol. imperial 4to, elegantly bound in morocco, gilt edges, price 3l. 3s.

*** *Also in Two Volumes, each complete in itself, and sold separately. Price of each volume: Imperial 4to, elegantly bound in red morrocco, gilt edges, 2l. 2s.; or in Atlas 4to, with proof impressions of the plates on India paper, price 3l. 3s.*

FINDEN'S BEAUTIES OF MOORE.
SINGLE ENGRAVINGS.

PRICE OF EACH PORTRAIT:

Beautifully Coloured, after the Original Paintings, Imperial 4to . . . . } *Half-a-Crown.*

Proofs, on India Paper, Atlas 4to . . . . *Two Shillings.*

Prints, Imperial 4to . . . . *One Shilling.*

1. Black and Blue Eyes.	17. The Coming Step.	33. Kathleen.
2. Lesbia.	18. St. Jerome's Love.	34. The Last Rose of Summer.
3. Norah Creina.	19. Ninetta.	35. The Hamlet's Pride.
4. Holy Eyes.	20. The Sleeping Beauty.	36. The Planet.
5. Irish Girl.	21. Theresa.	37. O'Donohue's Mistress.
6. Young Kitty.	22. The Vesper Hymn.	38. The Desmond's Love.
7. Laughing Eyes.	23. Zelica.	39. The Lute.
8. The Stricken Deer.	24. The Grecian Maid.	40. The Garland.
9. The Exile.	25. Anna.	41. The Casket.
10. Morning of Life.	26. The Wreath.	42. The Sunflower.
11. The Mountain Sprite.	27. The Cottage Maid.	43. The High-born Ladye.
12. The Garden Flower.	28. The Indian Maid.	44. Lalla Rookh.
13. Love's Summer-Cloud.	29. Rich and Rare.	45. The Peri.
14. Young Jessica.	30. The Rival Sisters.	46. Hinda.
15. The Evening Star.	31. Eveleen.	47. Nourmahal.
16. The Pensive Thought.	32. Young Love's Dream.	48. Lea.

"A charming publication. The portfolio redolent of beauty; and every single picture so bewitching that it deserves a frame, and the whole series to adorn a gallery. The work is one of the fairest promise; and in these days of admiration for the really superior productions of art must be a very popular public favourite."—*Literary Gazette.*

BARONIAL HALLS & PICTURESQUE EDIFICES OF ENGLAND.

From Drawings made expressly for the Work, by

J. D. HARDING.	H. L. PRATT.	G. F. SARGENT.
G. CATTERMOLE.	C. J. RICHARDSON, F.S.A.	S. RAYNER.
S. PROUT.	J. GENDALL.	J. S. DODD.
J. HOLLAND.	F. W. FAIRHOLT, F.S.A.	J. C. BAYLISS.
W. MÜLLER.	J. G. JACKSON.	J. DAFFORNE.
T. ALLOM.	F. W. HULME.	J. A. HAMMERSLEY.
LAKE PRICE.	G. H. HARRISON.	A. E. EVERITT.
W. L. WALTON.	WILLIAM RICHARDSON.	HENRY MOGFORD.

Executed in Lithotint, under the Superintendence of Mr. HARDING.
With Descriptive Letter-press, embellished with numerous Engravings on Wood. Edited by S. C. HALL, F.S.A.

In 2 vols. half-bound in morocco extra, cloth sides, gilt edges. **Prints,**
imperial 4to, price 7l. 7s.; or Proofs, Colombier 4to, price 10l. 10s.

CONTENTS.

A PROOF EDITION *of the Plates has also been prepared, in One Volume, im*
rial folio, to range with " NASH'S MANSIONS," *and other Works of the same*
of which a very limited number has been struck off, accompanied by a Volu
Letter-press, columbier 4to, uniformly half-bound in morocco, gilt top, price

MRS. PERKINS'S BALL;

Depicted in Twenty-three Plates; containing Portr
of the principal Personages present, with their C
racters.

By MR. M. A. TITMARSH.

THIRD EDITION, *foolscap 4to, ornamental boards, price 7s. 6d.;*
or with the Plates coloured, 10s. 6d.

"If Mr. Titmarsh had never done any thing more than this, he would be well entitled to his reputation. The humour is rich and graphic, and goes direct to its mark, without a particle of ill nature. The book is quite mirable in its way—perfectly true to middle class it depicts, and running with pleasantry and fun."—*Atlas.*

COSTUME IN ENGLAND:

A History of Dress, from the Earliest Period until
Close of the Eighteenth Century; with a Glossary
Terms for all Articles of Use or Ornament worn abo
the Person.

By F. W. FAIRHOLT, F.S.A.

With upwards of 600 Engravings drawn on Wood by the Autho
In one thick vol. 8vo, cloth, 31s. 6d.

"One of the most useful and interesting books we have seen for a long time."—*Literary Gazette.*

"A book for the eye and mind, for casual inspection and for permanent study or reference."—*John Bull.*

"The prettiest book of costume, and, at the same time, the most compact and complete, with which we are acquainted. It manifestly been a labour of love. There learning in the book, without pretence; a miliarity with the abstruser points of the ject, without a display of hard words; altogether as much modesty as merit."—*aminer.*

THE HOME OF SHAKSPERE

ILLUSTRATED AND DESCRIBED.

By F. W. FAIRHOLT, F.S.A.

AUTHOR OF "COSTUME IN ENGLAND," &c. &c.

With Thirty-three Engravings.
Small post 8vo, price 2s. 6d.

"*An elegant little book, delineating with pen and pencil all that is noteworthy of the birth-place and resting-place of our great and well-beloved poet.*"—*Britannia.*

"This publication is both profitable pleasing, and one from which the best person about Shakspere will learn so thing."—*Athenæum.*

THE ARCHÆOLOGICAL ALBUM;
Or, Museum of National Antiquities.
Edited by THOMAS WRIGHT, M.A., F.S.A.

With a beautiful Illuminated Frontispiece and Title-page, in Chromolithography, Twenty-six Etchings on Steel of Remarkable Buildings and Antiquities, and above One Hundred Engravings on Wood, all drawn by F. W. FAIRHOLT, F.S.A.

Post 4to, cloth, price 32s.

" A perfect treasure to the antiquary."—*Cambridge Chronicle.*

SERIES OF DIAGRAMS,
Illustrative of the Principles of Mechanical Philosophy and their Application. Drawn on Stone by HENRY CHAPMAN, and Printed in Colours by C. F. CHEFFINS. With Descriptive Letter-press. Under the Superintendence of the Society for the Diffusion of Useful Knowledge.

One large folio vol., cloth, price 2l. 12s. 6d.

THE ART-UNION JOURNAL
OF THE FINE ARTS, AND THE ARTS DECORATIVE AND ORNAMENTAL.
Extensively illustrated by Engravings on Steel and Wood.
Published on the First of every Month.

" On more than one occasion, incidentally, we have noticed this publication with favour. It seems to us, on the whole, excellently adapted to its professed objects, and very honest and zealous in the pursuit of them. Practically, its success must do good. Its engravings (which are selected with taste, very well executed, and given in surprising abundance) cannot fail of promoting both knowledge and taste in this direction. Its papers are sensible and various; it has the occasional attraction of very graceful literature; its information is carefully collected; and its attention to ornamental and decorative art, as well as to the branches of design in connexion with manufactures, have made it a really important ally to the Government schools."—*Examiner.*

POETRY.

THE CHILD OF THE ISLANDS.

A POEM.

By THE HON. MRS. NORTON.

SECOND EDITION, 8vo, cloth, price 12s.; or in morocco gilt, 18s.

"There can be no question that the performance bears throughout the stamp of extraordinary ability — the sense of easy power very rarely deserts us. But we pause on the bursts of genius; and they are many."— *Quarterly Review.*

"We find in almost every page some bold burst, graceful allusion, or delicate touch— some trait of external nature, or glimpse into the recesses of the heart,—that irresistibly indicates the creating power of genius."— *Edinburgh Review.*

ONE HUNDRED SONGS OF BERANGER.

With Translations in English Verse, on the opposite page.

By WILLIAM YOUNG.

18mo, cloth, price 5s.

"A set of translations which are every way faithful—often, very often, extremely happy." —*Morning Chronicle.*

"A pleasant volume, executed in a true spirit. Several of the translations we may compare with those of Mr. Mahony (the 'Father Prout' of *Fraser's Magazine*), and

we know of nothing better in this way."— *Examiner.*

"Mr. Young has given a faithful, in some instances a spirited, version of each song, and produced a book that must be acceptable to every class of readers."—*Observer.*

SONGS AND BALLADS.

By SAMUEL LOVER.

SECOND EDITION, with ADDITIONS, small 8vo, cloth, price 5s.

*** This Edition contains the Songs sung in Mr. Lover's "Irish Evenings."

THE COUNTRY HOUSE, AND OTHER POEMS.

By JAMES PRIOR, F.S.A., M.R.I.A., &c.

AUTHOR OF THE "LIFE OF BURKE," "LIFE OF GOLDSMITH," &c.

Small 8vo, cloth, price 6s.

"This poem belongs to a class which can never go out. Simplicity of diction, quiet truthfulness of description, and sound moral feeling, are essential merits in the treatment

of such themes; and here, easy versification and kindly sentiments will render this little volume acceptable to a large circle of readers."—*Atlas.*

MEMOIRS OF SIMON LORD LOVAT, AND DUNCAN FORBES OF CULLODEN.

From Original Sources.

By JOHN HILL BURTON, Advocate,

AUTHOR OF "THE LIFE OF DAVID HUME."

Post 8vo, cloth, price 9s.

"The best book on Jacobite history that has been written."—*North British Review.*

"A perfect storehouse of important facts."—*Inverness Courier.*

"A volume of singular interest and ability, rich in historical reminiscences."—*Glasgow Citizen.*

"As interesting as a romance, and as improving as historical biography ever is when written by a well-informed and able man."—*Tait's Magazine.*

"High commendation is due to Mr. Burton for the fidelity and ability with which he has made use of his materials."—*Fraser's Mag.*

THE LIFE OF MOZART;

Including his Correspondence.

By EDWARD HOLMES,

AUTHOR OF "A RAMBLE AMONG THE MUSICIANS OF GERMANY," &c.

Post 8vo, cloth, price 9s.

"A clear, complete, and judicious view of Mozart's life."—*Blackwood.*

"In every respect a most admirable piece of Biography."—*New Monthly Mag.*

"We cannot conceive a more fascinating story of genius."—*Examiner.*

"More rich and complete in the assemblage of its materials than any previous publication on the subject."—*Athenæum.*

"This is decidedly the best and most complete Biography of the great composer that we have ever seen."—*Westminster Review.*

THE LIFE OF GEORGE CANNING.

By ROBERT BELL,

AUTHOR OF THE "LIVES OF THE POETS," &c.

Post 8vo, cloth, price 9s.

"We think Mr. Bell's *Life of Canning* will become generally and permanently popular. Unquestionably it is written with great ability, and contains much with regard to Canning's early history but very little known. There is also a great deal of pleasant literary gossip relating to books and authors of the last century towards its close. We have no

hesitation in recommending his *Life of Canning* as an extremely interesting work, and as the production of a man of talent."—*John Bull.*

"We think Mr. Bell's estimates of the conduct of Mr. Canning, in the important and salient points of his noble career, are extremely impartial, just, and correct."—*Literary*

OLIVER CROMWELL'S LETTERS AND SPEECHES.

With Elucidations and Connecting Narrative.

By THOMAS CARLYLE.

SECOND EDITION, WITH NUMEROUS ADDITIONAL LETTERS, and a Portrait of Cromwell, from an Original Miniature by COOPER. 3 vols. 8vo, cloth, price 1l. 16s.

*** The Additional Letters, separately, to complete the First Edition, 8vo, cloth, price 5s.

THE LIFE OF FRIEDRICH SCHILLER:

Comprehending an Examination of his Works.

By THOMAS CARLYLE.

SECOND EDITION, with a Portrait, small 8vo, cloth, price 8s. 6d.

THE AUTOBIOGRAPHY OF HEINRICH ZSCHOKKE.

8vo, cloth, price 6s.

" Will be read with intense interest; with all the interest of a work of fiction. It is a beautiful picture of a good man's life, of a good man's struggles, of a benefactor of the human race."—*John Bull.*

" A vivid picture of the mind and life of a man worthy to be known—one who has striven with success, by speculation and by action, to improve the condition of his fellow-man."—*Morning Chronicle.*

" One of the best autobiographies ever published."—*Chambers' Journal.*

TRUE AND FAYTHFULL RELATIONN

Of a *Worthye Discourse,* held, *June* 'yᵉ eleauenth, in yᵉ Yeare of Grace 1643, betwene yᵉ late Colonell *HAMPDEN, Knighte* of yᵉ *Shire* for yᵉ Countye of *Buckingham,* in yᵉ presente *Parliament,* and Colonell *OLIVER CROMWEL, Burgesse* for yᵉ Towne of *Cambridge,* in yᵉ same.

Foolscap 4to, in appropriate binding, 8s.

This work is preceded by an explanatory preface, in which it is stated that it purports to be written by the Reverend Dr. Spurstowe, Chaplain to John Hampden's Regiment of Foot called the " Green Coats," and author of " Wells of Salvation," 1655, and " The Spiritual Chymist," 1666.

" *A* remarkably clever imitation of the political and oratorical literature of the age of Hampden and Cromwell, and obviously the work of a writer to whom its books and men are familiar."—*Examiner.*

THE FRENCH REVOLUTION: A HISTORY.
By THOMAS CARLYLE.

Vol. I. The Bastille; Vol. II. The Constitution; Vol. III. The Guillotine.
THIRD EDITION, 3 *vols. post 8vo, cloth, price 1l. 11s. 6d.*

HISTORY OF THE EIGHTEENTH CENTURY;
And part of the Nineteenth, with particular reference to Mental
Cultivation and Progress, Literary and Political.
By F. C. SCHLOSSER.

6 vols. 8vo, cloth, price 3l. 7s.

" Schlosser is, as an historian, second to none of his contemporaries. We possess in England no writer between whom and himself it would not be mere irony to institute any comparison. We must look to countries where literature is thought its own reward for his competitor. Ranke among German, and Thierry among French historians, may enter the lists with him. In the depth and variety of his attainments, and the range and compass of his view, he is superior to them, and, among modern writers, quite unrivalled. In vigour of expression, sagacity of judgment, and complete command of his materials (which are like the spear of Achilles, which its owner alone can wield), he is fully equal—and it is a praise of which any historian might be proud —to those great writers."—*Westminster Rev.*

HISTORY OF GERMANY,
From the Earliest Period to the Present Time.
By F. KOHLRAUSCH.

8vo, cloth, price 14s.

HISTORY OF TEN YEARS: 1830-1840.
France during the Three Days, and under Louis-Philippe.
By LOUIS BLANC.

2 vols. 8vo, cloth, price 1l. 6s.

" This is a remarkable work. The ten years 1830-1840 were troubled, stirring, and important times to every European nation—to none so much as France. * * * 'L'Histoire de Dix Ans' is one of those works so often libelled by being called as interesting as a novel. It is a narrative of events, real, striking, absorbing—the subjects of immense interest to all readers — the style unusually excellent."—*Foreign Quarterly Review.*

HISTORY OF FRANCE. BY M. MICHELET.
Translated by WALTER K. KELLY.

2 vols. 8vo, cloth, price 1l. 8s.

" Whatever subject M. Michelet touches, he treats it in a style peculiarly his own. Of all historians he is the most poetic and picturesque. His description of the physical aspect of France is one of the finest examples of eloquence applied to geographical illustration ever penned. It is quite original in conception, and is certainly unrivalled in grasp of subject and luxuriance of language."—*Britannia.*

WORKS OF GENERAL INTEREST AND UTILITY.

RECREATIONS IN SHOOTING;
A PRACTICAL GUIDE FOR YOUNG SPORTSMEN.

With Notices of the Game of the British Islands, including full Directions to the Young Sportsman for the Management of Guns and Dogs.

By "CRAVEN."

With Seventy Illustrations of Game and Sporting Dogs, from Original Drawings by WILLIAM HARVEY; engraved in the first style of the art by F. W. BRANSTON.

Post 8vo, cloth, price 12s.

"Every young Sportsman who wishes for sound and valuable advice on the subject of Shooting would do well to possess himself of this really clever and useful book."—*M. Chron.*

CHESS FOR BEGINNERS,

In a Series of Progressive Lessons. Shewing the most approved Methods of beginning and ending the Game, together with various Situations and Checkmates.'

By WILLIAM LEWIS.

THIRD EDITION, with 24 Diagrams printed in Colours.
Small 4to, cloth, price 5s. 6d.

THE COUNTRY YEAR-BOOK:

Descriptive of the Seasons; Birds, Insects, and Quadrupeds; Rural Scenes and Amusements.

By THOMAS MILLER,

AUTHOR OF "BEAUTIES OF THE COUNTRY," "RURAL SKETCHES," &C.

With One Hundred and Forty Illustrations on Wood, and Eight Coloured Plates.

In two vols. small 8vo, cloth, sold separately, price 5s. each; or complete in one volume, morocco gilt, price 12s.

This work comprises the four volumes on the Seasons, published in "The Boy's Own Library."

"A work more suited to the right direction and improvement of youth we could not wish to be placed in their hands."—*Literary Gazette.*

"Nothing can be more beautiful, and at the same time substantial; it is made for use as well as show, and is, considering the vast number of its embellishments, and its really lovely title-pages and frontispieces, one of the cheapest works we know."—*Howitt's Jour.*

ATLASES AND MAPS.

SHARPE'S CORRESPONDING MAPS.

Now publishing, to be completed in TWENTY-SEVEN PARTS, *each containing Two Maps in a Wrapper, Price* EIGHTPENCE *plain,
or* ONE SHILLING *coloured,*

A Series of Modern Maps,

Constructed upon a system of Scale and Proportion, from the most
recent Authorities.

By JOHN SHARPE.

And engraved on Steel by J. WILSON LOWRY.

*** *In order to expedite the completion of this Atlas,* TWO PARTS *are
now published* MONTHLY.

LIST OF THE MAPS TO BE COMPRISED IN THIS ATLAS.

1. The World—Western Hemisphere.
2. The World—Eastern Hemisphere.
3. The World—Mercator's Projection.
4. Europe, with the Mediterranean.
5. Great Britain and Ireland.
6. England and Wales—Railway Map, North.
7. England and Wales—Railway Map, South.
8. Scotland.
9. Ireland.
10. France—Belgium—Switzerland.
11. Belgium and Holland.
12. Prussia, Holland, and the German States.
13. Switzerland.
14. Austrian Empire.
15. Turkey and Greece.
16. Greece.
17. Italy.
18. Spain and Portugal.
19. Northern Sweden and Frontier of Russia.
20. Denmark, Sweden, & Russia on the Baltic.
21. Western Russia, from the Baltic to the Euxine.
22. Russia on the Euxine.
23. Russia on the Caucasus.
24. Russia in Europe.
25. Northern Asia—Asiatic Russia.
26. South-Western Asia—Overland to India.
27. South-Eastern Asia—Birmah, China, and Japan.
28. Australia and New Zealand.
29. Egypt and Arabia Petræa.
30. Nubia and Abyssinia to Babel Mandeb Strait.
31. Asia Minor.
32. Syria and the Turkish Provinces on the Persian Gulf.
33. Western Persia.
34. Eastern Persia.
35. Affghanistan and the Punjab.
36. Beloochistan and Scinde.
37. Central India.
38. The Carnatic.
39. Bengal, &c.
40. India—General Map.
41. North Africa.
42. South Africa.
43. British North America.
44. Central America.
45. United States—General Map.
46. United States—North-East.
47. United States—South-East.
48. United States—South-West.
49. Jamaica and Leeward and Windward Islands.
50. Mexico and Guatemala.
51. South America.
52. Columbian and Peruvian Republics, and Western Brazil.
53. La Plata, Chili, and Southern Brazil.
54. Eastern Brazil.

A copious Consulting Index will be published on the completion of
the Series.

For Commercial Purposes, and for General Diffusion in Public, National, and other Schools, the Maps will be sold in separate Sheets, at
FOURPENCE *each plain, or* SIXPENCE *coloured.*

PORTFOLIOS to hold these Maps may be obtained from all Booksellers
price 7s. 6d. each.

Sharpe's Railway Map

of England and Wales, with part of Scotland.

Comprising all the Railways for which Acts of Parliament have been obtained; distinguishing those in operation from those in progress.

Mounted on Cloth, in a Case, price 2s. 6d.

Sidney Hall's Pocket County Maps.

New Editions, with all the Railways correctly laid down.

Printed on CHAPMAN's Patent Paper-cloth.

Bedfordshire	England	Lancashire	Shropshire
Berkshire	Essex	Leicestershire	Somersetshire
Buckinghamshire	Gloucestershire	Lincolnshire	Staffordshire
Cambridgeshire	Hampshire	Middlesex	Suffolk
Cheshire	Herefordshire	Monmouthshire	Surrey
Cornwall	Hertfordshire	Norfolk	Sussex
Cumberland	Huntingdonshire	Northamptonshire	Warwickshire
Derbyshire	Isle of Wight	Northumberland	Westmoreland
Devonshire	Isles of Man, Jersey,	Nottinghamshire	Wiltshire
Dorsetshire	and Guernsey	Oxfordshire	Worcestershire
Durham	Kent	Rutlandshire	

On a Sheet, price 6d. ; or in a case, price 9d. and 1s. each.

Double the size of the above,

Yorkshire	Ireland	Scotland	Wales

On a Sheet, price 1s. ; or in a case, 1s. 6d. each.

A Pocket Travelling Atlas

Of the English Counties, with all the Coach and Rail-Roads accurately laid down and Coloured.

ENGRAVED BY SIDNEY HALL.

NEW EDITION, *Bound in roan, with a tuck, price 16s.*

" The best Atlas we have seen for neatness, portability, and clear engraving. The Maps are quarto size, but fold in the middle, so that the whole, when closed, forms a moderately thick octavo volume, exactly the size, without being too bulky, for the pocket of a greatcoat."—*Westminster Review.*

Sidney Hall's New County Atlas ;

prising the above Maps, bound flat in 4to, for the Library or Desk.

Cloth, price 10s.

WORKS IN GENERAL LITERATURE.

Diary and Notes of Horace Templeton, Esq.
LATE SECRETARY OF LEGATION AT ———

In two volumes, post 8vo.

A BOOK FOR A PRESENT.

Charles Boner's Book.

For those who 're young and those who love
What's natural and truthful;
If old in years, yet young in heart,
'Tis THAT which must be youthful.

With numerous Illustrations, from Designs by COUNT POCCI.

In one volume, small 8vo.

Shakespeare Proverbs;
Or, the *Wise Saws* of our Wisest Poet collected into a *Modern Instance.*

By Mary Cowden Clarke,
AUTHOR OF " THE CONCORDANCE TO SHAKESPEARE."

Elegantly printed in a pocket volume.

NEW WORK BY LEIGH HUNT.

A Book for a Corner.
Selections from favourite Authors, with Introductory Notices.

By Leigh Hunt.
With numerous Illustrations, from Designs by F. W. HULME.

In two volumes, small 8vo.

" This compilation is intended for all lovers of books, at every time of life, from childhood to old age, particularly such as are fond of the authors it quotes, and who enjoy their perusal most in the quietest places. It is intended for the boy or girl who loves to get with a book into a corner—for the youth who on entering life finds his advantage in having become acquainted with books—for the man in the thick of life, to whose spare moments books are refreshments—and for persons in the decline of life, who reflect on what they have experienced, and to whom books and gardens afford their tranquillest pleasures." *Introduction.*

Happy Ignorance; or, Church and State.

A Religious Adventure. With Notes by the Editors.

Small 8vo, cloth, price 5s.

"An undeniably clever book."—*Church and State Gazette.*

"This little book might have been written by the wise and good Dr. Arnold. It has many of the peculiarities of his opinions, and is full of his large-hearted tolerance and Christian charity. * * * That the author is a clergyman of the Church of England, we can hardly doubt."—*Examiner.*

Hours of Meditation and Devotional Reflection;

upon Various Subjects connected with the Religious, Moral, and Social Duties of Life.

By Heinrich Zschokke.

Translated from the Twenty-third German Edition.

SECOND EDITION, *small 8vo, price 5s. cloth; or in morocco gilt, 9s.*

"We can scarcely find terms adequate to express the gratification we have experienced from the perusal of this admirable volume. Never did philosophy appear more amiable, never more exalted, than in these devout reflections. They are irradiated by the light of heaven and the divinest spirit of religion. On the Continent, thousands have testified to the merits of this admirable author. We are convinced that this portion of his writings has only to be known in this country to be equally appreciated."—*Atlas.*

The Book of Symbols.

A Series of Seventy-five Short Essays, on as many different Subjects, in Connexion with Morals, Religion, and Philosophy; each Essay illustrating an Ancient Symbol, or Moral Precept.

SECOND EDITION, *post 8vo, cloth, price 6s.*

"The Essays are sensible and judicious. * * * We recommend the book to our readers, as the production of a learned and thinking mind."—*John Bull.*

Irish Diamonds;

or, a Theory of Irish Wit and Blunders; combined with other kindred Subjects.

By John Smith.

With six Illustrations by "PHIZ."

Small 8vo, cloth, price 5s.

"The book is a cluster of brilliants."—*Chambers' Journal.*

"A pleasant, gossiping book this,—a famous companion for the fireside,—fitted to be read on winter nights, when the bleak prospect without contrasts so charmingly the light and warmth which animate the circle or festive board."—*Nottingham*